TECHNOLOGY COMPENDIUM

SIR ARTHOUR'S GUIDE TO THE NUMENERA

CREDITS

Writer/Designer Monte Cook
Additional Writing Bruce R. Cordell, Shanna Germain, Rob Schwalb
Creative Director Shanna Germain
Editor & Proofreader Ray Vallese
Cover Artist Kieran Yanner
Graphic Designer Sarah Robinson

Artists

Brenoch Adams, chrom, Dreamstime.com, Jason Engle, Erebus, Guido Kuip, Eric Lofgren,
Patrick McEvoy, Mike Perry, Roberto Pitturro, Lee Smith, Hugo Solis, Prospero Tipaldi, Shane Tyree,
Cathy Wilkins, Ben Wootten, Kieran Yanner

Monte Cook Games Editorial Team

Scott C. Bourgeois, David Wilson Brown, Eric Coates, Gareth Hodges, Ryan Klemm, Jeremy Land,
Laura Wilkinson, George Ziets

TABLE OF CONTENTS

INTRODUCTION: SIR ARTHOUR HIMSELF

The Torein family was preparing to move to a new home in a land that would allow them "prosperity equal to their standing." House Torein had dwelt in the Crumbling Waste too long. While the fields that had once been a vast, ancient city had served as profitable scavenging grounds—cypher gathering had been the main source of income for Torein, and the house's sifters and cobblers were among the best in Matheunis—nothing could grow there. Discoveries and device troves became fewer and fewer with each year.

Young Arthour Torein regretted leaving this realm of lore and technology, and he had no interest in farms. Thus, he sat in the back of one of the moving caravan's wagons and sulked as they made their way to the first of many safe bases of operation that house agents had established along the road. All roads in the Ninth World were dangerous, and Arthour's father, Renault, fretted over his family's vulnerability.

The attack, however, came from within. The very wagons that carried the Torein family, their servants, and all their possessions rose up, wood and steel flowing and flexing like flesh and muscle. People cried out that demons had possessed the vehicles. That sorcery from the wilderness had befallen them, and that some dark curse would be their deaths. Even as the cries of crushed servants and dying guards rose around him, Arthour knew that what he was seeing was molecular control, the result of technology and science. He knew that it would have required a complex and lengthy process performed well ahead of time. It had to have started before they left.

Arthour tried to flee, but one of the animate wagons, standing like a humanoid giant with massive fists now red with blood, struck a blow that sent the young man flying into the dirt.

Arthour awoke days later, the only survivor of the massacre. He will not tell you what happened next. He does not relate how he survived in the wilderness, or how he spent the next six years tracking down those that had betrayed his family and took their wealth. He will not speak of how he learned to use his knowledge and affinity with the numenera to become a weapon of vengeance.

Today, he will speak only of his later years, having settled down in the southern reaches of the Steadfast and built one of the greatest laboratories anyone has ever seen. How his library of books about the numenera—many of which are penned by his own hand—has few rivals. How an entire university has grown around his home, although the classrooms and students are all but ignored by him so that he can focus on his research and experiments.

Some say the blow that Arthour took to the head made him "not quite right." Others put the blame on an early life filled with violence and vengeance without pity. Whatever the case, he is perhaps the Ninth World's greatest expert on the numenera, flaws and all.

The technology compendium you hold in your hands is a collection of cyphers, artifacts, and oddities for use in any and all Numenera games. It supplements and greatly expands upon the items found in the Numenera corebook. Before we get to those, however, the first chapter describes some of the various types of numenera that can be found in the Ninth World and how they might be used in a game—not just as equipment and items for characters, but as the basis for encounters and adventures. It is a starting point for those interested in the impossibly advanced science of the prior worlds. Like the man it is named after, this guide is informative and more than a little dangerous.

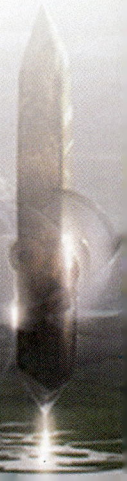

CHAPTER 1

USING TECHNOLOGY IN YOUR NUMENERA GAME

"The numenera, as most call it, shapes every aspect of our lives. It is the solution to all our problems, but the source of many dangers if we are not careful. Only the most learned and intelligent among us should tamper with it. Oh, uh, now where did I put that container of flesh-reshaping nanobots?"

~Sir Arthour

Throughout this book, you'll see page references to various items accompanied by this symbol. These are page references to the Numenera corebook, where you can find additional details about that item, place, creature, or concept. It isn't necessary to look up the referenced items in the corebook, but doing so will provide useful information for character creation and gameplay.

Look for this symbol throughout the book for real-world science and technology search terms. Delving into these topics can further inspire your gameplay.

The very name of the game, Numenera, comes from what the people of the Ninth World call the incredible technologies of the past (and the effects that technology has on the world). Thus, in many ways, technology is literally the name of the game. While the obvious expression of the numenera comes from cyphers, artifacts, and oddities, which this book is filled with, it's worth taking a step back to look at the bigger picture. How can incredibly advanced technology shape locations, adventures, creatures, and characters in the Ninth World? In other words, in this chapter we look at the forest rather than the trees.

The chapter is written for the game master (GM) and from the point of view of someone in the 21st century, as opposed to someone in the Ninth World. Still, it avoids overusing terms that wouldn't be used in the Ninth World, except where called out. Instead, in the margins you'll find "search terms." These are real-world, cutting-edge technological terms that can start you on your journey of learning more about some of the topics in the chapter. You don't have to know a thing about holographic data storage to have crystals with weird powers in your campaign. However, if you're interested, you might find further research informative and perhaps inspiring.

It's difficult to think of something that would be magical that can't be replicated with advanced technology. Things like telepathy, precognition, shape changing, teleportation, or telekinesis are possible via technological speculation of the 21st century. The numenera can go well beyond things that we can even speculate are possible.

For the sake of examination, this chapter breaks down the types of technologies into categories. These are not comprehensive or definitive. Instead, they are meant to be inspiring and thought-provoking. The chapter also presents ideas and suggestions for discoveries and encounter or scenario starting points dealing with the various types of numenera.

ELECTRONICS

The buzz and whir of unknown devices. A few flashing lights near a glass panel glowing with mysterious symbols. The smell of ozone and metal. An arc of blue lightning.

"Electronics" is a terribly inadequate word. We use it, however, to cover any sort of basic device that requires power (although it's possible that the power is not electric at all). It's certainly not a Ninth World term. Instead, Ninth Worlders might say "powered device," but that term might be too broad. In the end, for the purpose of examination of technologies, "electronics" means any device that uses energy that isn't mechanical (energy associated with the motion and position of an object, such as that of pistons, gears, and so on). A voice communicator, an energy weapon, a climate-control device, and a holographic image projector would all fall into this category, as would many, many other devices. In many ways, this is the "everything else" category, covering the most basic types of devices, but also including some amazing tools and weapons.

The archetype of this category would be a handheld device of synth or metal with buttons and a screen, or perhaps a screen with touch-activated controls. It might be a palm-sized handheld device, a rod with control studs, a bracelet, a large device with multiple complex control arrays, or a weird cube with controls hidden behind sliding panels. It could also be something very small, like a ring that's activated by brain waves, vocalizations, or gestures.

Not all devices of this nature are hard metal objects or soft, smooth plastic. A communicator, light source, or energy shield projector could be a cloth headband, a patch on a shirt, or the shirt itself. An energy weapon, a sonar range finder, or a teleporter could resemble what a 21st-century person might think of as a "temporary tattoo"—an electronic device that adheres to the skin and is controlled by brain waves, body heat, or simple muscle action.

Energy Walls: The interior (or a portion of the interior) of an ancient complex might use energy walls rather than walls composed of matter. In addition to being effective barriers, such walls might be dangerous to touch, inflicting their level in damage on anyone who

so much as brushes up against them. This is not so much of a problem in a standard exploratory mission, but if a fight or other action-focused encounter (like a chase) occurs amid these walls, it might be hard to avoid touching them (the occasional Speed defense roll would be appropriate, with the difficulty based on the situation, not the level of the wall).

The walls might also be transparent or translucent, allowing explorers to see what discoveries lie on the other side, close but still out of reach—or, conversely, what dangers or other weirdness lie ahead.

Mind-Reading Defenses: Electronics can key into brain waves just like any other kind of transmissions, allowing for automated defenses in an ancient ruin that react to intruders in an uncomfortably intimate way. The obvious way to do this is to have detectors that sense the presence of intruders by their thoughts, or have slugspitters or hunter/seekers fire at where the target plans to move rather than where it is (increasing the difficulty of the target's Speed defense tasks by two steps).

More invasive defenses might include analyzing memories and projecting realistic hologram "visions" of great horror or shame,

Electric energy is carried by free electrons from a source to a load. Also, it is the potential energy of a stationary charge. Other types of energy include (but are not limited to): mechanical, sound, gravitational, thermal, chemical, radiant, and nuclear.

Slugspitter, page 311

Hunter/seeker, page 287

Search Terms: *types of energy, flexible electronics, e-textiles, silicon tattoo grafts*

Search Term: *apergy*

Zero gravity, page 98

Search Terms: *rail gun, high EMF effects, Faraday cage*

or new scenes of loved ones in danger, drawing the intruder into a trap or a reverie from which she cannot escape. Only an Intellect defense roll allows a character to ignore such things.

Subject-Sensitive Tools: Designed for who-knows-what reason, a complex scanner conducts automated activities based on some element of a subject who enters a locale created in a prior world. This means that when one person enters the area, tools build him a form-fitting suit of advanced polymers, but when his friend comes along, she is bombarded with radiation designed to alter her DNA in a specific way—but since she is not the subject the machine was designed for, it has a very different effect, harming or even mutating her.

FUNDAMENTAL FORCES
Smooth, curved synth panels with the pale glow of touch-sensitive symbols embedded within them. Lights growing in intensity as a low hum slowly becomes a high-pitched whine. The hairs on your neck and arms standing straight as the tingling of energy starts deep in your gut and spreads outward.

For our purposes here, the term "fundamental forces" describes technology that harnesses things we normally think of as simply being a part of the natural landscape of the universe: gravity, magnetism, sound, light, and time, primarily. Such technology can seem to be the most godlike sort of numenera, keeping floating cities aloft, making impossibly twisted mountains rise into the air, or changing the very orbit of the Earth itself.

GRAVITY
Control over gravity means, of course, the ability to float or fly through the air, perhaps indefinitely. However, it also means the ability to increase and decrease the perceived weight of objects. In a way, then, it's a complete control of motion through space.

In the Ninth World, Aeon Priests and scholars use the term "apergy" to mean the opposite of gravity. A floating platform uses apergy to push against and ultimately overcome gravity so that it can hover in midair.

Gravity can be increased rather than lessened or negated. An object can be made to crush itself under its own artificially inflated weight as the force of gravity is increased. A

particularly nasty weapon might selectively increase gravity and apergy on the same target, ripping it apart as half is crushed to the ground and the other half flies into the air. Carefully manipulated gravity could dramatically increase the range of a physical ranged weapon (like an arrow or a slug from a slugspitter). For example, an arrow could fly toward its target under the effects of reduced gravity, and then significantly increase gravity at the last moment to bring it down with even greater force. Tracing the trajectory of such a missile would reveal an arc nothing like a conventional arrow's path.

A gravity shield could ground such attacks before they reach their target by rapidly and dramatically increasing gravity's pull. Such a shield would also be harmful to those attempting to charge through it in close-quarters combat.

Gravity Alteration Tunnel: If explorers pass through a long, round tunnel, the orientation of gravity could shift subtly as they make their way along. At the end, they might be standing on the "ceiling" without realizing that anything had changed.

Transport Tube: In a large, mostly buried ancient complex, explorers might find a maze of tubes. Through sheer manipulation of gravitic forces, someone (or something) entering a tube can be carried to a designated destination, as if propelled along in a (far more low-tech) pneumatic tube. If one had an encounter in such a tube, either with a foe or with some obstacle (such as an onrush of debris that got caught up in the tube system going the opposite way), that encounter would be handled using the zero-gravity rules.

MAGNETISM
More than simply pulling at metal objects, magnetism is a versatile force that can be harnessed in many ways. Magnetism is a part of the electromagnetic spectrum, of course, but that concept is likely lost on many Ninth World scholars. To them, magnetism is its own separate force.

Electromagnetic Ghosts: It's worth mentioning that extremely intense fields of electromagnetic energy can have varied and adverse effects on creatures and objects. For example, if deep in the wilderness some travelers came upon a structure like an obelisk

that produced intense electromagnetic fields (at varying frequencies), at first they might not realize that anything was amiss. Soon, however, around that obelisk the travelers might see (or feel) objects move in violent fashion. They might hear voices, feel intense emotions (fear being chief among them), experience nausea, hallucinate, and even fall unconscious. To a Ninth Worlder, this might seem like the activities of ghosts or spirits.

Magnetic Sphere: A swirling mass of powerful and precisely manipulated magnetic fields could create a sphere of orbiting metal objects, such as jagged, razor-sharp blades. This would be an interesting and effective way of protecting a valuable treasure, a large machine's inner core, or even a creature. Inversely, it could also be a horrific prison cell.

SOUND
Sound manipulation can control the volume and intensity of sound waves. Numenera devices involving sound can even change the speed of sound, so that it takes much longer, for example, to reach the ears of people who are nearby.

Some devices can create "sonic holes." These are areas without sound—perfect for

someone attempting to sneak past a group of guards or silence an alarm. A sonic hole is also an effective counter to a sonic weapon.

Sound as a Weapon: Concentrated sound can be blasted like any other sort of energy ray, making an effective ranged weapon. A blast of sonic energy is a powerful bludgeon that can knock a target backward or tear through it like a mighty stab. A simple loud sound can deafen (perhaps permanently), and a very loud sound can kill, disrupting the target's brain.

Different frequencies of sound can also be more subtle weapons. Sound can be used to manipulate emotions in imperceptible ways. A subsonic device planted on a person might make those around her happy (and thus feel more positive about her) or fill them with terror (forcing them to flee before her). A possibly more overt acoustic weapon could daze and disorient those in an area, perhaps in a radius around the source or in a more focused ray or cone.

Solid Sound: Sound waves can be made to remain stationary—a standing wave—rather than travel. This application of sonic energy can be used to make solid objects of pure sound, such as blades, shields, barriers, and

Search Terms:
anechoic chamber, emoacoustics, sonic weapons, sonic hole

Be sure to refresh your memory with the technology chapter in the Numenera corebook, pages 276 to 277. In particular, the section called "The Appearance of Numenera Devices" is useful in fully realizing all sorts of the numenera in your campaign.

so on. Many force fields might actually be sonic constructs, and even far more precise objects can be made out of sound. While crude sonic technology might involve creating a rather unstable, flickering plane of sound, more advanced machines could make sonic objects that had any property of solid matter. An explorer could have clothing made of sound, an ultrasharp scalpel made of sound, or a cushiony bed made of sound. With a moderate adjustment of the controls, the sonic clothing could become armor, or it could disappear altogether in the blink of an eye.

LIGHT

Bringing light to the dark is perhaps one of the most basic forms of technology. Glowglobes, for example, are ubiquitous throughout the Ninth World, and many people have learned to manufacture them.

As much as it might seem like sorcery, ancient technology can drain illumination as well as produce it, creating areas of unnatural dim light or absolute darkness.

Light as Mind Attack: Ray projectors are obvious ways to turn light into a weapon. Light, and specifically color, can affect the minds of those who view it, changing their mood and emotion, forcing Intellect defense rolls. Bursts of light can cause seizures and unconsciousness, also requiring Intellect defense rolls to resist.

Search Term: *photonic molecule*

Hard Light: A photonic molecule is fabricated matter, created artificially by changing the qualities of light in a fundamental way. In short, this process turns light into solid matter: an object or structure made of hard light. With the flip of a switch, something exists where nothing did before, and the object can be switched off just as easily, making it disappear as the photonic molecules return to their energy state and dissipate.

TIME

"Fiddle with time and it will fiddle with you." ~Sir Arthour

Time manipulation is perhaps one of the most uncommon and least understood (if such a thing can even be determined) types of numenera. But the existence of various devices shows that time can be stopped (locally or broadly), sped up, slowed down, and reversed. Time can be a defense, a weapon, or a tool.

Wave of Ages: An explorer brings home a strange device he found. When he and his family awaken the next morning, they all feel weary and generally ill. The same is true the next day. In a few days, the explorer's hair is noticeably whiter, and his face wrinkled. Only then does he realize that everyone in proximity of the device is aging very quickly. It's not an illness but a rapid passing of time, and it comes in waves. He's got to get rid of this thing and put it far outside the reach of anyone else.

Time Dilation Maze: In a noble's tower, built within and around a far older structure, lies a maze of corridors. Within each corridor, time moves at a different rate, so that if one explorer goes left and another goes right, and they return after one minute, the first might arrive back three minutes before the other. If an explorer wanders long enough through this maze, she might catch sight of her past self about to enter a corridor she has already entered.

GM Advice on Time and Time Travel: Time can mess with your campaign in a big way. Keep in mind that places where time moves at different speeds, while quite fun, can be exploited by clever players. For example, if the PCs have access to an extradimensional space where time moves very quickly in relation to the real universe, they could go there in the middle of a dangerous encounter, rest and recuperate, and then come back into the middle of the encounter, just moments later in normal time. This is great for a one-shot ability, but making it available long term drains a lot of the tension out of things.

Time travel presents a host of challenges. Going back in time to undo something that happened in the campaign might cause you to create "retroactive continuity" (retcon) to explain the changes that cascade up to the present due to that tinkering with time. Going into the near future may require you to develop what will likely happen in the campaign before it happens. Both of these problems can be dealt with by stating that the time travel option available to the PCs—whether they realize it or not—involves going to the past or future of parallel universes. Thus, the past can be altered, but it's not actually the past of the PCs' proper universe.

Travel to the distant past involves detailing one or more of the prior worlds and ultimately should be as weird and incomprehensible as going to an alien world or another universe altogether. Remember, too, that revealing too much about the past can take some of the mystery and wonder out of the setting. That said, with some care and thought, time travel can be a very fun part of a scenario.

ARTIFICIAL LIFE

The flexing hiss of motors and the smell of oil and synth. A soft whir as steel caresses steel. Metallic fingers clench. Artificial eyes glow red.

Whether it be a mind or a body, numenera facsimiles of living things (or portions of living things) exist in an array of forms and purposes. Usually, it appears that the goal of such things is to do biology one better. Mechanical arms are stronger, mechanical minds think faster, mechanical legs run faster, and so on. In other cases, the mechanical version possesses an ability that the original never had, such as mech eyes that see through matter or blast destructive rays.

AUTOMATONS

The Ninth World is filled with automatons—what a 21st-century person might call robots—of all kinds. Some pose threats, like Oorgolian soldiers, disassemblers, or dread destroyers. Others are innocuous, either completely depowered or still carrying out ancient directives that have little bearing or meaning in the current world.

Despite the name, many automatons are free-willed, thinking beings. Many, for example, have escaped to a refuge in the Beyond called the Weal of Baz to keep far from humans and other organic beings that often mistreat them.

Automaton Suicide: At the top of a cliff, a number of humanoid automatons stand dutifully, waiting until a living creature of their size or so comes along, at which point they attempt to grab the creature and throw themselves off the cliff. Perhaps this is some kind of strange quasireligious ceremony, or simply a malfunction.

Replicants, but of What?: In a region of the southern Steadfast, people occasionally come upon humanoid creatures with three arms and long, three-eyed faces. These creatures don't seem to speak any language known to humans, and no one has ever been able to communicate with them. Stranger still, it

has been revealed that at least some (and perhaps all) of these beings are mechanical automatons made to look like living creatures. These, then, are carefully designed replicants, but the creatures that they were designed to look like are now long gone.

FUSION OF BODY AND MACHINE

Artificial life is a technology that also involves fusing the organic with the inorganic, usually with the latter mimicking the former in some way. Thus, we have characters with machine arms, mech eyes, or other implants that replace or augment conventional biological systems. Characters who fuse flesh and steel are such "cyborgs," but that term is not frequently used. In fact, mechanical implants

Oorgolian soldier, page 250

Disassembler, page 238

Dread destroyer, page 239

Weal of Baz, page 198

Fuses Flesh and Steel, page 64

"The binding of the mechanical to the organic, or the creation of inorganic, mechanical life (or at least intelligence), in many ways carries with it the most weight of any type of technology. Because what is more potent—and more dangerous—than stretching the very definition of life?"

~Sir Arthour

Search Terms:
bioresorbable devices, silicon tattoo grafts

Peerless: level 5, Numenera and repairing as level 7. For full details, see The Ninth World Bestiary, page 97

Mount Zanlis, page 177

Black Riage, page 177

Decanted: level 4, stealth as levle 6 when using visual distortion field. For full detials, see The Ninth World Bestiary, page 34

are common enough that there really is no single term for the numenera enhancements or those who use them. The distinction is that these characters adopt mechanical parts on a permanent basis, and the devices are meant to be incorporated into an organic host. Thus, these are not simple cyphers or tools to be used and tossed away. They become a part of a character, as much as any part the person is born with.

Incorporating such technology into a campaign is just a matter of description. An NPC passes by on artificial legs or stares at the PC with whirring mech eyes. The fusion can be more subtle, with the implants hidden subdermally, covered with artificial flesh, or just placed so that the person's clothing usually conceals them. And it can also be far more overt and far weirder. The PCs might meet a character whose head can detach from his body thanks to devices sealing his neck (and antigravity hover devices built into his lower cranium). Or they might come upon a woman with enormous metal legs, like those of a spider, jutting from an artificial lower abdomen bristling with strange devices. Or an NPC might just be a head, like a decanted.

There are many ways to create a subtle fusion of inorganic with organic. For example, tiny implants—narrower than a human hair and only a centimeter long—could be implanted in a person's body, perhaps without his knowledge. Such an implant might grant the ability to interface directly with another machine, or it might cure a malady in the body. It could rewrite DNA, serve as a homing device, or perform any of a thousand other functions.

But such interfaces can get subtler yet. A device might not need to be implanted at all. It could be swallowed by a creature or—in the case of very tiny machines—inhaled. Such devices might be bioresorbable, eventually broken down harmlessly and flushed from the system when their work is done.

The Unwanted Interface: A character is implanted with a device without his knowledge. This almost microscopic transmitter allows him to interact with and control the actions of a larger machine like an articulated automaton with arms and various functions. However, interaction and control are very difficult. At first, the character might not even realize that the things the automaton does are the result of his actions or thoughts. Only over time and with some careful deduction can he learn that he is in control and how to exert that control in deliberate ways. One might imagine that in the distant past, such implantation and interface could have been a process conducted with young children, but what the young child of a prior world could easily deal with passes all understanding in the Ninth World.

The Steel Chiurgeon: Within the back alleys of a large city there exists a woman simply called the Steel Chiurgeon who has mastered the numenera to the degree that she can add artificial parts to willing (and wealthy) subjects. Mechanical limbs, brain enhancements, armor, built-in weaponry—she can design these parts to order and give them to those who wish to "upgrade" their own biological forms.

MACHINE INTELLIGENCE

Rarer still are the disembodied machine intelligences such as Peerless or whatever is inside Mount Zanlis in the Black Riage. These typically are not housed in a single mechanical body but instead in a more permanent locale, remotely controlling many mechanical bodies.

The Machine God: A powerful machine intelligence shares so many of the same qualities of a god—vast knowledge, extraordinary powers and influence, the ability to observe and hear a number of lesser beings—that it is not difficult to see how one might become worshipped. The surprising part comes from the idea that the machine would desire such a thing. It is possible that, over time, even a machine can go mad. Such might be the case for one wishing the adoration and supplication of others, even though there is very little logical reason for it.

A machine god's temples might be communication stations where those who have been properly sanctified can directly interact with their deity. The avatar-priests

would be mechanical figures that the god could directly control. The rites and ceremonies of such a religion might be very different from those created by humans, involving the implantation of mechanical parts as a quest toward perfection. Brain implants might allow more frequent communion and even possession by the god.

It is also possible that a machine god might serve as the deity only for other thinking machines. As an inverse of the standard worshipper/deity relationship, however, the worshippers would be the ones that take care of the deity. In fact, they might have created it. Still, as the machine god is so much more advanced than they are—for that's how they designed it—it is still worthy of veneration and adoration.

The Displaced Intelligence: A machine intelligence could be hosted within a swarm of molecule-sized processing and storage units spread out over a wide region. This would, in effect, allow the intelligence to be omnipresent. Such an entity would have no central core, and it would look upon the world as its body. The displaced intelligence

would have a vast amount of knowledge and awareness, but little or no ability to affect the world around it. Finding a way to communicate with the entity (if one even became aware of its existence) would be tricky, but the attempt would likely prove worthwhile.

NEW DESCRIPTOR: ARTIFICIALLY INTELLIGENT

You are a machine. Not just a sentient machine, but a *sapient* one. Your origins may hearken back to an earlier age, but memories of such a time are long lost. Alternatively, you might be a far more recent creation of some tinkerer or Aeon Priest.

Artificially intelligent characters have machine minds of one type or another. This can involve something that a 21st-century person might call an advanced computer brain, but it could also be as different as a liquid computer, a quantum computer, or a network of smart dust particles creating an ambient intelligence. You might even have been an organic creature whose mind was uploaded into a machine.

Your body, of course, is also a machine. This means that most people will refer to you as

An Artificially Intelligent character who Fuses Flesh and Steel would be an automaton who has organic parts added to its body.

Fuses Flesh and Steel, page 64

Search Terms: *smart dust, quantum computing, ambient intelligence, liquid computing*

an automaton, although you know that term doesn't describe you very well, as you are as free-willed and free-thinking as they are.

You gain the following characteristics:

Superintelligent: +4 to your Intellect Pool.

Artificial Body: +3 to your Might Pool and Speed Pool.

Shell: +1 to Armor.

Limited Recovery: Resting restores points only to your Intellect Pool, not to your Might Pool or Speed Pool.

Mechanics, Not Medicines: Conventional healing methods, including the vast majority of numenera restorative devices, do not function to restore points to any of your Pools. You can recover points to your Intellect Pool only by resting, and you can recover points to your Speed and Might

Organic/Biotech Devices table, page 155

Healing, page 103

Search Terms: *bioengineering, synthetic biology, biopolymers*

Pools only through repair.

Machine Vulnerabilities and Invulnerabilities: Damaging effects and other threats that rely on an organic system—poison, disease, cell disruption, and so on—have no effect on you. Neither do beneficial drugs or other effects. Conversely, things that normally affect only inorganic or inanimate objects can affect you. Effects that can disrupt machines affect you.

Uncanny Valley: You have a hard time relating to organic beings, and they don't react well to you. The difficulty of all positive interaction tasks with such beings is increased by two steps.

BIOTECHNOLOGY

A sour, almost acrid smell. A gelatinous substance slowly bubbling as it spreads across the floor. A tangle of metal and synth tubes pumping nutrient solutions. Something squirms in a clear tank of thick greenish fluid, avoiding the light. In the darkness, something makes soft noises, like an infant.

Although technology can mimic or perhaps redefine life, biotechnology creates (or shapes) actual life. Using artificial means to create or modify organic life, biotechnology can be smelly, slimy, and squirmy where more conventional technologies are cold, clean, and hard—soft tech versus hard tech, so to speak. Hallmarks of this kind of numenera include creatures and parts of creatures grown in vats or plugged into nutrient tubes.

Biotechnological numenera sometimes self-repair by healing the way that natural creatures do. They grow and move. Often, they don't need power—they need nutrients. These nutrients can come from immersive or injected solutions (the aforementioned tanks and tubes), or they can be drawn from another creature, like a parasite feeding on a host.

One strange expression of biotech numenera comes in the form of tailor-made viruses. These viral organisms enter the body of a living creature and make alterations. These changes can be something as simple as resistance to disease or other unwanted conditions, or as complex as subtle behavior modification or a complete physical restructuring of the host's body.

BIOENGINEERING

The so-called sorcery of the past enables the creation of living creatures in their entirety, grown from just a few raw materials.

Eric lofgren

Sometimes these are creatures that, once fully grown, can exist entirely on their own. Others have special requirements, such as nutrient or energy injections, some of which might be difficult to obtain in the Ninth World. Some of these beings are merely copies of creatures that already exist—clones or replicants. Others are unique, often designed in ways that evolution probably would never have allowed—battle creatures with almost unwieldy claws, teeth, and armor; flying creatures built for speed but incapable of landing safely; sentient plants that take root each night; and so on. Not all bioengineered creatures are quite so untenable, of course. Bioengineering is the origin of many of the creatures that now dwell in the wilds of the Ninth World.

This means that some bioengineered creatures are able to reproduce on their own, producing natural offspring. That further means that, given time—and the history of the Earth in the Ninth World has time in abundance—evolution can and does take over. Thus, many of the creatures in the Ninth World are actually the evolved forms of genetically engineered creatures from the past. They are examples of nature being overtaken by science, which in turn has been retaken by nature.

The technology to create new bioengineered creatures still exists amid the wreckage of the past. So among the species originally engineered (or re-engineered) and grown long ago, there are brand new specimens as well. But it's not just wild or monstrous beasts. Biotechnology can create intelligent beings, which includes humans. Some learned philosophers wonder, in fact, if the origin of Ninth World humanity as a whole doesn't have its roots in bioengineering.

Some bioengineered creatures are referred to as biomechanical—creatures grown with an inherent dependence on mechanical parts. In some cases, these vat-produced creatures are literally grown around mechanical parts that fuse with their organic systems. But the far more advanced biotechnologies can actually create organic mechanical parts that are born with the offspring and grow alongside the living portions of the organism. This blurred line between organic and inorganic almost makes the words meaningless in this case, but nevertheless the results are evident. The Ninth World has biomechanical creatures with internal scanners, ray projectors, force fields, and other "mechanical" devices existing as a part of their "natural" physiology. (Words like "natural" and "artificial" begin to lose their

It's tempting to have machine intelligences or intelligent automatons from the past relate specific details or descriptions of the prior worlds to allies in the Ninth World who ask about them. Such details might undermine some of the general conceits of the setting, so straightforward descriptions should be avoided. Instead, either the intelligence no longer possesses clear data on the events of literally millions of years ago, or the meaningful communication of such details is very difficult. In the latter case, imagine trying to explain today's society, with all its advancements, to an ancient Sumerian. This would be far harder.

meaning in these contexts as well.)

The Ithsyn Prototype: The ithsyn that hunt in the wilds of the Ninth World are the evolved descendants of creatures designed and produced in the distant past. But now the numenera that produced the original creatures has been recovered. If curiosity cannot be held in check, the process will result in a new creature that vaguely resembles the ithsyn, but the gas it produces has wildly different effects on those nearby. The progenitor was not a dangerous hunter at all, but was engineered to produce mind-altering gas that allows those breathing it to mentally transcend to another level of nonphysical reality altogether.

Ithsyn, page 241

Living Furnishings: A wealthy noble has employed a team of experts to create furniture that is alive. So far, they've produced a soft, shaggy creature in the shape of a bed, a pair of chairs that come when called, a table that can reshape itself to fit the needs of the day, a storage chest in the kitchen that grows meat inside itself, and more.

Sun Worshippers: Three hundred years ago, a group of explorers found an ancient facility that could create creatures by design. These explorers, and the nearby villagers that they eventually brought with them to the discovery, decided as a group to produce a generation of children that would never know hunger. Thus, today, the facility lies at the heart of a small, isolated town of people who don't need to eat or breathe, gaining all they need from the rays of the sun, like plants. Originally, sexual reproduction was forbidden, and all children were produced by the engineers in the facility whose knowledge was handed down from the first explorers. Today they have found that the photosynthetic qualities in the population breeds true. However, these natural offspring have green-tinted flesh, hair, and eyes.

Aldeia, page 134

The Beyond, page 174

REMAKING

By tapping into the genetic codes at the heart of any biological creature, the numenera can literally remake that creature into something else. In modest cases, this might simply involve making a creature more resistant to disease (perhaps a disease she already has contracted) or repairing a wound. In more extreme cases, it can involve anything from regrowing lost limbs to a complete redesign of the creature's anatomy to include armored plates, a rearrangement of limbs, eyes that can

Technologies are not exclusive or exclusionary. For example, biotechnology involves advanced chemistry and often nanotechnology.

see in the dark, gigantic claws, and so on.

The Rejuvenator: A traveling merchant has two creatures pulling a large, iron-wheeled wagon in her caravan. Beneath its tarpaulin, she keeps a coffinlike device that will literally remake any adult placed inside it for two hours, restoring the body to late adolescence. The merchant moves on, however, before the side effects take hold. Some of the remade people continue to grow, until a year later they are almost 8 feet (2 m) tall. Others develop a scaly exterior (+1 to Armor) over the course of a few months. After three years, all of them begin to bud. They reproduce asexually, as a bulge in their side eventually (and painfully) grows into an infant humanoid creature with blue scales and gills.

GRAFTS

Some creatures are engineered to be symbiotic "tools" for other creatures, grafted onto the host and providing a special function. Grafts can replace a missing body part, such as a hand, an eye, or a leg, or they can become entirely new body parts, such as an extra arm or an eye on a stalk grafted onto the back of someone's head. The advantage of grafts is that they are ready-made and instant use, removing the need to wait for a bioengineered body part specifically tailored for the recipient.

The Hive: In a small aldeia in the Beyond, discoveries have allowed some scholars and mechanics to grow a wide array of symbiotic creatures that serve as grafts—insects with large wings that merge with a human's back to allow her to fly, insect carapace armor, stinger bugs that graft onto the back of one's hand to form a weapon, and more. The people of this isolated place now look more like insects than humans, and they have abandoned their traditional homes to begin building a large nest.

ORGANIC SUBSTITUTES

Simple tools and weapons can be grown rather than made. A grown sword might look like the sharpened claw of a massive beast, a grown shield might look like an animal's shell, and a grown saw might resemble the serrated tooth of a huge scavenger. But such things are as useful and sturdy as more conventional items, if not more so.

Biological "machines" can replace more conventional ones. Rather than a slugspitter, a character could wield a creature that grows

and projects spines from its back. A pair of nightvision goggles might instead be an insectlike thing that perches on someone's forehead and lowers its wings over her eyes, granting her the ability to see in the dark. Any device can be organic. It doesn't even need a biological appearance. Something that appears to be metal or synth might actually be a superhard secretion or a smooth shell. Certain inorganic substances can be replicated by advanced biotechnology as well. Living steel, for example, is as strong as or stronger than metal but can move and grow like flesh. Biosynth and organic crystals are also known. Imagine the surprise when an explorer realizes that the detonation or ray projector that he has found is actually a living thing.

Weapons Pod: As a defensive measure, Aeon Priests have grown a large pod that looks a bit like a large insect nest outside the entrance to their clave. If someone approaches the entrance without giving the proper passphrase, the pod launches poisoned quills and exploding nodules, all grown inside itself. The pod also begins to shriek an alarm to warn the priests of intruders.

CHEMISTRY

Bubbling liquid in clear backlit tubes. The air thick with something so potent it burns your nose and throat. Bottles of powders, liquids, and pills crowding cramped shelves. Somewhere, something drips. Somewhere else, a blue flame burns, bringing the liquid in a steel canister to a boil.

In many ways, the simplest, most straightforward type of numenera is the injector, the pill, or the vial of liquid that has some beneficial property to the imbiber. Pop a pill and instantly feel better as you regain energy. Inject yourself in the arm with something and feel stronger or faster for a while. Most chemicals of this sort are temporary, one-use items. Thus, there are far more chemical cyphers than chemical artifacts.

Not all pills and injections are strictly chemical. Some involve engineered viruses or nanotechnology. But the bulk of them are simply drugs or chemical admixtures. This is interesting primarily in that it is a form of the numenera most easily replicated by Ninth World dabblers and experimenters. For example, it's not uncommon for a clave of Aeon Priests to know how to create a handful of drugs and concoctions, which have all manner of strange results. Some of these

Slugspitter, page 311

Nightvision goggles, page 308

"Some of my contemporaries insist on calling it alchemy. Eh, whatever. Just don't mix the blue powder with the red liquid. Never did grow that eyebrow back. At least not naturally." ~Sir Arthour

Search Term: *DNA data storage*

are minor—blemish removers, tooth polishers, and the like—but some can be quite potent. Indeed, there are villages in the Beyond where all the inhabitants live to be 250 years old thanks to all the drugs and chemicals available from their ingenious Aeon Priests. In other villages, similar chemical discoveries (and manufacturing) have made all the people highly resistant to burns (+5 to Armor against fire and heat), able to learn specific new skills at a fantastic rate (one dose grants training in a specific skill), or capable of breathing underwater.

On the one hand, a pill or injection is the quintessential cypher—single use, easy to understand, and easy to carry and use. On the other hand, they're unlike most other cyphers. Many types of cyphers require power of some sort, but chemical-based cyphers do not. That means that they are immune to effects that drain or negate the power in another item (you can't absorb the power out of a pill).

Pain Free: A large quantity of a drug is discovered and brought to a nearby city. The drug seems to alleviate all pain and is highly sought after. However, it slowly deadens nerve endings altogether, and those who use it soon have no sense of touch at all. Plus, the drug is quite addicting, and nefarious elements are attempting to replicate its effects. Some are hucksters who want to sell this "pain medicine" to dupes, while others want to get people hooked on it and then offer it for sale at whatever price they choose.

Slickstick: A chemical compound is found in a barrel. It possesses an odd quality in that it is extremely slick, except to itself. When applied to a surface, at first touch it is very slippery. An object is almost impossible to hold onto. A floor is extremely difficult to walk across. (These are difficulty 6 Speed tasks.) However, if the same person tries again (with a tiny bit of residue on him from the first time), the substance becomes a powerful adhesive. Prying oneself away from the coated surface is a difficulty 5 Might task, and it inflicts 2 points of damage that ignores Armor.

Eric Lofgren

Iron Wind, page 135

Search Terms:
artificial spider silk, molecular superglue, quantum spin liquid, smart fluid

Because pills and injectors are so simple and have no stored energies, some GMs might be tempted to make them exempt from the character limits for carrying cyphers. That's fine if that level of scientific verisimilitude is important, but who can say how some extremely advanced chemical compounds might act in the presence of other devices with their own strange radiations? Perhaps it's not so far-fetched to include pills and injectors in the cypher limit after all.

CHEMICAL WEAPONS

Not all chemicals are helpful drugs in pill or injection form. Some are weaponized—poisons, acids, or other toxic substances. These can come in the form of detonations, chemical sprayers, or canisters of gas, as well as injectors, pills, or liquids. Injectors for chemical weapons of this nature are often hidden in rings, the pommels of swords, or other surreptitious places.

The Ever-Changing Mist: A cloud of chemicals is released from an ancient, unknown storage facility. Carried by the winds, this complex cocktail of chemicals interacts with living creatures in a variety of seemingly random ways. Almost like a minor version of the Iron Wind, this cloud is sometimes a boon and sometimes a bane, healing, hurting, and sometimes wildly mutating every living thing it comes across.

CHEMICAL POWER

Rarely, a device—usually a cypher—can be powered by chemicals rather than by some other, more sophisticated sort of energy. Imagine a ray projector that produces a harmful ray when two or more chemicals are activated in its interior. Most of the time, this nuance isn't particularly important. Many characters won't even notice the difference. However, certain effects and devices disrupt or drain power from other items. A chemically powered cypher is likely to be immune to such things.

MATTER

Metal flows like liquid. Synth stretches and grows. Liquid takes on a form and motion, like a thing alive. Crystals glow with different colors as they are arranged in different formations.

Material science has to do with the various properties of any number of materials. Just as the ancients wielded energies that confound people today, they shaped and reshaped matter in ways that seem mysterious and magical to anyone who tries to understand. With their knowledge, the people of the prior ages made almost indestructible metals, crystals that store and control vast energy and information, synth that moves like flesh, liquid that holds its shape like a solid while remaining fluid, and even greater wonders. The very fact that objects from prior worlds are still around proves the value of this science. The most recent of these ancient civilizations might have disappeared as much as a million years ago or more, yet the things they made remain.

METAL

The most obvious thing about numenera metal is its durability and strength. It's not at all out of line to rate the shell of an ancient structure or craft as level 10. In fact, it's not out of line to simply state that it is utterly and unequivocally indestructible.

But superscience can do more with metal than simply make it tough. Transparent metal, superlight metal (almost lighter than air), and metal as flexible as soft cloth are all possible. Explorers might find metal that exists in a foamlike state, that is in a liquid state at room temperature, or that alternates between being flexible and firm (or firm and brittle) depending on conditions. For example, a metal's qualities might change when exposed to different magnetic fields (or other radiations). With the flick of a switch in its handle, a metal whip might become a hard pole. Alternatively, a metal's qualities can change based on what is interacting with it. A metal can go from pliable (to the point of being almost fluid) to utterly rigid upon impact. Thus, a suit of metal clothing might suddenly harden into light adamant armor when struck.

LIQUID

A remarkable interaction of special fluids and energy fields creates liquid devices, tools, and weapons. A spurt of liquid shoots from a wrist-mounted container, and a solid shield appears to protect you. A bit of liquid comes out of a small, pommel-like handle and hardens into a razor-thin, ultrasharp knife at the end. Liquid walls, liquid bridges, liquid rope, liquid armor—these are all possible. The advantage, of course, is that a small cylinder of special fluid is far easier to carry than the ladder that it can turn into.

Some smart fluid technology is so advanced that the liquid can be formed into any desired shape. Most comes in a predetermined size

For comparison, very, very few of our own 21st-century creations would still be around in a million years— mostly just a few types of plastic.

Search Terms:
graphene aerogel, mu-metal, titanium foam, aluminum bubble wrap, programmable matter, fullerene molecules

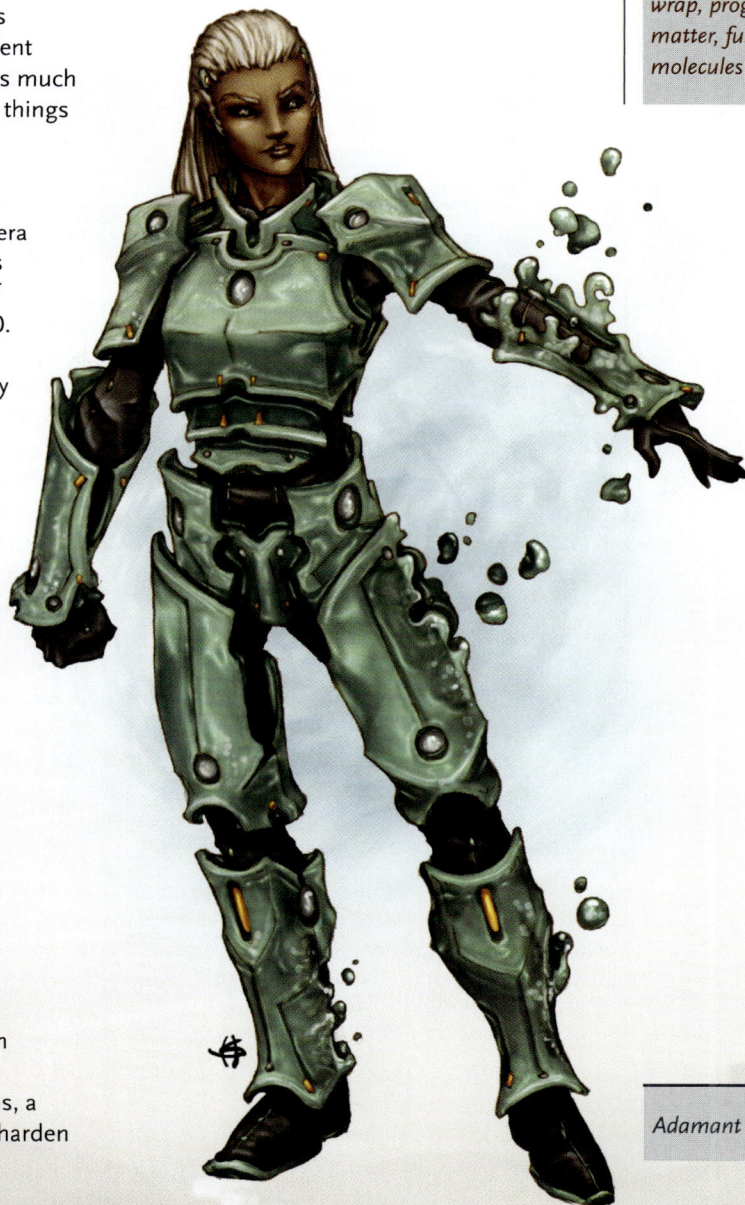

Adamant silk, page 77

and shape, usually with a fairly straightforward application. However, even then—because it's fluid—its shape can adapt. So liquid armor forms snugly around any wearer, a liquid wall conforms to the space it can occupy, and so on.

Most of the time, smart fluid creations are simple—no moving parts—and temporary. Neither of these truths is absolute, however.

CHANGING MATTER

Sometimes, matter can be made to shift and change as needed, perhaps in a predetermined pattern. For example, a numenera item might look like a silver sphere. But if one approaches it without a predetermined brain wave pattern, the metal sphere transforms into a whirling blade or a chemical bomb.

Certain types of processes can take ordinary matter and make it extraordinary. A fine molecular spray can render an object that appears to be flammable (cloth, for example) almost entirely heat resistant. Another can make wood as hard as steel, or steel as light as a feather.

The Doors of Mist: An entire structure in the middle of a town appears to be made of solid greenish stone with no doors or windows. However, the right notes played on a flute or lyre can make portions of the wall transform into gas for a time, allowing someone to pass through as if it were a veiled doorway.

The Reactive Sculpture: An abstract metal sculpture rises high into the air in the wilderness. Like a flower, the sculpture reacts to the appearance, movement, and setting of the sun, changing shape and position as it moves across the sky. That's only the beginning, however. Portions of the mass of unknown metal take on the features of any creature that approaches, moving as the creature does (although the sculpture as a whole does not move from where it rests).

CRYSTALS

At some point in the past, a civilization made use of crystals as the basis for an entire system of technology. These crystals store energy and information with great efficiency and thus can produce a variety of effects. Most of the time, crystal devices are simple—a set amount of stored energy is released in a specific fashion. More complex crystal devices likely involve a collection of different crystals. Rather than pushing buttons or flipping switches, the device is activated and controlled simply by arranging the crystals in different patterns.

It's likely that the prior world that developed an array of technology based solely on crystals was a particularly alien one.

Crystal Harvesting: Deep underground, a cave glistens with growing crystals. However, they are not entirely natural. Instead, they grow based on precise specifications of someone from the ancient past. This means that these crystalline structures already hold the capacity to become potentially useful or dangerous numenera devices, if the one who discovers them can determine how to infuse them with power.

Crystal Icons: Within an ancient ruin, pedestals hold tall crystals engraved with symbols. Likewise, the walls of the place glisten with symbols carved into them and inlaid with crystal. These symbols and icons are not merely decor. They have a variety of functions, some of which are defensive, such as projecting protective force walls and blasting intruders with rays. Other crystals have functions that may not have been defensive originally, but that still bring mayhem and weirdness to explorers entering the ruin. For example, intruders may find that the crystals modify their equipment, their bodies, and even their minds in strange ways.

BIZARRE MATTER

Most Ninth World scholars understand that some aspects of the world cannot be seen with the naked eye. An even passing familiarity with a nano's esoteries suggests that. These scholars also understand that the matter that can be seen can be broken down into very tiny units, grasping the idea of what a 21st-century scientist would call molecules and atomic structure. The rarest among them knows that some particles of matter are far stranger than the simple things that make up the air around them and the ground at their feet. Use of these particles can warp time and space, cause matter to move out of phase, or react in different ways to things like psychic abilities. For example, strange particles can react in interesting ways to telekinesis, making it easier to use, resisting it, or setting up varied reactions. In an ancient structure where the builders had access to telepathy and telekinesis, certain walls might show special

messages, turn transparent, or phase away with the right telepathic or telekinetic key. However, the wrong application of psychic power might trigger a trap that targets the psionic intruder.

Other types of bizarre matter interact with energy in various ways. In fact, some of them begin to blur the lines between matter and energy. For example, one material might store almost limitless amounts of energy within its own structural lattice, while another remains utterly immune to almost every sort of energy.

NANOTECHNOLOGY

Nothing. Then, as if moved by invisible hands, a metal box slides across the floor. It turns to mist and then reforms as a leather bag filled with gemstones. Someone in the room whispers, "sorcery."

By its very nature, nanotechnology represents the creation and use of "devices" so small that they cannot be perceived by most methods available to Ninth Worlders. It's no wonder that most people consider it to be the work of ghosts or magic. Nanites are molecule-sized machines. Each has a very limited function, but together—a cloud of trillions of them, for example—they can accomplish almost anything that can be imagined. First and foremost, nanotech can move, reshape, and build matter on the molecular level. That means the air can be transformed into a glass vase, that vase can be shattered, and the pieces can be reassembled and fused—all by nanites, and all in just a few seconds.

If atoms and molecules are the building blocks of matter, nanotechnology is the way to change matter on its most fundamental levels. As the alchemist dreams, it can transform lead into gold. Or it can turn steel into mist, or turn a box of hammers into a thick, juicy steak. The real truth is that most of the applications of nanotechnology in the Ninth World (especially the esoteries of the nanos) don't even scratch the surface of what is possible. Representing potentially complete control over matter and energy, they can explain almost any strange occurrence the GM wants to introduce (but in such a case, they should be used carefully and sparingly).

The Iron Wind is a good example of the dangers of such godlike power. It is nanotechnology gone awry, and it is one of the greatest threats to life in the Ninth World.

Search Terms:
holographic data storage, condensed matter physics, tachyonic antitelephone

Iron Wind, page 135

Bonding Surface: A patch of ground adheres instantly and powerfully to anything that touches it, trapping wind-borne debris, animals, and even people that realize too late where they are walking. Just as quickly, the surface begins breaking down the molecular bonds of the matter that it is holding fast. Living creatures move one step down the damage track per round while trapped, although a successful Might defense roll will stave off this effect for one round.

TRANSDIMENSIONAL TECHNOLOGY

A rent in the air opened as if torn wide by unseen claws. The space hidden between the spaces well known. Colors and shapes unknown. Air around the rent bubbling like the spittle of a madman. A single tentacle reaching through, gently exploring.

At least some of the inhabitants of the prior worlds discovered and explored other universes—realms beyond our own, dimensions above those we can perceive, and other realities that we can barely comprehend. In so doing, they didn't just challenge the

Exists Partially Out of Phase, page 60

fundamental laws of physics—they went beyond to places where our physics have no meaning. And some of the doorways are still open. Doorways that work both ways.

Transdimensional numenera involves more than just gateways to other universes. By accessing higher states of being, this technology creates new ways for matter and energy to interact in our own reality. Transdimensional technology bypasses physics by going around it. For example, a transdimensional device might be able to deliver objects through a warp in space, moving hundreds or thousands (or quadrillions) of miles instantaneously.

PHASING

By using technology that changes the way some discrete amount of matter—such as a person—interfaces with the rest of the universe, that matter can pass through other matter. There may simply be two phase states: normal and "out of phase." On the other hand, there may in fact be many phase states, and only one is able to interface directly with physical matter. Typically, when a creature or object is out of phase, it is more difficult to see and hear, but it is not invisible or silent. However, this can vary with the means by which the creature or object moved out of phase, or perhaps with the differing phase states.

Phase Doors: A tower in the wilderness has no visible doors at all, inside or out, and every room appears to be entirely sealed and without exits. Stairs go up to solid ceilings. The truth, however, is that a section of the walls can be knocked out of phase temporarily, allowing matter to pass through them. Finding the means to activate a phase door can sometimes be very tricky and involves looking for nearly invisible switches, sometimes activated in specific sequences.

Phase Weapons: Weapons sometimes have a precise control over their phase, allowing, for example, a projectile to pass through a wall to strike a target on the other side, phasing out and back again in fractions of a second. Likewise, a sword blade could pass through armor and even a portion of a creature while out of phase, and then materialize (coming back into normal phase) inside the foe's guts. Such a weapon might even be of use against foes who are out of phase, essentially doing the opposite of their normal function by moving out of phase just as they penetrate the target, so as to be in sync with the target's phase.

EXTRADIMENSIONAL SPACES

Extradimensional spaces are spaces that exist where space should not be. A room bigger on the inside than the outside. A pocket that holds far more than its size would suggest. A corridor 15 feet (5 m) long that requires a minute and a half to traverse. These spaces are sometimes called "no rooms" or pocket dimensions. Obviously, they are useful for storage purposes, but they also create secret places, often ones that no one would even think to look for. Due to the warping of space involved, extradimensional spaces are sometimes out of reach of things like scans, teleportation, or other effects (this varies from one extradimensional space to another).

And these spaces have other uses as well. Imagine a warping of space but only in one direction, so that there is more distance to traverse going north to south than south to north on the same path. Defensively, an enemy would take longer to reach where they are going than their opponents would. If the space were dramatically altered, enemy ranged weapons could not reach the defenses, while the defenders' weapons could reach the attackers.

However, in the same way that warping can create more space, it can also create less space between two points than perception or logic would indicate, resulting in distances that take less time or even literally no time to cross. This kind of space warp is useful for communication across vast distances (distances that are mostly beyond the concern of Ninth World humans), but it primarily exists for instantaneous transport or travel. For example, this is how most teleportation devices work, although other methods are used as well.

Warped Space: Wandering through the wilderness, explorers discover an ancient doorway set into a hilltop. They pass through and come out the door they thought they went in, but now there are two doorways. Going in one of these means instantly coming out the other. What happened is that entering the initial door took them into an extradimensional space inside the hill so large that it appeared they emerged outside again. This space has a similar hill within it, but this new hill has two doors. These doors are connected by a space warp that

allows travelers to pass through one and out the other. Beyond the hill, the pocket dimension is miles of wilderness, with no animal life except that which might have wandered in like the explorers did. Reaching one end of the pocket merely shifts the traveler around to the other end, so if she walks long enough, she ends up where she started—by the hill with the doors.

The only way to escape the pocket dimension is to burrow into the hill, which, after a foot or so of digging, brings the digger through to the outside of the original hill. The hole repairs itself in just a few rounds, returning the hill to normal.

OTHER UNIVERSES

Most sages and scholars refer to other universes as other dimensions, which is probably technically inaccurate. Creatures from other universes are referred to as ultraterrestrials.

The Bizarre Dimensions: Although the prior worlds are incomprehensible, many transdimensional worlds are even stranger. The inhabitants of these places aren't just not human—they might not even be composed of matter or energy as we understand them. Things like mass, direction, or temperature might have no meaning there. Traveling to such a place might destroy the mind of the sojourner (requiring a Might defense roll upon arrival and perhaps more rolls as time passes and the different physics and nature eat away at the context of his consciousness).

The Parallel Universes: Not nearly as strange as some ultraterrestrial worlds, a parallel Earth can be just as disconcerting, for while it is like the Ninth World that we know and understand, it can be vastly different. In one universe, the Earth was never saved from the growing luminosity of the sun millions of years ago, leaving it a world capable of barely supporting microbial life and nothing more— no plants or animals. It's simply too hot and too bright this close to the oppressive sun in the sky.

In another parallel universe, one of the prior worlds still flourishes, making the Earth unrecognizable to Ninth World travelers. In fact, they probably wouldn't understand that what they have found is a version of their own world.

In yet another parallel, the Ninth World flourishes as expected. In fact, travelers might not realize that they are not home. But as time passes, the differences begin to make themselves known. People who are dead are not dead, and vice versa. Buildings in the travelers' city are different or located in different places.

THE DATASPHERE

Glass screens alive with moving lights, forming symbols and pictures that have no meaning. Tubes thrumming. Wires connected to temples and foreheads. Hands resting on synth panels. Voices and images seeping into awareness. Long-buried mechanisms seething with tidal waves of knowledge.

The Earth is wrapped in information, like an invisible blanket that most people don't even know exists. In the past, one or more civilizations created a vast data network that stored enormous amounts of information and allowed instant communication across the world. At least some of this network (or networks) still exists, stored and transmitted in secret stations or in constructs orbiting high above the Earth. The problem is accessing it, which requires the knowledge and understanding that it exists, as well as the ability and tools to tap into it.

Glimmers are examples of the datasphere accessing people, rather than the other way around. At least a part of the datasphere, as it exists now, can interact directly with a biological mind, with no need for a mechanical interface. Again, the problem is awareness and understanding. But sometimes, the datasphere—for mysterious reasons, some of which may be entirely accidental—contacts the person's mind.

SAMPLE GLIMMERS

- Colors flash. A three-fingered hand made of light caresses your face. Three voices speak at once, each clearly in a different language, yet each layered as if they complement each other like instruments in an orchestra. You get the general impression that you should go north in three hours' time.

- An eye made of smaller eyes looks at you, and you can tell that it sees both your past and your future, but perhaps not your present. You feel numbing cold, and a steady stream of symbols and lines that seem meaningless cascade all around you. Even if you could decipher them, you would need eyes all around your head to see them all.

- You get an overwhelming urge to eat toasted bread, severely burnt, with lots of oregano. You've never tasted oregano before and have no idea what it is or where it comes from.

- You grow to enormous size and can see for miles around, but the landscape in the distance is not the one you know to be there (at least, not in the present).

- Your body is suddenly covered with worms, all of which explain to you in unison how to build a machine that will produce tools specifically designed for a purpose you cannot begin to comprehend.

USING THE DATASPHERE

Accessing the datasphere usually requires specific devices, which either allow for some kind of manual input (such as asking a question verbally or inputting data on a touchscreen) or have a more direct mental interface. Many of these are impossible to use without access to languages that no one alive remembers, but some are sophisticated enough to go beyond language or operate on a basis of pure thought.

Still, unless the device allows for a direct question, navigating through the oceans of information can be difficult. Doing so would require multiple difficult Intellect-based tasks, depending on the information sought.

The datasphere is both alien and ancient. It is likely incomplete, disjointed, and damaged after all this time. It may or may not be updating its information, although the answer most likely is neither straightforward nor simple. Satellites and other machines tied into the network probably still track global positions and may even take in new input on their own. But this data is about a world that has changed over millions of years, as interpreted by alien devices made aeons earlier by civilizations now dead. In other words, the datasphere might have information about such modern things as—for example—the Jagged Dream, the city of Qi, or the rituals of a small religion in the Beyond, or it might not. And even if it does, that information would likely be incomplete and at least somewhat misunderstood and full of errors.

The datasphere can be used as a communication medium for two people who have direct access to it. Instantaneous communication is possible, using not only

It is possible that glimmers come from nanobot contamination. A living creature absorbs, inhales, or ingests nanites that have some kind of connection to the datasphere, which then manifests as a glimmer in that creature's mind.

The Jagged Dream, page 224

Qi, page 148

The Beyond, page 174

words but all senses. Messages can also be left for those that know how to find and access them.

The datasphere can be used in a more limited fashion as well. For example, an ancient complex might have its own individual datasphere that links all of its devices, sensors, defenses, thinking machines, and other numenera. Accessing this limited datasphere would be very similar to accessing the larger datasphere, and in fact it might be possible from within the worldwide datasphere (and thus from thousands of miles away from said complex). Those who succeed at this difficult task could activate, deactivate, or control the systems within the complex. However, the limited datasphere might have its own defenses that could result in lost access or direct Intellect damage.

ENTERING THE DATASPHERE

The datasphere is not simply the Internet, to use a 21st-century term. It exists on far more levels and represents far more senses, including taste, touch, smell, hearing, spatial awareness, and very likely other senses that Ninth World humans don't possess. In a way, fully accessing the datasphere might be like

entering a universe all its own, with virtual constructs, icons, and representations taking the place of real matter or energy. This is a "place" with its own laws that have nothing to do with the physical world.

Entire exploratory scenarios could take place within the datasphere itself. Such adventures would involve traveling across surreal landscapes—virtual constructs made by inhuman minds from 100 million years in the past. Almost anything is possible except that which is easily comprehended. The object of such a quest would very likely be finding information that is lost in a maze of other data and, depending on the information, might be guarded by defensive constructs that attack the will, intellect, and virtual existence (in the datasphere) of any intruders.

The journey would be akin to an out-of-body experience. The physical bodies of the explorers would not—could not—enter the datasphere. However, suffering Intellect damage there is as real as suffering it in the real world, and like any kind of damage, it can carry over to the characters' other stat Pools until they are both virtually and physically dead.

It may be useful to remember that the datasphere is a matrix of potentially many information networks, some of which are entirely incompatible and inaccessible from each other.

CHAPTER 2

CYPHERS

Cyphers, page 278

Creating new cyphers, page 317

Ray emitter, page 82
Energy siphon, page 51
Biometric reference, page 35

There are two kinds of cyphers:

Anoetic cyphers are easy to use—just pop a pill, push a button, pull a trigger, and so on. Anyone can do it.

Occultic cyphers are rarer, more complicated, and more dangerous. They are devices with multiple buttons, switches, knobs, keypads, touchscreen controls, wires, and so on. They have many different settings, but only one produces an effect. Occultic cyphers count as two cyphers for the purpose of determining how many a PC can carry and use at one time.

Cyphers are the most common form of the numenera recovered from ancient ruins by explorers. Some are clearly ancient devices that—due to the fantastic materials and construction techniques—still function (at least one more time). Most, however, are bits torn from larger devices by those with an eye for such things. With a few tweaks and the addition of a few other small pieces scavenged from the world, a crystal-tipped rod from the inner workings of a large control panel can be used as a ray emitter or an energy siphon.

Cyphers are the backbone of Numenera, which is why the system behind the game is sometimes called the Cypher System. Cyphers enable PCs to get their hands on incredible powers, but only for a moment, so no single ability will ever throw the game out of whack. They also give the GM the ability to play a small role in determining what a character can and can't do. Most of all, however, since cyphers are dangerous to hoard, they provide an ever-changing variety to a character's available abilities.

All cyphers have a level. Sometimes the level suggests the amount of time the cypher works. Other times, it relates to the amount of damage or healing provided.

They also have different forms based on three types: internal, wearable, and usable. Internal cyphers are things you ingest or inject. Wearable cyphers are articles of clothing, jewelry, or other things you wear on your physical body. Usable cyphers are basically anything else.

Most cyphers can exist in more than one form, but all forms work the same way. For example, a biometric reference can be found in the form of a pill, an ingestible liquid, a temporary tattoo, an amulet, a headband, a crystal, or a small handheld device. But they all provide the user with the same effect. GMs can choose a form for flavor or roll randomly. If a cypher form is not listed, the cypher only rarely comes in that form. However, nothing is impossible. If the GM wants a pill that allows anyone swallowing it to

teleport, then it exists.

For more information on finding, identifying, and using cyphers, as well as—perhaps most important of all—the dangers involved with hoarding cyphers, see chapter 18 of the Numenera corebook.

In this section, you'll find four hundred new cyphers for your game. Added to the almost one hundred cyphers in the Numenera corebook, and considering that many of them come in many different forms, with different variations on their effects, you have far more cyphers than you'll ever need in your campaign. With so many interesting choices, however, you'll want to incorporate them all.

GM INTRUSIONS: THE MALFUNCTION

Not all GM intrusions, even those triggered by a roll of 1 on the die, should be fumbles or malfunctions. A GM intrusion can be anything that potentially changes the course of the action or the storyline. However, when the intrusion involves the numenera, sometimes a malfunction is in order. Here are some suggestions:

- The device triggers its effect on an unintended target.
- The device's effect is reversed, if possible. A restorative effect becomes damaging. An attack becomes something that aids or heals.
- The device's effect is triggered in an unexpected or undesirable way. The user is not in control of the device. A belt that grants the ability to hover sends the wearer careening off in a random direction, probably to crash into a wall or the floor. A ray emitter fires wildly or explodes. An injector sprays its contents into the user's eye, causing pain and temporary blindness.
- The device explodes, inflicting damage equal to its level on all within immediate range.
- The device reaches out telepathically and obeys the commands of another creature within long range instead of the commands of the user.
- The device inexplicably sprouts metallic, spiderlike legs and scurries away, never to be seen again.
- The device negates gravity in immediate range for one round.
- The device releases a pulse that stuns everyone in immediate range for one round, during which they can take no action.
- Energy feeds back into the user, who suffers damage equal to the device's level.
- The device and 1d6 other nearby devices are permanently depowered.
- The device loses all power, but another device within long range gains extra power.
- A spatial warp is created, leading to a place very far away (or another universe entirely). It remains open for only a few rounds.
- The device gains intelligence and telepathic abilities and wishes to negotiate with the user in order to activate.
- All within immediate range are filled with irrational fear for one round and flee at top speed.
- The device fuses with one or two other devices in the user's possession and becomes an entirely new artifact.

CYPHER LISTS

To choose cyphers at random, first roll a d20 to figure out which table you should roll on.

01–04	Cypher List A
05–08	Cypher List B
09–12	Cypher List C
13–16	Cypher List D
17–20	Cypher List E

* Items marked with an asterisk are from the Numenera corebook.

CYPHER LIST A

01 Access glasses
02 Access token
03 Adamant foam
04 Adhesion clamps*
05 Airfins
06 Alarm worm
07 Amplification parasite
08 Analysis daemon
09 Analysis scanner
10 Anchor stone
11 Antipathy field emitter
12 Antivenom*
13 Anxiety engine
14 Armor patch
15 Artificial leech
16 Atmospheric hyperskin
17 Attractor*
18 Awareness enhancer
19 Banishing nodule*
20 Battle vapor
21 Beauty mask
22 Bezoar discharge
23 Biofeedback glove
24 Biological transpiercer
25 Biometric reference
26 Biomorph
27 Blinking nodule*
28 Blood boiler
29 Blood magnet
30 Bloom (fireflower)
31 Bloom (serpent)
32 Bloom (spore)
33 Blue crystal
34 Body enhancer

35 Bone dress
36 Brain lightning
37 Breather symbiote
38 Buoyancy
39 Burrowing bubble
40 Butterfly drone
41 Cable projector
42 Camouflage screen
43 Camouflage spray
44 Catholicon*
45 Catseye*
46 Caustic storm
47 Chemical factory*
48 Chitin colony
49 Cicerone
50 Clamp trap
51 Cleaner
52 Cloaking pin
53 Clone tank
54 Cloud seed
55 Cloudskimmer
56 Colorless grease
57 Communication disks
58 Complex fluid wall projector
59 Comprehension graft*
60 Concrete casting
61 Conflict advisor
62 Construction foam
63 Contingent Subroutine
64 Controlled blinking nodule*
65 Countermeasure (magnetic)
66 Countermeasure (membrane)
67 Countermeasure (Technological)

68 Crystal virus
69 Cyberflesh
70 Cypher replicator
71 Cypher seed
72 Data flood
73 Data merge
74 Data mine
75 Data spike
76 Data vault
77 Datasphere siphon*
78 Deadly mist
79 Death messenger
80 Deficiency detector
81 Demonsphere
82 Density nodule*
83 Deployer (atmospheric)
84 Deployer (hypersound)
85 Deployer (muscular)
86 Deployer (optical)
87 Desiccation bag
88 Detonation*
89 Detonation (coma)
90 Detonation (crystal)
91 Detonation (desiccating)*
92 Detonation (distress)
93 Detonation (electromagnetic)
94 Detonation (filament)
95 Detonation (flash)*
96 Detonation (flashfire)
97 Detonation (flesh warping)
98 Detonation (foam)
99 Detonation (gravity)*
00 Detonation (healing)

CYPHER LIST B

01	Detonation (living metal)	38	Electronic nose	78	Frigid wall projector*
02	Detonation (massive)*	39	Emoacoustic weapon	79	Fungal garden
03	Detonation (matter disruption)*	40	Energy module	80	Gas bomb*
04	Detonation (plant transformation)	41	Energy siphon	81	Gel suit
04	Detonation (plant transformation)	42	Energy token	82	Ghostly duplicate
05	Detonation (pressure)*	43	Eraser	83	Ghostly intruder
06	Detonation (singularity)*	44	Erosion ray	84	Ghostly veil
07	Detonation (smoke)	45	Essence transfer	85	Glass flame pellets
08	Detonation (sonic)*	46	Exalted vapor	86	Glass scorpion
09	Detonation (spatial warping)	47	Explosive nodule	87	Glowing tracker
09	Detonation (spatial warping)	48	Extra time	88	Goss
10	Detonation (spawn)*	49	Eye in the sky	89	Grasshopper
11	Detonation (stasis)	50	Eyebug	90	Gravity dampener
12	Detonation (suggestion)	51	Eyestalk graft	91	Gravity nodule
13	Detonation (tendril)	52	Fact finder	92	Gravity nullifier*
14	Detonation (web)*	53	Fallback clone	93	Gravity-nullifying spray*
15	Detonation delay	54	Fangs of the reaver	94	Ground orb
16	Detonation trigger	55	Faraway ear	95	Grow ray
17	Device enhancer	56	Fast hail	96	Growth harness
18	Dimensional sheath	57	Fertility barrier	97	Growth serum
19	Dimensional trap	58	Firebreather	98	Growth stimulator
20	Disintegration gel	59	Fireproofing spray*	99	Grub armor
21	Displacement cloak	60	Flame catcher	00	Gyre loop
22	Disrupting nodule*	61	Flame hand		
23	Dissonance cube	62	Flame-retardant wall*		
24	Distance activator	63	Flesh eater		
25	Distortion field emitter	64	Floating bubble		
26	Doomsday device	65	Flow		
27	Drastic propulsion	66	Flowstone		
28	Dreamachine	67	Fluttering recorder		
29	Dry water	68	Flying cap		
30	Duplicator	69	Foam limb		
31	Dynamic hourglass	70	Foam sprayer		
32	Eagleseye*	71	Fool killer		
33	Ear worm	72	Force cube projector*		
34	Echo crystal	73	Force nodule*		
35	Ecstasy glass	74	Force screen projector*		
36	Effulgent body	75	Force shield projector*		
37	Ejection nodule	76	Freeze inducer		
		77	Friction-reducing gel*		

CYPHER LIST C

01	Habiliment mirage
02	Hand of the conqueror
03	Hanging cocoon
04	Harassing companion
05	Head transference collar
06	Healing nodule
07	Health symbiote
08	Health viewer
09	Heartbeat lock
10	Heartburst
11	Heartlink
12	Heat nodule*
13	Heat sensor
14	Heat sheath
15	Heat stone
16	Heatvision lenses
17	Heliolithic halo
18	Helping hand
19	Hidden reviver
20	History tap
21	Homunculus

22	Hover disk
23	Hover module
24	Hunter/seeker*
25	Image caster
26	Image projector*
27	Indestructible oil
28	Inertia shield
29	Inferno wall projector*
30	Infiltrator*
31	Inflatable companion
32	Inflatable suit
33	Insanity mask
34	Instant boat
35	Instant companion
36	Instant guardian
37	Instant servant*
38	Instant shelter*
39	Instant shield
40	Instant weapon
41	Instant wings
42	Intellect enhancement*
43	Interaction advisor
44	Internal detector
45	Invisibility nodule*
46	Invulnerable mesh
47	Jolter
48	Jonah ice
49	Kinetic rod
50	Knowledge enhancement*
51	Leap belt
52	Lie eater
53	Life sensor
54	Light binder
55	Light flyer
56	Light shield
57	Light steed
58	Light writer
59	Lightning lance
60	Lightning wall projector*
61	Living solvent*
62	Living weaponmaster nodule

63	Lobal sheath
64	Lotus paste
65	Lutin (bioengineered insects)
66	Lutin (combos)
67	Lutin (engineered spores)
68	Lutin (light drops)
69	Lutin (metal shrapnel)
70	Lutin (nanites)
71	Machine control implant*
72	Magnetic attack drill*
73	Magnetic boots
74	Magnetic ink
75	Magnetic master*
76	Magnetic shield*
77	Magnetic winch
78	Malady maker
79	Mass destructor
80	Mass nodule
81	Matter converter
82	Memory cube
83	Memory dust
84	Memory gel
85	Memory lenses*
86	Mental coupling
87	Mental director
88	Mental scrambler*
89	Mental thieves
90	Message capsule
91	Message detonation
92	Metal death*
93	Metal patch
94	Metamagnetizer
95	Mind control implant
96	Mind killer
97	Mind module
98	Mind oculus
99	Mind sled
00	Mini gate

CYPHER LIST D

01	Miniaturized weapon	42	Pleasure center	82	Repair unit*
02	Mist animator	43	Poison (emotion)*	83	Reproductive bud
03	Mist energizer	44	Poison (explosive)*	84	Repulsion field
04	Mist producer	45	Poison (mind-controlling)*	85	Reset
05	Momentum dampener	46	Poison (mind-disrupting)*	86	Retaliation nodule*
06	Monoblade*	47	Portable biolab	87	Revealer dart
07	Mood patch	48	Portable steed	88	Reviver
08	Motion activator	49	Portable vortex	89	Root spike
09	Motion sensor*	50	Portal ring	90	Rynrad skin
10	Muscle cart	51	Power siphon	91	Sanity assassin
11	Mystery box	52	Prismatic field projector	92	Screaming madness
12	Navigator daemon	53	Projectile module (homing)	93	Second sight symbiote
13	Nectar dispenser	54	Projectile module (mind-blasting)	94	Secret finder
14	Needle sphere			95	Secret pocket
15	Needleburst	55	Projectile module (poison)	96	Security clamp
16	Neuron disruptor	56	Projectile module (teleport)	97	See you goggles
17	Nevermind	57	Psychic communiqué*	98	Seed boat
18	Numbing oil	58	Psychic focus	99	Seed of knowledge
19	Numenera analyzer	59	Purgspitter	00	Sense record
20	Numenera net	60	Purity		
21	One perfect cut	61	Pushpull beam		
22	Orbital armor	62	Pyrolytic pulser		
23	Orbital launcher	63	Quadraturin		
24	Organ patch	64	Radiant web		
25	Ostracized vapor	65	Ranged protector		
26	Overwatch defender	66	Ranged retaliator		
27	Overwatch slayer	67	Ray emitter*		
28	Pain inverter	68	Ray emitter (molecular rearrangement)		
29	Panoramic capture ball				
30	Parous cypher ball	69	Ray emitter (numbing)*		
31	Parous oddity box	70	Ray emitter (paralysis)*		
32	Perma-damp	71	Reality spike*		
33	Permanent handle	72	Reanimator		
34	Personal environment field*	73	Regrow		
35	Phase changer*	74	Rejuvenating shield		
36	Phase disruptor*	75	Rejuvenation field		
37	Photon igniter	76-77	Rejuvenator*		
38	Photonic fabricator	78	Remake		
39	Photonic hand	79	Remote scarificator		
40	Photonic smasher	80	Remote sensorium		
41	Piezoelectric engine	81	Remote viewer*		

CYPHER LIST E

01	Sensory disruptor	40	Stone guts	76	Transposer
02	Sexual alteration device	41	Stone melt	77	True speak
03	Shadow net	42	Store-all	78	Truth inducer
04	Sheen*	43	Strength boost*	79	Variable tool
05	Shock nodule*	44	Stronghold	80	Verdant nectar
06	Shocker*	45	Subdual field*	81	Visage changer*
07	Shrink ray	46	Summoning staff	82	Vision subjugator
08	Shudder stones	47	Swarm herder	83	Visual displacement device*
09	Sidestep portal	48	Sweeping glove	84	Vocal changer
10	Signal detector	49	Synth corroder	85	Vocal translator*
11	Skill boost*	50	Talio's compass	86	Volcanic heart
12	Sleep inducer*	51	Targeting oculus	87	War mites
13	Sleep watch	52	Task drone	88	Warming pouch
14	Sleeper spray	53	Telepathy implant*	89	Warmth projector*
15	Smart bugs	54	Teleport seal	90	Water breather*
16	Snake eye	55	Teleport trap	91	Water repellant plates
17	Snake in the grass	56	Teleporter (bounder)*	92	Water weapon
18	Snow lens	57	Teleporter (mass)	93	Way back
19	Solar reviver	58	Teleporter (traveler)*	94	Weaver drone
20	Solid light gloves	59	Temporal sheath	95	Wing symbiote
21	Solid light retribution	60	Temporal viewer*	96	Wish disk
22	Sonic hole*	61	Tendril gloves	97	Witless powder
23	Sound amplifier	62	Tether	98	Wrist launcher
24	Sound dampener*	63	Third man	99	X-ray extractor
25	Sparkle	64	Three-part alarm	00	X-Ray viewer*
26	Spatial distorter	65	Time auger		
27	Spatial warp*	66	Time capsule		
28	Speed boost*	67	Time delay		
29	Speed heal	68	Time dilation nodule (defensive)*		
30	Spike balls				
31	Spine spheres	69	Time dilation nodule (offensive)*		
32	Standstill				
33	Stasis field emitter	70	Tracer*		
34	Stealthy serpent	71	Tranquility pod		
35	Steel sentinel	72	Transdimensional gate		
36	Still field	73	Transference beam		
37-38	Stim*	74	Transformation torque		
39	Stone form	75	Transient inscriber		

Access Glasses

Level: 1d6 + 1
Wearable: Goggles plus gloves or rings
Effect: The user can see through up to half an inch of solid material and can pass his hands and anything his hands are holding through that solid matter. Once the area to be looked and passed through is chosen—about 18 inches by 18 inches (46 cm by 46 cm)—a new area cannot be chosen. However, the effect lasts for an hour.

Access Token

Level: 1d6
Wearable: Gloves, ring, false fingernail
Usable: Tiny metal device
Effect: Automatically unlocks one locked door or container within short range.

Adamant Foam

Level: 1d6 + 1
Usable: Small spray canister
Effect: The foam in this canister is extraordinarily light—almost weightless, lighter than a soap bubble—and virtually invisible. It's possible, in fact, to have this foam in your hand and not even realize it. And yet the foam, which dries on contact with the air, is superstrong. While pliable, it's as unbreakable as steel mesh. The canister has enough foam to coat an area 6 feet by 6 feet (2 m by 2 m) with a thin layer.

Although this foam has many uses, if sprayed on a living target, that target has +2 to Armor.

Adamant foam disintegrates after 28 hours.

Airfins

Level: 1d6
Wearable: Long gloves with forearm fins
Effect: Through gravity manipulation, the wearer can swim through the air as if it were water for one hour. Training or specialization in swimming aids in movement.

Alarm Worm

Level: 1d6
Usable: A bloated worm about 1 foot (0.3 m) long
Effect: Six minutes after activation, the worm inflates and excretes 1d6 wet, shuddering eggs at a place the user designates. After laying the eggs, the worm slithers back to the user and coils around one of his limbs, gripping tightly. For the next seven hours, whenever a creature approaches within 5 feet (2 m) of the eggs, the worm tightens and exudes a thick orange slime that reeks of rotten meat. When the effect ends, the worm relaxes its grip, falls, and expires messily.

Amplification Parasite

Level: 1d6 + 4
Internal: Living fish, beetle, or worm that must be ingested
Effect: Upon eating the parasite, the user chooses one stat and the GM chooses a different stat. The difficulty of any roll related to the user's chosen stat is reduced by two steps, and the difficulty of any roll involving the GM's chosen stat is increased by two steps. The parasite dies after 1d6 hours, and the effect ends when the user violently expels it from her body.

Analysis Daemon

Level: 1
Internal: Pill, ingestible liquid
Wearable: Temporary tattoo, amulet, headband, crystal worn on temple
Usable: Small handheld device, crystal
Effect: The user examines a cypher or an artifact and then taps into the datasphere. The user automatically identifies the device.

Although some people might use the access glasses to peer into a locked box and remove the contents, many have found that it's most useful to those who work with the numenera by allowing them to pass through the outer casing of a device to get at the workings inside. Doing so can offer up to two levels of assets in repairing or tinkering with a device with many internal components.

Analysis Scanner

Level: 1d10
Wearable: Bracelet
Usable: Handheld device
Effect: This device scans and records everything within short range for one round and then conveys the level and nature of all creatures, objects, and energy sources it scanned. This information can be accessed for 28 hours after the scan.

Anchor Stone

Level: 1d6
Usable: Lump of oddly shaped stone or metal
Effect: Submerging the device in water causes it to swell into a boulder about 5 feet (2 m) in diameter that weighs 500 pounds (227 kg).

Antipathy Field Emitter

Level: 1d6
Wearable: Mask, amulet worn around the neck, temporary tattoo
Usable: Small handheld device, node that can be attached to a weapon or armor
Effect: When activated, the device emits an invisible energy field for one hour. The field extends out to immediate range. Any living creature in the field other than the user experiences nausea and physical discomfort. The difficulty of all tasks performed by an affected creature is modified by one step to its detriment.

If you cobble together an antipathy field emitter and a duplicator (task difficulty 5), you create a cypher that forms a solid dome of stonelike matter with a 10-foot radius around the user. The dome is level 7 and disintegrates after 28 hours.

Duplicator, page 49

Anxiety Engine

Level: 1d6 + 2
Usable: White sphere with a glowing red orb
Effect: Fills a 5-foot (2 m) cube with a cloud of shadowy mist that lingers for one hour. The mist cannot be dispersed and remains despite the environmental conditions. Whenever a creature moves to within a short distance of the mist and can see it, the creature sees the cloud transform into something terrifying and horrific, its worst nightmares come to life. While the creature remains within a short distance of the cloud, the difficulty for all its tasks is modified by one step to its detriment.

Armor Patch

Level: 1d6
Wearable: Sewn-on patch, self-stick fabric, metallic swatch

Effect: After being applied to armor of any kind, this patch activates when firmly slapped, sending tiny nanowires through the armor's material to provide greater benefit.

01–50	Nanowires add a repellent layer to the material. Gain +1 to Armor against ranged, piercing, fire, or beam attacks for 28 hours.
51–75	Nanowires create greater flexibility in the material. Gain a +2 bonus to Speed defense rolls for 28 hours.
76–00	Nanowires create a tough outer coating to the material. Gain a +2 bonus to Might defense rolls for 28 hours.

Action to attach to armor. Activation can be combined with another action.

Artificial Leech

Level: 1d6
Usable: Handheld device
Effect: When used at the site of an infected or poisoned wound, the device draws out as much of the infection or poison as it can without injuring the surrounding tissue. The device restores a number of points equal to the cypher level to the user's Might Pool.

Atmospheric Hyperskin

Level: 1d6
Wearable: Adhesive patch of clear or flesh-colored substrate, temporary tattoo, sticky bundle of bare nanowires
Effect: When applied to any part of the body, nanowires penetrate the surface of the skin, allowing the user to sense a wider-than-normal range of atmospheric, geologic, and aqueous pressures, sensations, and vibrations. The user becomes trained in geology, biology, climatology, and perception for 28 hours.

Awareness Enhancer

Level: 1d6
Internal: Pill, injector
Wearable: Headband
Effect: For the next 28 hours, the user is more aware of his surroundings through telepathic and telekinetic means. He can feel objects move within short range and can mentally hear thinking beings within long range. This is an asset for all perception and initiative tasks.

Battle Vapor
Level: 1d6
Usable: Small metal canister
Effect: Releases faint red vapor that fills an area within long distance within two rounds. The vapor persists for ten minutes unless natural conditions (such as wind) suggest otherwise. All energy weapons used in the area inflict 2 additional points of damage as the vapor intensifies them.

Beauty Mask
Level: 1d6
Usable: Paste
Effect: Once applied to the user's face and left to dry for ten minutes, this paste removes blemishes and wrinkles. The user appears much younger and more attractive. This effect is permanent.

Bezoar Discharge
Level: 1d6
Usable: Explosive device (thrown, short range) or handheld projector (long range)
Effect: Explodes in an immediate radius, giving everything and everyone within it a sticky, powdery coating that provides +1 to Armor against poison, chemical, and fire damage for 28 hours.

Biofeedback Glove
Level: 1d6
Wearable: Single glove made of synth and nanowires
Effect: For the next hour, each time the wearer uses the gloved hand to perform an action, the glove sends a biofeedback response regarding the action. After wearing the glove for one hour, the wearer may choose one of those actions (such as wielding a weapon, crafting, working with numenera devices, and so on). She becomes temporarily trained in that skill. For the next 28 hours, the difficulty of all tasks related to that skill is reduced by one step.

Biological Transpiercer
Level: 1d6 + 2
Usable: Biological needle or spike that is inserted under the skin
Effect: Once inserted beneath the user's skin, the transpiercer releases a slow-acting biological compound that begins to mix with the user's blood, causing one of the following effects:

01–04	Allows the user to see in the dark for one hour
05–08	Causes the user to go out of phase for one hour
09–12	Increases Might Pool by 5 for one hour
13–16	Increases Speed Pool by 5 for one hour
17–20	Increases Intellect Pool by 5 for one hour
21–25	Restores a number of Might Pool points equal to cypher level
26–30	Restores a number of Speed Pool points equal to cypher level
31–35	Restores a number of Intellect Pool points equal to cypher level
36–45	Increases Might Edge by 1 for one hour
46–55	Increases Speed Edge by 1 for one hour
56–65	Increases Intellect Edge by 1 for one hour
66–75	Creates a random beneficial mutation for one hour
76–85	Creates a random powerful mutation for one hour
86–95	Creates a random distinctive mutation for one hour
96–00	Creates a random cosmetic mutation for one hour

Biometric Reference
Level: 1
Internal: Pill, ingestible liquid
Wearable: Temporary tattoo, amulet, headband, crystal worn on temple
Usable: Small handheld device, crystal
Effect: Activating the device allows the user to connect with the datasphere to identify one creature he can see. The user learns the creature's level, motivations, health, damage inflicted, armor, and movement, plus a detail about how it fights in combat.

Biomorph
Level: 1d6 + 2
Internal: Pill, ingestible liquid
Usable: Injector
Effect: Causes the user to gain a mutation. Roll to determine the type of mutation:

01–20	Harmful mutation
21–40	Cosmetic mutation
41–60	Beneficial mutation
61–80	Distinctive mutation
81–00	Powerful mutation

While using a biofeedback glove, if you choose a skill that you are already trained in, you become temporarily specialized in that skill instead. The difficulty of related tasks is reduced by two steps instead of one.

Blood Boiler

Level: 1d6 + 1
Internal: Pill, ingestible liquid
Effect: Causes an increase in blood flow to any stimulated body parts. Adds 1 to Might Edge for one hour.

Blood Magnet

Level: 1d6
Wearable: Glove, wristband
Usable: Syringe
Effect: The user injects the biological magnet into his own blood or that of another living creature within close range. The hemoglobin of the injected creature gains strong ferromagnetic properties for one hour. Roll d100:

01–50	Attracts metallic objects to the creature (can move an object up to the weight of the creature within long range)
51–75	Repels metallic objects from the creature (can move an object up to the weight of the creature within long range)
76–00	Causes the creature's blood to become overly magnetized, decreasing the flow of oxygen to the cells (does damage equal to the cypher level)

For some reason, blood magnets—also known as meat magnets or mutant magnets— seem to work especially well on mutated blood. They are rumored to be a favorite weapon of the Angulan Knights in their war against mutants.

Bloom (Fireflower)

Level: 1d6 + 4
Usable: Ceramic, glass, or other breakable material in the shape of a flower or seed pod with a fuse stem (lit and then thrown or launched, long-range)
Effect: Ten seconds after the fuse is lit, the device explodes, sending shards of red-hot glass out into the pattern of a flower. Any living creature that comes into contact with falling or spraying shards suffers burn damage equal to the cypher level.

Blooms are a special type of detonation that explodes into specific, often elaborate, shapes. Floristas—those who create blooms—take great pride in their craft, attempting to make not only the most beautiful, but also the most lethal, explosions.

Bloom (Serpent)

Level: 1d6 + 2
Usable: Ceramic, glass, or other breakable material in the shape of a coiled snake with a fuse tongue (lit and then thrown or launched, long-range)
Effect: Ten seconds after the fuse is lit, the device explodes, sending out electrified wireworms in the pattern of a long, gyrating snake. As the snake pattern slides through the air, it explodes a second time, sending the electrified wireworms out in a wider pattern. Any living creature that comes into contact with the wireworms is electrified, taking damage equal to the cypher level and becoming dazed for one round, during which time the difficulty of all tasks it performs is modified by one step to its detriment.

Bloom (Spore)

Level: 1d6 + 4
Usable: Moss-wrapped ball filled with small pressure-activated detonator and propellant spores
Effect: Ten seconds after the ball is firmly squeezed (to activate the detonator), the device explodes, sending spores out in foliage patterns. Any living creature that breathes in the falling or spraying spores takes damage equal to the cypher level.

Blue Crystal

Level: 1d6 + 1
Usable: Small blue crystal
Effect: When one gazes through a blue crystal, for a brief moment she can view a spot corresponding to her current position in a parallel universe. Moreover, the view is set a few moments in the future. However, since the crystal shows a parallel universe, the future seen may or may not be an accurate reflection of her reality. The user, then, sees a possible future. Normally, there is about a 30% chance that the glimpse is entirely accurate and a 30% chance that it is partially accurate, but these numbers depend on the circumstances.

Body Enhancer

Level: 1d6
Usable: Tube of malleable material
Effect: Adjusts to match the user's skin color and temperature, can be shaped into any form, and affixes itself to the user's body for up to two hours. Single action to shape and affix.

Bone Dress

Level: 1d6
Usable: Squeezable tube filled with liquefied bone
Effect: The material can be squeezed into a pattern of protection around anything, living or nonliving. Within a few seconds after application, the bone hardens in the established pattern, providing a cage of armor around the selected object or creature. The cage is malleable, allowing movement, and offers +1 to Armor for one hour.

Application takes ten seconds or one round.

Brain Lightning

Level: 1d6
Wearable: Electrical headband
Usable: Handheld device, long-needled syringe
Effect: Provides a short, low-level burst of electrical stimulation directly to the brain, increasing awareness and cognitive function. As a result, the user moves one step up the damage track for ten minutes. This is a temporary effect that doesn't change the status of her Pools. If she is hale (or becomes hale), the device has no effect.

Breather Symbiote

Level: 1d6 + 2
Wearable: A gelatinous mask that must be pressed onto the face
Effect: Activating the symbiote causes the device to forcefully inject a long tendril down the user's throat until it reaches his lungs, where it lodges in the fleshy material. The symbiote provides him with breathable air for one hour, letting him breathe in the absence of air. However, while the symbiote is activated, the user can't speak. If the symbiote is removed, the user takes 4 points of damage.

Buoyancy

Level: 1d6
Internal: Pill, ingestible liquid
Wearable: Full bodysuit, harness worn about the chest
Usable: Injector
Effect: For one hour, the user cannot become submerged in any liquid.

Burrowing Bubble

Level: 1d6 + 4
Wearable: Ring, bracelet, headband
Usable: Handheld device
Effect: Upon activation, for ten minutes, the user is surrounded by a bubble of energy that projects incredible heat outward, but not inward. This bubble floats 1 foot (0.3 m) in the air, inflicts 6 points of damage to all within immediate range, and inflicts 3 points of damage to all within short range. Further, it instantly melts the material directly below (of lower level than the cypher), and the bubble sinks an immediate distance into the new hole it created. This continues for the duration of the effect, so a user who stands on the ground when activating this cypher ends up about 800 feet (244 m) underground when it finally stops.

If the user concentrates, she can force the bubble to move an immediate distance in any direction she chooses as an action.

The user cannot penetrate the bubble, and neither can forces from the outside. Not even ambient damage gets through. Dealing at least 50 points of damage to the bubble (which has no Armor) destroys it. Damaging the bubble does not harm the user inside until the bubble is destroyed, at which point she falls from whatever height the bubble was at, which is at least 1 foot (0.3 m) in the air.

For a time, explorers found blue crystals in great numbers throughout many regions. They are more rare now.

The GM should decide what a PC sees through a blue crystal based on what is most likely to happen, and then allow actual play to determine whether what was seen was entirely accurate, partially accurate, or inaccurate.

Bone dresses are often used by those who wish to protect their companions in combat. It's not uncommon to see seskii wearing intricate bone dresses before battle.

Damage track, page 93

Butterfly Drone

Level: 1d6
Usable: Fingertip-sized winged insect built of synth and biological elements
Effect: This voice-controlled cyberbug travels in a designated direction and distance. There, it holds its position, flying around in the area for ten minutes, recording sound and images. After that time, it returns to the user. To decipher the information, the user must ingest the bug, which then relays the recording via mechanical impulses to her brain. She sees and hears the recording only once.

Cable Projector

Level: 1d6
Wearable: Wrist-mounted projector
Usable: Handheld device
Effect: Projects a cable or rope (if the PC has one) attached to a powerful spike up to long range. The projected rope embeds itself solidly into most surfaces, and the cypher can retract the rope later or pull it extremely taut. If desired, the device can easily be spiked into a surface so that the rope attaches to something solid at both ends.

Camouflage Screen

Level: 1d6 + 4
Usable: Handheld device
Effect: Projects an opaque, two-dimensional screen of light that is 12 feet (4 m) high and 20 feet (6 m) across. It lasts up to 28 hours. The screen bears an animate image appropriate to the surrounding area, such as trees and brush in a forest, sandy dunes in a desert, and so on. Thus, anything behind the screen is easily hidden from visual observation unless the viewer is within immediate distance (and even then it may be obscured, depending on the circumstances).

Camouflage Spray

Level: 1d6 + 1
Usable: Canister
Effect: An inanimate object (or group of objects) small enough to fit into a cube that is 10 feet by 10 feet by 10 feet (3 m by 3 m by 3 m) can be quickly coated so that its color and texture blend into its surroundings perfectly.

If you cobble together a camouflage screen and a pushpull beam (task difficulty 7), you create a cypher that fires a beam up to long range that encapsulates a target in a bubble of solid light about 8 feet (2 m) across. The target can't take physical actions or perceive through the bubble for ten minutes.

Pushpull beam, page 81

Caustic Storm

Level: 1d6 + 4
Usable: Handheld device
Effect: When activated, the cypher surrounds the user with a nimbus of energy, giving him +10 to Armor that works only against caustic damage. This lasts for one round, and the Armor is ablative, which is to say that each point of damage that it absorbs destroys 1 point of the Armor.

The cypher also releases fourteen hailstone-sized motes of roiling caustic fluid that fly toward and attack all targets (including the user) within immediate range, one mote per target. If there are not fourteen targets within immediate range, the motes fly out to short range. If there are not fourteen targets within short range, they fly out to long range. If there are not fourteen targets within long range, the targets within long range get attacked twice (or more times) each, starting with those in immediate range.

Chitin Colony

Level: 1d6
Usable: Small container filled with metal shavings
Effect: The shavings sprout sharp legs and rush out of the container to completely encase the user's body. Each piece locks with another piece to form a flexible mesh. The user gains +1 to Armor for one hour.

Cicerone

Level: 1d6
Usable: Handheld automaton
Effect: The user activates the device, points the automaton's face in the general direction he wishes to go, and states a general distance. The device suggests the easiest and quickest way to travel that route, taking into account terrain, weather, potential threats, and existing paths. It functions for 28 hours and then dies, speaking a single bit of useful information about the route ahead when it does so.

Clamp Trap

Level: 1d6 + 1
Usable: Mouthlike metal clamp
Effect: When activated, this device becomes a pressure-plate trap that clamps around anything that triggers it. The device is similar to a bear trap, except that when it is fully activated, it becomes invisible. Once triggered,

it inflicts damage equal to the cypher level, plus 1 additional point of damage per minute until it is removed.

Cleaner
Level: 1d6
Wearable: Wristband projector (immediate range)
Usable: Metal container filled with what looks like metal filings
Effect: When activated, the device dissolves the remains of one dead human-sized creature into a small pile of salts and other minerals.

Cloaking Pin
Level: 1d6 + 2
Usable: Metal disk that has been made into a lapel pin
Effect: When activated, this creates a cloaking field that effectively makes the user invisible and completely silent for one minute. While invisible, the user is specialized in stealth and Speed defense tasks. This effect ends if he does something to reveal his presence or position—attacking, performing an esotery, using an ability, moving a large object, and so on. If this occurs, he can regain the remaining invisibility effect by taking an action to focus on hiding his position.

Clone Tank
Level: 10
Usable: A large glass and metal tank filled with pink slime
Effect: To activate this device, the user must place a few drops of blood, strands of hair, nail clippings, or a piece of flesh in the slime. The slime hardens around the organic material to form a cyst. Over the next 3d6 months, the device rapidly grows a person from the material. At the end of this time, a full-grown creature, identical in every physical way to the donor creature, emerges from the tank, and the device deactivates. The clone is a level 1 creature. It can communicate in a language known to the user, but otherwise it understands nothing of the world. It becomes a unique character that develops a personality, objectives, and nature of its own.

Cloud Seed
Level: 1d6 + 4
Usable: Handheld projector (5 miles or 8 km)

Effect: This device can be activated only outdoors and with a clear and unobstructed path to the sky. Once activated, a bright white mote flies up from the device into the sky and explodes, throwing grey tendrils out for 1 mile (2 km) in all directions. After one minute, the tendrils become dark clouds, and after another minute, the skies open up and drench the ground below with heavy rains. In freezing temperatures, the precipitation is sleet, ice, or snow. With the rain comes lightning and thunder. The storm moves with the prevailing winds and dissipates 1d6 hours later.

Cloudskimmer

Level: 1d6 + 2
Usable: A lightweight box large enough to hold four human-sized creatures
Effect: The lid of the box opens, and ten small bags rise from within and spend the next five minutes filling with a lighter-than-air gas. As they inflate, they rise above the box, revealing an empty compartment. A sturdy cord tethers each balloon to the box. When the balloons finish inflating, they lift the box and anything in it into the air at a rate of 100 feet (30 m) per minute until it reaches a maximum altitude of 1,000 feet (305 m). The device remains airborne for seven hours. After this time, it loses 100 feet (30 m) of altitude every ten minutes until it lands. The device moves in whatever direction the winds are blowing.

Colorless Grease

Level: 1d6 + 4
Usable: A metal container filled with thin, colorless grease
Effect: There's enough grease in the container to cover a human-sized creature or an object that can fit inside a 5-foot (2 m) cube. Rubbing the grease onto the target causes it to reflect no color and become invisible for as long as the grease remains. The grease wears off after 1d6 hours. Heat can cause the grease to melt and run, revealing the concealed target early.

Communication Disks

Level: 1d6 + 1
Usable: Small synth disks
Effect: These cyphers usually come in pairs (although each is its own cypher). They allow verbal communication between their users at any distance. Both cyphers must be activated at the same time, and they function for 28 hours.

Complex Fluid Wall Projector

Level: 1d6 + 2
Usable: Handheld device
Effect: Creates a wall of complex fluid up to 30 feet by 30 feet by 1 foot (9 m by 9 m by 0.3 m). It inflicts damage equal to the cypher level on any out-of-phase creature that passes through it. Breaking through or puncturing the wall is a task equal to the cypher level.

The wall conforms to the space available. It lasts for one hour.

Concrete Casting

Level: 1d6
Usable: Compound
Effect: When mixed with water, this compound turns into malleable paste. If molded around a piece of armor, a body part, or another object and allowed to harden for ten minutes, the paste gives it an additional layer of protection, granting +3 to Armor. The paste lasts for one hour before it begins to disintegrate.

Conflict Advisor

Level: 1d6 + 2
Internal: Pill, ingestible liquid
Wearable: Temporary tattoo, amulet, headband, crystal worn on temple
Effect: The device allows the user to access the datasphere to analyze opponents and anticipate their actions. For one hour, the user has an asset on all attack rolls and Speed defense rolls.

Construction Foam

Level: 1d6 + 1
Usable: Large canister
Effect: The canister produces a vast amount of foam. This foam can easily be shaped into whatever form the user wishes that equals about four 10-foot (3 m) cubes—the size of a small house or a wall that's 1 foot (0.3 m) thick, 10 feet (3 m) high, and 400 feet (122 m) long. This probably takes about twenty minutes. The foam dries quickly (in about a half hour) and hardens to the strength of steel, but it remains fairly lightweight. The entire mass of hardened foam weighs about 200 pounds (91 kg).

Contingent Subroutine

Level: 1d6
Internal: Pill, ingestible liquid, inhalable powder
Wearable: Temporary tattoo, dermal patch
Effect: The device automatically activates if the user becomes debilitated or dies. The device downloads special instructions from the datasphere that cause the body to take steps to protect and repair itself. During the next minute, the user is under the GM's control and on each of the user's turns, even if he is dead, he takes an action to move away from danger by the safest available route. At the end of this time, he makes a recovery roll—again, even if he is dead. The recovery roll does not count against the limit on recovery rolls that he can make in a day.

Countermeasure (Magnetic)

Level: 1d6 + 2
Usable: Handheld device
Effect: This device creates an invisible field that fills an area within short range and lasts for one minute. The field scrambles magnetic fields, making any device or power involving magnetism unusable. The effect lasts as long as the device or power remains within the field.

Countermeasure (Membrane)

Level: 1d6 + 2
Usable: Handheld device
Effect: This device creates an invisible field around up to three living creatures that lasts for one minute. The field scrambles all effects of incoming technological devices, ricocheting the effect back toward the initiator. It has no effects on technological devices used inside the field.

Countermeasure (Technological)

Level: 1d6 + 2
Usable: Handheld device
Effect: Two rounds after being activated, the device creates an invisible field that fills an area within short range and lasts for one minute. The field scrambles the electronic processes of most technological devices and makes them inoperable. Intelligent devices cannot take actions during this time. The effect lasts as long as the devices remain within the field.

Crystal Virus

Level: 1d6 + 3
Wearable: Crystal that affixes to forehead
Effect: When placed on a human's forehead, this cypher immediately takes effect by permanently grafting itself in place (no longer counting against the person's cypher limit). Within 1d10 + 2 days, the wearer's flesh begins to take on a crystalline appearance in patches. In three times that number of days, her entire body becomes organic crystal, flexible enough to move without hindrance, but hard and cold like crystal. She has +1 to Armor permanently but is no longer capable of sexual reproduction.

Further, at the time of complete transformation, she produces a new crystal virus cypher, which can be used by another human.

It's possible to remove the crystal before complete transformation, but it requires surgery and the task difficulty is equal to the cypher level. Doing so ensures that the creature's flesh returns to normal. This will not work after complete transformation occurs.

Cyberflesh

Level: 1d6 + 2
Internal: Pill, injection
Wearable: Spray-on mist
Effect: A character covered in cyberflesh has many advantages. The metallic coating offers +1 to Armor. The character also can use an action to touch any numenera device and automatically learn its function and how to use it (if possible). Cyberflesh lasts for ten minutes.

Cypher Replicator

Level: 1d6
Usable: An orb created from a series of synth blocks in various shapes that connect to each other via male and female tabs

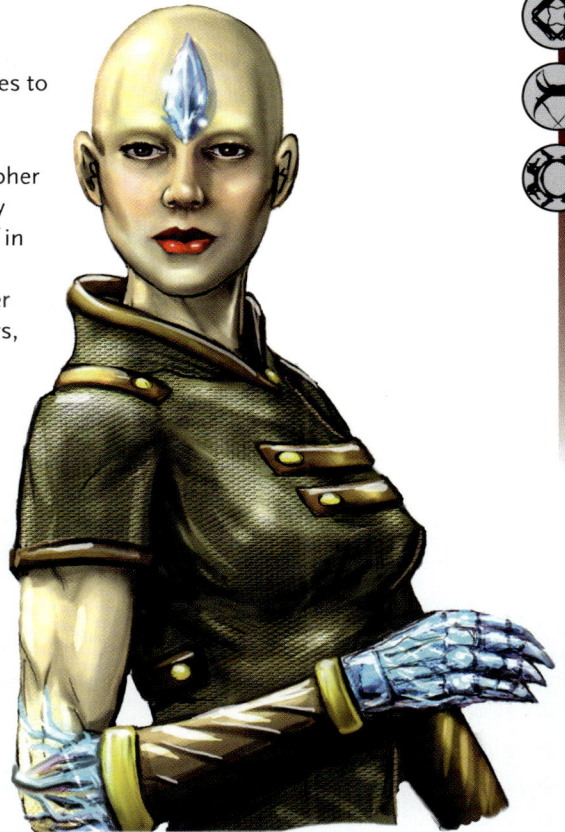

There are isolated communities in the Beyond where the entire population is infected by the crystal virus. The transformation might be done for practical, protective reasons or as part of a religious ritual.

Effect: The user can dismantle the orb and use the individual blocks to replicate the shape of a weapon, bit of armor, or piece of equipment that is in her line of sight. Even if the duplicate is not identical, the finished object gives a viewer the sense that it is. In fact, for most people, it would be hard to tell the two objects apart.

Creating the duplicate takes two actions. The replicated item works exactly as the original does, except that it disintegrates in one hour.

Cypher Seed

Level: 1d6
Usable: Tiny metal and synth chip
Effect: If affixed to another cypher that is a handheld device, it infuses that cypher with additional circuitry like roots from a plant. In 28 hours, it transforms the cypher into an artifact. The GM determines whether the new artifact retains the same ability (but now with potentially multiple uses) or whether it becomes a different artifact of the handheld-device variety.

Data Flood

Level: 1d6 + 2
Internal: Pill, ingestible liquid
Wearable: Dermal patch that must be worn and tapped to be activated
Effect: Activating the cypher enables the user to connect her mind to the datasphere for one hour. Until the connection is broken, the difficulty is reduced by one step for her Intellect defense rolls and Intellect tasks to identify objects, creatures, and places.

Datasphere, page 24

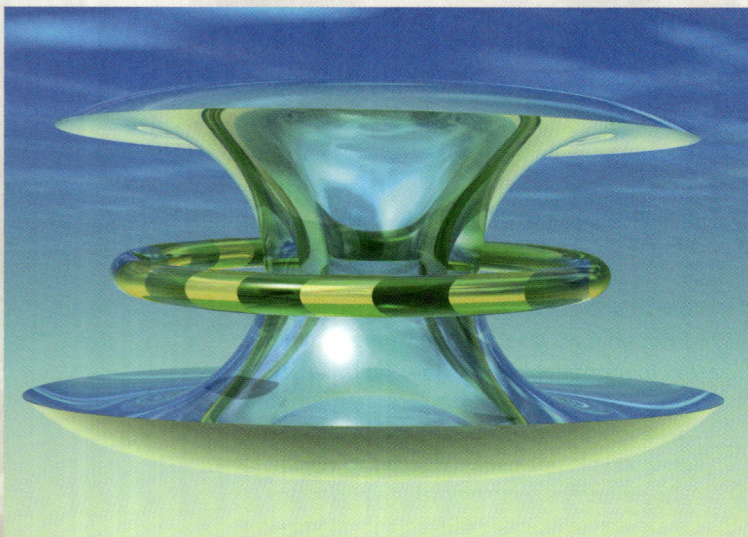

Data Merge

Level: 10
Internal: Pill, ingestible liquid
Wearable: Temporary tattoo, amulet, headband, crystal worn on temple
Usable: Small handheld device, crystal
Effect: The user uploads his mind into the datasphere, where it becomes a being of pure thought. His body becomes catatonic and remains that way until he downloads his consciousness back into his body. If his body dies, he becomes trapped in the datasphere and is forever lost.

While the user is merged with the datasphere, the difficulty of his Intellect rolls is reduced by two steps.

In addition, the user can project a solid light hologram anywhere he chooses in the world. The hologram acts as a level 5 creature under the user's control. He can perceive and communicate through the hologram and decide how it acts and moves. If the hologram is reduced to 0 health, the user must wait at least one hour before he can create a new one.

Data Mine

Level: 1d6
Usable: Small disk that attaches to forehead, electronic bracelet, thick collar, stretchy gloves
Effect: Allows the user to tap into the mind of anyone in visual range and steal the target's knowledge of a skill that it is trained in. The user becomes trained in that skill for one hour. During that time, the target loses its own training in that skill.

Data Spike

Level: 1d6
Internal: Tiny spike
Effect: A user activates the device by inserting it or having another character insert it into the base of his neck, angled upward so that it enters the brain stem. Installing the spike and removing it at a later time inflicts 1 point of damage that ignores Armor. A user can benefit from only one data spike at a time.

Once the spike is installed, the user immediately connects to the datasphere and downloads information about a randomly determined skill into his mind. He becomes trained in that skill for a number of hours equal to the cypher level. If he is already trained in the skill, he instead becomes specialized.

When a data spike is found, the GM can choose a skill or roll a d20 to determine the skill(s) randomly.

1	Astronomy
2	Balancing
3	Biology and botany
4	Climbing and swimming
5	Deceiving
6	Escaping and lockpicking
7	Geography and geology
8	Healing
9	History
10	Identifying
11	Intimidation
12	Leatherworking, metalworking, and woodworking
13	Numenera
14	Perception
15	Persuasion
16	Philosophy
17	Pickpocketing
18	Repairing
19	Riding
20	GM's choice

Data Vault
Level: 1d6 + 2
Usable: Hourglass-shaped synth device with a ring around the center
Effect: The device scans one object (chosen by the user) that can fit inside a 10-foot (3 m) cube and is within a short distance. The object then dissolves, its substance drawn into the device. Activating the device again causes it to create an identical copy of the object using solidified light at an open spot within a short distance.

Deadly Mist
Level: 1d6 + 2
Wearable: Wrist-mounted sprayer
Usable: Canister with a short hose
Effect: This cypher sprays a mist of exotic fluid at one or more targets within immediate range (potentially all targets in range, if the user desires). The mist condenses on the targets and gathers into a thick liquid that begins to form hard, razor-sharp edges, needles, spikes, and barbs that inflict damage equal to the cypher level. Affected targets suffer half the damage on the next round as well before the fluid turns back into mist and evaporates.

Death Messenger
Level: 1d6 + 2
Usable: A pair of metal or organic wings on a frame that can be attached to any detonation cypher
Effect: To activate the device, the user places a bit of skin, hair, nail, or some other material from a living creature inside a compartment positioned between the wings. The wings begin to flap, causing the device to lift into the air and fly off toward the creature whose materials were used to activate it. The device uses the datasphere to locate the creature and speeds off toward it by the shortest and fastest available route. The device flies about 30 mph (48 kph) and maneuvers around obstacles. If blocked by a solid object, it goes out of phase, along with the cypher it carries, and moves through the object until it emerges into an open space. The device activates its detonation cypher when it reaches the target or after 28 hours, whichever comes first.

Deficiency Detector
Level: 1d6
Usable: Two small disks. One attaches to the user. The other, when thrown, seeks out and attaches to the nearest living creature in long range.
Effect: When the disk hits its target and attaches, it relays information about the target's weakness to the user. This information decreases the difficulty of the user's next interaction with the target by one step. If the user relays the weakness to others, the difficulty of their next interaction with the target is also decreased by one step.

Demonsphere
Level: 1d6 + 4
Usable: A 6-inch (15 cm) orb of steel lattice with a reflective red sphere in the center
Effect: This is a dangerous cypher to use, perhaps giving rise to its name. When activated, it creates a horrific sound, a combination of shrill shrieks and low rumbling (which also might account for its name). At the same time, red streaks of energy lance out at a number of intelligent targets within short range equal to the cypher level. If there are more targets than streaks of energy, the targets are determined randomly, meaning that the user could be a target.

Detonation cypher, page 284

Deployers are complex numenera devices that are almost always fashioned rather than cobbled or scavenged. Their main purpose is to simplify the process of arranging or moving things strategically for the user. Deployers can arrange everything from cells and light waves to sentient, living creatures into specific, complicated patterns and reactions. Think of them as a Ninth World equivalent of an app—someone else has done all the complicated coding for you, and all you have to do is push a button or pop a pill.

Because deployers are always anoetic but they do the complex work of an occultic device, they're good choices for characters who have a lower cypher limit or a limited knowledge of the numenera.

Fashioned, cobbled, and scavenged, page 277

The Truth, page 133

The streaks of energy are extradimensional conduits tying the targets to an ultraterrestrial intelligence with a level equal to the cypher level. The intelligence attempts to control the targets' actions for one round per cypher level. (Eligible targets include machine intelligences or any living creature more substantial than an insect.) The ultraterrestrial intelligence has a motive and understanding all its own, but it is utterly alien. Thus, it can do almost anything, but if desired, roll d100 each round instead:

Roll	Target's action
01–10	Scream
11–20	Make incomprehensible gestures
21–40	Attack the nearest creature
41–55	Attack the nearest object
56–60	Attack the ground
61–65	Activate the nearest numenera device
66–75	Run off as fast as possible
76–80	Begin speaking in an unknown language
81–83	Speak in the Truth and ask strange, random questions
84–85	Speak in the Truth and demand obedience
86–88	Examine a random object
89–90	Try to eat a random creature or object
91–93	Access unknown energies and teleport away
94–95	Access unknown energies and create a force field around itself
96–97	Access unknown energies and use them to attack all nearby
98–00	Access unknown energies and open a transdimensional portal

Deployer (Atmospheric)
Level: 1d6
Wearable: Wristband projector (long range), arm- or shoulder-mounted launcher (long range)
Usable: Handheld projector (long range)
Effect: Once initiated, the device collects the most widely available atmospheric aerosols within long range (such as drit dust, water droplets, pollen, bacteria, or smoke). It brings those aerosols together in a whirling tornado that centers around the device itself. Anything in close range of the tornado takes damage equal to the cypher level.

Deployer (Hypersound)
Level: 1d6
Usable: Handheld device

Effect: Once initiated, the device causes all audible sound waves within long range to gather in a single wave of inaudible hypersound. This wave then carries the sound directly to the ears of the user, allowing him to hear everything while at the same time creating absolute silence for everyone else in long range.

Deployer (Muscular)
Level: 1d6
Internal: Injector, pill
Usable: Needle projector, blow gun (short range)
Effect: Once the material enters a living body, it begins to rearrange the skeletal muscle tissue of the creature in an orderly fashion to allow muscles to be used at their maximum capacity. For the next ten minutes, the difficulty of all Speed-based tasks (including Speed defense) is decreased by one step.

Deployer (Optical)
Level: 1d6
Usable: Handheld device
Effect: Once initiated, the device manipulates the path of electromagnetic radiation through specific parts of the light spectrum. In doing so, it shields the user from view, essentially rendering her invisible, for one hour.

Desiccation Bag
Level: 1d6
Usable: Small synth bag approximately 1 foot by 1 foot by 3 inches (0.3 m by 0.3 m by 8 cm)
Effect: Completely dries out any object placed in the bag within ten minutes. Living creatures put into the bag take damage equal to the cypher level.

Detonation (Coma)
Level: 1d6 + 4
Usable: Explosive device or ceramic sphere (thrown, short range), handheld projector (long range)
Effect: Explodes in a patterned flash of pale yellow gas in an immediate radius. Living creatures in the area fall unconscious for a number of rounds equal to the cypher level, or until violently slapped awake or damaged.

Detonation (Crystal)

Level: 1d6 + 3

Usable: Crystal shard the size of a fist (thrown, short range)

Effect: Explodes with wild energy and crystal shrapnel. The shrapnel strikes in a short radius, inflicting damage equal to the cypher level. The energy extends to a long radius and inflicts 4 points of damage that ignores Armor.

Detonation (Distress)

Level: 1d6

Usable: Explosive device or ceramic sphere (thrown, short range), handheld projector (long range)

Effect: Explodes in an immediate radius with blue vapors. Anyone in the area becomes nauseated and spends one round per cypher level vomiting and incapacitated in pain, unable to take actions.

Detonation (Electromagnetic)

Level: 1d6 + 4

Usable: Explosive device or ceramic sphere (thrown, short range), handheld projector (long range)

Effect: Explodes and releases a potent wave of electromagnetic energy in a short radius. Numenera devices in the area when it explodes do not function for one hour.

Detonation (Filament)

Level: 1d6

Usable: Explosive device or ceramic sphere (thrown, short range), handheld projector (long range)

Effect: Bursts into a swirling mass of hundreds of extremely thin metal filaments that slice through flesh and objects in an immediate radius, inflicting damage equal to the cypher level. Further, the razor-sharp filaments remain in the area, difficult to see but dangerous. Anyone entering the area suffers damage as if they were caught in the initial explosion. The area of filaments collapses after ten minutes.

Detonation (Flashfire)

Level: 1d6 + 3

Usable: Explosive device or ceramic sphere (thrown, short range), handheld projector (long range)

Effect: Explodes with radiation in an immediate area. The radiation burns so quickly that things affected by it char (taking damage equal to the cypher level) but never catch fire.

Detonation (Flesh Warping)

Level: 1d6 + 3

Usable: Explosive device or ceramic sphere (thrown, short range), handheld projector (long range)

Effect: Explodes in an immediate radius with strange energies. Those within the area suffer damage equal to the cypher level and are afflicted by a harmful mutation that fades after 1d6 + 1 weeks.

Detonation (Foam)

Level: 1d6 + 2

Usable: Explosive device or ceramic sphere (thrown, short range), handheld projector (long range)

Effect: Explodes with foam in an immediate area. The foam inflicts no damage but hardens immediately, filling the area with resilient, spongy matter. Those trapped in the foam can break free only by using their Might or perhaps a cutting tool (which would take at least a minute). The foam disintegrates after one hour.

Detonation (Healing)

Level: 1d6 + 4

Usable: Explosive device or ceramic sphere (thrown, short range), handheld projector (long range)

Effect: Explodes to release a burst of warm energy in a short radius. The energy restores a number of points equal to the cypher level to the Pools (or health) of everyone in the area.

Detonation (Living Metal)

Level: 1d6 + 3

Usable: Metal sphere (thrown, short range)

Effect: Explodes in a short radius, spraying shards of liquid metal that inflict damage equal to the cypher level. The shards then drop to the ground or other nearby surface and slither along toward the point of detonation, where they rejoin. This process takes about three rounds. If it is not somehow prevented, the detonation explodes again, inflicting 1 fewer point of damage than before.

Detonation cypher, page 284

Harmful mutation, page 124

Detonation (Plant Transformation)

Level: 1d6 + 2

Usable: Explosive device or ceramic sphere (thrown, short range), handheld projector (long range)

Effect: Explodes in an immediate radius with a grey mist. Living creatures affected in the area begin to transform into plants. Player characters exposed to the mist must attempt three Might defense rolls (any Effort used on one roll is applied to all three). The final result depends on the result of the rolls:

No successes: Over the course of ten minutes, the character's flesh turns green and begins to sprout shoots. He permanently turns into a human-shaped plant.

One success: Over the course of ten minutes, the character's flesh turns green and begins to sprout shoots. Her body stiffens and she cannot move for 28 hours as she takes root. At the end of that time, she becomes a human-shaped plant. However, if someone keeps her from taking root, she returns to normal over the course of another 28 hours, during which time she can take no actions.

Two successes: Over the course of ten minutes, the character's flesh turns green and begins to sprout shoots. This is a painful process. At the ten-minute mark, he moves one step down the damage track, and he remains that way until he returns to normal 28 hours later.

Three successes: The character is not affected at all.

NPCs in the area who are one level lower than the cypher are affected as if they had two successes. NPCs who are two or three levels lower are affected as if they had one success. NPCs who are four or more levels lower than the cypher are affected as if they had no successes.

All plants in the area gain a permanent +1 level boost.

Detonation cypher, page 284

Detonation (Smoke)

Level: 1d6 + 2

Wearable: Wristband projector (long range)

Usable: Explosive device or ceramic sphere (thrown, short range), handheld projector (long range)

Effect: Bursts in a short radius, filling the area with thick smoke that lasts for one minute. A strong wind disperses it immediately. Treat the smoke as darkness, and the difficulty of melee attacks in the area is modified by one step in the defender's favor.

Detonation (Spatial Warping)

Level: 1d6 + 3

Usable: Explosive device or ceramic sphere (thrown, short range), handheld projector (long range)

Effect: Explodes in an immediate radius with strange energies. All creatures within the area are teleported (safely) to a different spot within short range of the detonation.

Detonation (Stasis)

Level: 1d6 + 4

Usable: Explosive device or ceramic sphere (thrown, short range), handheld projector (long range)

Effect: Explodes in an immediate radius with strange energies. All creatures within the area are held in temporal stasis for one minute, during which time they cannot take actions or be affected in any manner.

Detonation (Suggestion)

Level: 1d6 + 2

Usable: Explosive device or ceramic sphere (thrown, short range), handheld projector (long range)

Effect: Explodes in a patterned flash of multicolored lights and gas in an immediate radius. For all sentient creatures in the area, the difficulty of Intellect defense rolls to resist reasonably worded suggestions is increased by a number of steps equal to half the cypher level (round down). The effect lasts for a number of rounds equal to the cypher level.

Detonation (Tendril)

Level: 1d6 + 2

Usable: Explosive device or ceramic sphere (thrown, short range), handheld projector (long range)

Effect: Bursts into a swirling mass of dozens of animate tendrils that emerge from the point of explosion. The tendrils attack every creature and unattended object within immediate range. If successful, they hold their victim fast for up to six rounds unless the victim can break free (small or fragile objects are simply crushed and destroyed).

Detonation Delay

Level: 1d6

Usable: Small wired device

Effect: The device can be attached to almost any type of detonation cypher to delay its activation. The user can set the timer for one minute, ten minutes, or 28 hours. Provided that the delay or detonation is not found and dismantled ahead of time, the detonation explodes at the preset time.

Detonation Trigger

Level: 1d6
Wearable: Wristband transmitter (long range) and a small patch or bundle of nanowires
Effect: The nanowires can be attached to almost any type of detonation cypher. The user can then remotely trigger the device using the wristband transmitter. The detonation must be within long range, but it doesn't need to be in the user's vision.

Device Enhancer

Level: 1d6
Usable: Tiny metal and synth chip
Effect: If affixed to another cypher or artifact, that device is enhanced in one of the following ways (roll a d6):

1 The device now also inflicts 4 points of damage if used on a target other than the user. If the device already inflicts damage, the damage is increased by 2 points. If used on an artifact, this effect lasts for 28 hours after the first use.

2 The device, when activated, also projects a force field around the user that lasts for an hour. This field provides +2 to Armor. If the device already creates protective Armor, that Armor gains +1 instead. This functions once, regardless of whether the enhanced device is a cypher or an artifact.

3 The device, when activated, also adds 1 to the user's Might Edge, Speed Edge, and Intellect Edge for one hour. This functions once, regardless of whether the enhanced device is a cypher or an artifact.

4 If the device has immediate range, the range is increased to short. If short, it is increased to long. If long, it is increased to 200 feet (61 m). Such changes to the device last for 28 hours. If the device does not have a ranged effect, it instead affects the user when activated so that the user moves a long distance on an action for 28 hours. This latter effect can be used once.

5 The device, when activated, also makes the user invisible for an hour. While invisible the user is specialized in stealth and Speed defense tasks. This effect ends if he does something to reveal his presence or position—attacking, performing an esotery, using an ability, and so on. If this occurs, he can regain the remaining invisibility effect by taking an action to focus on hiding his position. This functions once, regardless of whether the enhanced device is a cypher or an artifact.

6 The device now also restores a total of 4 points each time it is activated. The user can allocate those points among his stat Pools as desired, but the Pools cannot go above their maximum. If the device already restores points to Pools, it restores 2 additional points. If used on an artifact, this effect lasts for 28 hours after the first use.

Dimensional Sheath

Level: 1d6 + 4
Wearable: Belt, headband, bracelet
Usable: Handheld device
Effect: User is enveloped in invisible energy for six hours. During this time, she has +1 to Armor against any type of energy attack (including those that normally ignore Armor) and is immune to any effect that would change her phase state, send her to another universe, teleport her, or do anything similar.

Dimensional Trap

Level: 1d6 + 4
Usable: Complex device
Effect: One creature or object within immediate range disappears and is drawn into the device, where it remains for 28 hours. When the effect ends, the target reappears in an open space (chosen by the user of the device) within immediate range.

Disintegration Gel

Level: 1d6 + 3
Usable: Synth tube containing gel
Effect: This tube produces a fist-sized amount of gel. When applied to a specific material, the gel vaporizes it at a rate of about 1 inch (3 cm) per round. The gel works for two rounds per cypher level. It has no effect on other materials. Roll d100 for the material affected:

01–35	Metal
36–39	A specific metal (GM's choice)
40–71	Stone
72–81	Metal or stone
82–98	Synth
99–00	Organic matter (inflicts damage equal to the cypher level on a living creature)

Displacement Cloak

Level: 1d6 + 4
Wearable: Cloak, cape, mantle
Effect: For the next ten minutes, the user disappears and an image of her appears somewhere within immediate range. The image is a perfect copy of the user and mimics her physical movements and actions. The difficulty of her Speed defense rolls is reduced by three steps until the effect ends.

Dissonance Cube

Level: 1d6 + 4
Usable: Complex device
Effect: Activation causes the device to emit a subsonic noise for seven hours. At the end of each hour, any metal object within long range of the device takes 4 points of ambient damage.

Distance Activator

Level: 1d6 + 1
Usable: Handheld device with a small, detachable nodule
Effect: When the nodule is detached and connected to any other cypher, the user of the distance activator can activate that cypher from a range of up to 1 mile (2 km).

Distortion Field Emitter

Level: 1d6 + 2
Internal: Subdermal injection
Wearable: Helmet, headband, metallic choker
Usable: Complex device
Effect: Activation creates an invisible field that extends out from the device to short range for the next hour. Numenera devices do not function while in the field.

Doomsday Device

Level: 10
Internal: Subdermal injection
Usable: Explosive device
Effect: When activated, the user sets a timer for up to one year. When the time runs out, the device explodes out to a range of 1 mile (2 km). The explosion inflicts 20 points of damage to everything in the area and saturates the air and ground with radiation that lasts for 5d20 years. Until the radiation dissipates, it inflicts 1 point of ambient damage for each minute a creature remains in the area.

Drastic Propulsion

Level: 1d6
Wearable: Small black box with a hook that attaches to a piece of clothing
Effect: When activated, the device propels the user quickly in the direction he desires, allowing him to cover twice the usual amount of ground each round. If the user is holding tightly to another person or creature, that

"Transdimensional technologies are some of my favorites. They force you to question your entire understanding of the laws that govern our universe."
~Sir Arthour

person or creature moves with him at the same speed. The effect lasts for one minute.

Dreamachine

Level: 1d6
Wearable: Hood, mask, head halo
Usable: Standalone device
Effect: The device creates pulsing light, sound, or some other combination of stimuli designed to alter the brain's electrical oscillations. When the user sits within close range of the device for at least ten minutes with his eyes closed, he enters a hypnagogic state. This allows his mind to open to the wonders of the datasphere, granting him the answer to a single question.

Dry Water

Level: 1d6
Usable: Tiny marble made from ceramic, stone, or glass
Effect: The device activates when exposed to water. It instantly expands into water with a volume of 1 gallon (4 L) per cypher level.

Duplicator

Level: 1d6 + 1
Usable: Synth cylinder etched with fine, glowing lines
Effect: When one end of the device is touched against a creature, a mass of gelatin sprays out the other end. Within three rounds, the gelatin creates what appears to be an exact living copy of the touched creature, including clothing and equipment, but it's a spongy facade. The copy is a level 1 creature with minimal intelligence that follows simple commands, but complex thought and emotions are beyond its capabilities. The copy lasts up to 28 hours, at which time it melts and evaporates.

Dynamic Hourglass

Level: 1d6
Usable: Handheld device
Effect: When the user activates the device, she disappears. She is removed from existence until the next round ends, at which point she returns to the same spot she left (or the nearest open space to that spot). At any time within the next 28 hours, she can take an extra action on her turn.

Ear Worm

Level: 1d6 + 2
Internal: A tiny worm covered in sharp hairs
Effect: The cypher activates when placed on someone's face. The worm crawls up the side of the user's face and enters his ear canal (or the closest thing to an ear canal the user has). It then embeds the bristles coating its body into the canal. For the next 28 hours, the user can understand any language he hears and has an asset for any task that involves listening. When the effect ends, a fleshy moth flies out of his ear.

Echo Crystal

Level: 1d6 + 4
Usable: Crystal nodule affixed to a melee weapon
Effect: When the device is activated, the crystal projects a second weapon in the air formed from solidified light. It follows the weapon it copies, floating through the air and mimicking the original's movements. Whenever the user takes an action to attack with the original weapon, he makes an additional attack with the copy as part of the same action. The

Using a dreamachine can have unexpected short-term side effects, including auditory and visual hallucinations, seizures, or nose bleeds.

second weapon inflicts the same damage as the original. After 28 hours, the copy dissipates into a cloud of sparkling motes.

Ecstasy Glass

Level: 1d6
Wearable: Spectacles, goggles, helmet with visor
Usable: Six joined glass spheres
Effect: The device takes over the user's senses for one hour and floods them with profound pleasure. The user cannot see, hear, smell, taste, or feel anything in her surroundings during this time. Instead, she experiences whatever she most desires, and she believes that she is engaged in an activity that produces great and lasting pleasure. The experience might be eating a sumptuous meal, engaging in a sexual act with one or more people she desires, or simply sitting comfortably in a beautiful landscape. When the effect ends, she feels restored and may immediately make a recovery roll. This recovery roll does not count against the limits on the number of recovery rolls that she can make in a day.

Effulgent Body

Level: 1d6
Internal: Syringe, pill, ingestible liquid
Effect: Injects a fluorescent protein gene into the user, causing her to glow with a bioluminescent light that illuminates the area around her (within close range) as though it were daylight. The effect lasts for one hour.

Ejection Nodule

Level: 1d6 + 1
Usable: Crystal nodule affixed to a melee weapon
Effect: For the next hour, each time the weapon the nodule is attached to strikes a solid creature or object hard enough to inflict damage (but no more than once per round), the target of the strike teleports to a random location within a radius of 100 × the cypher level in feet.

Electronic Nose

Level: 1d6 + 2
Wearable: Small nodule that affixes to nose, synth nose that attaches over a real one, clip-on nose ring

Effect: This device enhances the wearer's sense of smell, allowing him to detect odor signatures of various biological, biochemical, or chemical compounds for one hour. Those with knowledge of the numenera can attempt to "set" the nose to a desired substance just prior to using it (difficulty equal to the cypher level), or the GM can roll ahead of time:

01–10	Explosives or detonations
11–30	Disease
31–40	Blood
41–50	Poison
51–75	Chemical traps
76–00	User's choice

Emoacoustic Weapon

Level: 1d6 + 2
Wearable: Mask
Usable: Handheld device
Effect: This device allows the user to change the emotion of a single target in short range with a sonic burst that only the target will hear. The user can choose one of these emotions or states: anger, despair, fear, joy, calm, great hunger, and sexual arousal. This artificial state lasts for ten minutes (or as the situation afterward dictates).

Energy Module

Level: 1d6 + 2
Usable: Small metal and synth plate
Effect: This cypher must be attached to another cypher or artifact (a level 4 task) that produces energy, such as a ray emitter or a force shield projector. Once attached, it no longer counts against a character's cypher limit. The level of the device it is attached to is increased by 2.

The module cannot be removed from the device without destroying both the module and the device.

Energy Siphon

Level: 1d6
Usable: Small metal device
Effect: When activated, this small metal device hovers around the user, and any energy attack (such as a nano's force blast or a beam from a ray emitter) strikes the cypher instead. The device is not harmed by the attack. Once activated, the energy siphon functions for one hour.

If you affix an ejection nodule and a disrupting nodule to the same weapon, not only do both function, but the weapon inflicts 2 additional points of damage to any transdimensional creature it strikes.

Disrupting nodule, page 285

Energy Token

Level: 1d10

Usable: Glowing ball of energy

Effect: This cypher functions when it is touched by a living creature (perhaps even before it can be identified), although it can be manipulated by tools such as tongs and safely stored if well away from a creature. Normal gloves or a leather bag is not enough to keep it from activating. The ball bathes a living creature touching it with energy of a type and effect depending on its color (roll a d20):

1–2	*Blue:* Reorganizes brain connections; +1 to Intellect Edge for one hour.
3–4	*Red:* Restructures skeletal structure; +1 to Might Edge for one hour.
5–6	*Green:* Alters musculature; +1 to Speed Edge for one hour.
7–8	*Yellow:* Alters respiratory system; grants immunity to dangerous gases. User can also breathe a puff of poisonous vapor at a victim in immediate range that inflicts 2 points of Speed damage (ignores Armor) for a number of rounds equal to cypher level. The effect lasts for one hour.
9–10	*Orange:* Changes physical density; +1 to Armor, and user deals 2 additional points of damage with melee attacks.
11–12	*Violet:* Tunes dimensional phase of entire body; user can move through solid matter at a rate of 6 inches (15 cm) per round for ten minutes.
13–14	*Brown:* Alters cellular relationship with gravity; user can move through the air as easily as on a solid surface for ten minutes.
15–18	*Black:* Infuses cells with disruptive energy; inflicts 5 points of damage to user, and then user's touch inflicts 8 points of damage to others for ten minutes.
19–20	*White:* Alters ocular system; user gains x-ray vision and can see through up to 10 inches (25 cm) of matter for one minute.

Eraser

Level: 1d6 + 4

Usable: A small metallic device

Effect: Causes an object that can fit inside a 5-foot (2 m) cube or one creature it touches to instantly disappear from existence.

Erosion Ray

Level: 1d6 + 4

Usable: Handheld device

Effect: Emits a beam at an object within short range. The beam weakens an amount of material that can fit inside a 10-foot (3 m) cube. The target does not appear to change, but it assumes the hardness of thin paper. A creature can easily tear chunks from the object or punch through it. If the user targets a section of floor, anything weighing at least 5 pounds (2 kg) that moves across that section falls through it. The effect can also weaken structures such as bridges, walls, and the like at the GM's discretion.

Essence Transfer

Level: 1d6 + 2

Usable: Handheld device

Effect: Allows one willing character to transfer points from his Pools to another character's Pools. The transferring character can't reduce a Pool below 1, and the receiving character can't raise a Pool above its normal maximum.

Exalted Vapor

Level: 1d6

Internal: Electronic smoking implement

Wearable: Smoking mask

Effect: Allows the user to inhale a potent chemical that restores a number of points equal to the cypher level to one random Pool. Roll d100:

01–50	Might Pool
51–75	Speed Pool
76–00	Intellect Pool

Ray emitter, page 293

Force shield projector, page 286

Explosive Nodule

Level: 1d6 + 2
Usable: Crystal nodule affixed to a melee weapon
Effect: For the next 28 hours, each time the weapon the nodule is attached to strikes a solid creature or object, it releases a pulse of concussive force that throws the target a short distance away from the user. This force knocks the target and the user to the ground.

Extra Time

Level: 1d6 + 3
Wearable: Belt, ring
Usable: Handheld device
Effect: After using his action to activate this device, time slows down for the user, and he can take up to three additional actions while the rest of the world seemingly stands still. He can attack, move, make a recovery roll, or take any other allowed action. Actions are resolved normally. However, this process takes a toll. For every extra action he takes, the user suffers 3 points of damage.

Eye in the Sky

Level: 1d6
Usable: Handheld device
Effect: When activated, part of this device shoots 800 feet (244 m) into the air, projecting everything it sees onto a screen on the other portion of the device. The eye in the sky floats for an hour, all the while projecting what it sees.

Eyebug

Level: 1d6 + 2
Usable: Small mechanical insect and a small eyepiece lens
Effect: Once activated, this device moves on its own for one hour, following a single, simple verbal command with surprising intelligence. For example, if directed to find a way into the chamber to the south, it will search around, attempting to find the most direct path (if one exists), even one that is not known to the user. If told to find the nearest ithsyn, it will search around on its own until it finds the target (or until its hour is up). The device cannot be given multiple objectives, nor can it be given multistep directions. Most important, during the entire time, the user can see everything it can see through the eyepiece. The eyebug can see in the dark as easily as in the light.

Eyestalk Graft

Level: 1d6 + 1
Wearable: A large bulbous eye with a 6-inch (15 cm) stalk
Effect: This organic object grafts directly and immediately onto the flesh of the user's head. The eyestalk functions for 28 hours, during which time the user has an asset for all perception tasks and can look surreptitiously around corners.

Fact Finder

Level: 1d6
Wearable: Glove with a mechanical device in the palm, headband with mechanical device
Effect: When someone wears the device and it

Ithsyn, page 241

is activated, the wearer should be asked three simple questions. These questions allow the device's mechanics to calibrate to the wearer's response. After that, the device will shock the wearer (doing damage equal to the cypher level) every time he says something that is not true. The effect lasts for five questions (in addition to the original calibration questions).

Fallback Clone
Level: 10
Wearable: Two headbands
Effect: To activate this device, the user must place a few drops of blood, strands of hair, nail clippings, or a piece of flesh in a sealed, water-filled tank with one of the headbands and wear the other one. The headband in the tank facilitates the rapid growth of a clone in one month. The clone is a fully grown creature, identical in every physical way to the user. However, it has no consciousness and remains in a comatose state in the tank.

Once the clone has matured, if at any time the user dies while wearing the headband, her consciousness is transferred into the clone, regardless of distance. All skills, abilities, and knowledge are transferred.

The user does not need to wear the headband throughout the process (if, for example, she is worried about her cypher limit)—just at the beginning to spur the clone's growth. However, if she dies while not wearing the headband, no transfer occurs.

Fangs of the Reaver
Level: 1d6 + 1
Usable: 2-inch (5 cm) metal sphere
Effect: Upon activation, the sphere opens to reveal nasty metal teeth. It flies at a single target within short range that the user chooses, and it attacks as a creature of a level equal to the cypher level. It continues to attack that target for a number of rounds equal to the cypher level or until the target is dead, whichever comes first.

Faraway Ear
Level: 1d6
Wearable: Earring, helmet
Usable: Handheld device
Effect: When this device is activated, the user can pinpoint any spot she can see, up to 1,000 feet (305 m) distant, and hear whatever could

normally be heard (as soft as a whisper) at that location for ten minutes.

Fast Hail
Level: 1d6
Usable: Cooled capsule filled with pressurized compound
Effect: When firmly shaken and then projected via a ranged weapon of any kind, the capsule explodes, sending pressurized streams of large water droplets into the air. Within one minute, the droplets form hailstones about 2 inches (5 cm) in diameter. Everything within the hailstorm takes damage equal to the cypher level. The storm lasts for 10 minutes.

Fertility Barrier
Level: 1d6
Internal: Pill, ingestible liquid
Effect: Once ingested, it prevents conception for one week. If a fertility barrier is used by both parties, it *increases* the chance of conception (decreases the difficulty by one step) for the same amount of time.

Firebreather
Level: 1d6 + 2
Wearable: Mouth guard, mouth sprayer, long tube
Effect: The wearer breathes fire onto a foe in immediate range, doing damage equal to the cypher level. Inserting the device is an action. However, breathing fire is an Enabler and can be used in addition to a melee attack or movement.

Flame Catcher
Level: 1d6 + 4
Usable: Complex device
Effect: Causes all fire within a short distance to safely flow into the device. At any time within the next seven hours, anyone holding the device can release the stored flames in a stream about 1 foot (0.3 m) wide that extends out to short range. The flames inflict damage equal to the cypher level to one target within range.

Flame Hand
Level: 1d6 + 2
Wearable: Glove with a large metal device fitted over it
Effect: Although this cypher is a glove, the wearer cannot use his hand while wearing

It is a task with a difficulty of 6 to turn a flame catcher that has absorbed flame into a massive detonation that explodes with fire that inflicts damage equal to the cypher level.

it—a heavy metal device with a long tube on the end fits over the glove, encompassing his entire hand. When activated, this device sprays a stream of flaming liquid up to short range that inflicts damage equal to the cypher level. The wearer can spray this stream around to affect multiple targets and hit as many as are next to each other in range. (If he need not worry about hitting friendly targets, he could potentially attack all foes within range.)

Flesh Eater

Level: 1d6
Wearable: Wristband sprayer (long range)
Usable: Balloon or ceramic sphere (thrown, short range)
Effect: Bursts in an immediate radius, eating away any organic matter that it comes into contact with. Living creatures take damage equal to the cypher level.

Floating Bubble

Level: 1d6
Wearable: Ring, bracelet
Usable: Handheld device
Effect: Upon activation, the user is encapsulated in a bubble of force for ten minutes. This bubble floats at least 1 foot (0.3 m) in the air at all times but moves as the user wishes (requiring an action to do so, just like normal movement) vertically or horizontally, up to a short distance each round. The user cannot penetrate the bubble, and neither can forces from the outside. Not even ambient damage gets through. Dealing at least 50 points of damage to the bubble (which has no Armor) destroys it. Damaging the bubble does not harm the user inside until the bubble is destroyed, at which point he falls from whatever height the bubble was at, which is at least 1 foot (0.3 m) in the air.

Flow

Level: 1d6 + 1
Internal: Pill, ingestible liquid, ingestible powder
Effect: Enables the user to move more rapidly by harnessing momentum gained from movement. Once per round, when the user takes an action to move, she gains another action that she must use at once. She can use this action only to move. The effect wears off after one hour.

Flowstone

Level: 1d6
Usable: Steel or glass jar containing thick grease
Effect: The user activates the item by applying the contents to a stone surface. There is

enough grease to coat a 5-foot (2 m) radius area. It takes one minute for the stone to absorb the grease. At the end of this time, the stone gains the consistency of soft clay to a depth of 5 feet (2 m). The effect lasts for one hour. At the end of this time, the stone returns to its normal hardness.

Fluttering Recorder

Level: 1d6
Usable: Tiny insect made from metal
Effect: Activation causes the device to sprout tiny wings and flutter up into the air, waiting for instructions. The user can give the device specific directions to travel to a place within 3 miles (5 km) of where it was activated. The cypher follows the directions it was given, exactly as they were given, until it can travel no farther or it arrives at its destination. There, it waits for one hour, recording everything it sees and hears. At the end of this time, the cypher flies back to where it received the instructions and plays back the recording by projecting the images it witnessed onto a flat surface and playing the audio through the speakers in its body. It repeats the recording 1d6 times and deactivates.

Flying Cap

Level: 1d6 + 2
Wearable: Hat, helmet
Effect: Three metal poles extend out from the top of the device, which clamps onto the user's head and cannot be removed for the duration. Two poles fold down on either side of the user's head, while the third rises straight up and sprouts four blades that begin spinning. The blades function as a propeller and lift the user into the air. She can control the direction of the movement by using the poles to either side. The device allows her to fly by making a Speed roll (level 2) each round. She can fly a short distance each round in combat or about 1 mile (2 km) each minute. The device operates for 3d20 minutes before breaking up and deactivating. If the user is still in the air when it stops working, she falls.

Foam Limb

Level: 1d6 + 1
Usable: Canister
Effect: If sprayed upon a creature, the foam builds an arm with a hand that mimics one of the creature's existing limbs in appearance, if

possible. (If not applicable, the default limb is a long, sinewy arm with a three-fingered hand.) The foam arm hardens to the consistency of the creature's flesh and can be used by the creature as if it were its own. The new arm does not grant the creature additional actions or attacks in a round, but it can be useful for carrying things. If the arm is harmed, the creature suffers no ill effect. The arm lasts for 28 hours.

Foam Sprayer

Level: 1d6 + 1
Usable: Canister
Effect: This device sprays foam on a target within immediate range. There is enough foam to cover up to three humans standing next to each other (or one larger target). Different kinds of foam have different effects. Roll a d6 to determine the foam in a given canister:

1 *Hardens*: All movement is halved, and the difficulty of all physical actions is increased by two steps for ten minutes.
2 *Caustic*: The foam burns like acid, inflicting 4 points of damage on the first round and 2 points of damage on the second round before becoming harmless.
3 *Caustic and hardens*: All movement is halved, the difficulty of all physical actions is increased by two steps for ten minutes, and the target suffers 4 points of damage.
4 *Dampens energy*: If sprayed upon any numenera item (or if the target is in possession of numenera items), the item's effective level is lowered by 4 for ten minutes. If this effect reduces the level of the item to 0, the item will not function for that time. Nonpowered numenera items, like pills, are not affected.
5 *Dissolves metal*: The level of a metal item covered in the foam is lowered by 4 permanently. If this effect reduces the level of the metal to 0, the item is destroyed.
6 *Dissolves metal and dampens energy*: The level of a metal item covered in the foam is lowered by 4 permanently. If this effect reduces the level of the metal to 0, the item is destroyed. Numenera items coated by the foam also have their level effectively lowered by 4 for ten minutes. If this effect reduces the level of the item to 0 or less, the item will not function for that time. Nonpowered numenera items, like pills, are not dampened.

Fool Killer

Level: 1d6 + 3
Usable: 2-inch (5 cm) crystal tetrahedron
Effect: When activated, this crystal flies into the air and seeks the least intelligent sentient creature in long range, which takes one round. After finding its target, the crystal fires a bolt of energy similar to lightning at the creature. The bolt inflicts 10 points of Intellect damage (ignores Armor).

Freeze Inducer

Level: 1d6 + 3
Usable: Complex device, handheld device
Effect: This item is cold to the touch and may freeze to solid surfaces when not in use. The item is activated by being pressed against an object or creature weighing no more than 200 pounds (91 kg). Any liquid contained in the object freezes; a living creature takes a number of points of damage equal to the cypher level.

Fungal Garden

Level: 1d6 + 2
Usable: Vial filled with multicolored dust
Effect: When a user pours out the contents of the vial, the dust sinks into any earthen or sandy surface it touches. One hour later, a field of mushrooms grows from the ground in a long radius centered on the spot where the dust fell. The mushrooms grow until they reach about 10 feet (3 m) tall on average. Each mushroom has a wide, colorful cap that spreads out in a 6-foot (2 m) radius.

Touching a mushroom causes spores to fall from the cap onto anything below. Each time this happens, roll a d6 to see what the spores do to all creatures they touch.

Roll a d6 for effect:

1–2 *Bliss.* The target experiences profound feelings of joy and happiness for one day.
3–4 *Sadness.* The target experiences profound feelings of sadness for one day.
5–6 *Hallucinations.* The target experiences visual and auditory hallucinations for one day. The hallucinations increase the difficulty of any task that involves seeing or hearing by one step.

If the contents of a fungal garden are carefully mixed with the paste of a beauty mask (task difficulty 6), the resulting concoction is a cypher that can coat a surface or object about the size of a human. The stain left behind glows as bright as a glowglobe forever.

Beauty mask, page 35

Gel Suit

Level: 1d6 + 2
Usable: A large container filled with gel
Effect: To activate the device, the user must place his hand or foot into the container. The gel flows over his appendage and spreads across his body until it completely encases him. The gel retains its semiliquid consistency for 28 hours.

While the gel covers the user, it prevents him from taking damage from acid, cold, electricity, or fire. In addition, whenever he takes damage from being struck by an object, he temporarily gains +1 to Armor until the next round ends as the gel briefly hardens in response to the hit.

Ghostly Duplicate

Level: 1d6 + 1
Wearable: Bracelet, necklace, ring
Usable: Handheld device
Effect: When activated, an incorporeal duplicate of the user appears and remains for ten minutes. The duplicate does not have a mind of its own. Rather, the user controls both forms, but only one at a time. Switching consciousness between forms is an action. While the user's consciousness focuses on one form, the other stands motionless. The duplicate moves at the same speed as the user's normal form, but there is no limit to how far apart the two can be.

The duplicate is ghostly and translucent. It can pass through solid matter and cannot be harmed except by special transdimensional weapons and effects. It likewise cannot affect normal matter in any way. While moving as the incorporeal duplicate, the user gains an asset for all stealth tasks.

When the duplicate's duration ends (or it is somehow destroyed), the user's mind returns to his normal body. If the normal body is slain, the user stays in the duplicate, but only for the remaining duration.

Ghostly Intruder

Level: 1d6 + 3
Usable: Handheld device
Effect: Teleports the user to a location within sight and within long range. When she arrives, she is invisible for up to ten minutes. While invisible, she is specialized in stealth and Speed defense tasks.

This effect ends if she does something

to reveal her presence or position, such as attacking, performing an esotery, using an ability, moving a large object, and so on. If this occurs, she can regain the remaining invisibility effect by taking an action to focus on hiding her position.

Ghostly Veil
Level: 1d6
Usable: Metamaterial compound in a jar, tube, or box (enough for one application)
Effect: When applied to armor or a weapon, the metamaterial refracts light around the object, rending it nearly invisible for one hour. For anyone wearing veiled armor or using a veiled weapon, the difficulty of all tasks involving sneaking, being stealthy, and hiding is decreased by one step.

Glass Flame Pellets
Level: 1d6 + 1
Usable: Handful of glass pellets
Effect: If thrown—as a group—at the floor, the pellets burst into flame, filling the immediate area with fierce flames that burn for 28 hours, inflicting 6 points of damage to anyone in or passing through the area. There is just barely enough time for a character to drop the pellets and move out of the area of the fire in one action.

Glass Scorpion
Level: 1d6 + 1
Usable: Small scorpion made of glass
Effect: When activated, the glass scorpion immediately moves in the direction it is pointed until it comes upon a living creature at least the size of a hound. It then attacks with the needlelike stinger in its tail as a creature of a level equal to the cypher level. The scorpion injects a poison that inflicts 3 points of damage per round for a number of rounds equal to the cypher level.

Glowing Tracker
Level: 1d6
Wearable: Wristband projector (long range)
Usable: Handheld projector (long range); can be thrown against a hard object (short range)
Effect: The device explodes in a shower of gel filled with neon gas, covering everything within immediate range in brilliant green and

orange. The color can be seen in the dark up to 1 mile (2 km) away and lasts for one hour.

Goss
Level: 1d6
Usable: A small, moist tongue
Effect: To activate the cypher, the user must place it under her tongue and then speak for up to one minute. The device records everything she says. At the end of this time, she can place it anywhere she chooses. For the next day, the device repeats whatever she said in her voice and tone to anyone who moves within 10 feet (3 m) of it. Once the device repeats the recording, it makes no further noise until another creature approaches, at which point it begins the speech all over again. When the effect ends, the device breaks up into chunks of foul-smelling filth.

Grasshopper
Level: 1d6 + 2
Wearable: Wrist projector, shoulder launcher (launched, long range)
Usable: Firm synth ball (thrown, short range)
Effect: When thrown, the grasshopper bounces 1d6 times about 5 feet (2 m) apart, setting off an explosion of shrapnel in each place it lands. Each explosion deals damage equal to the cypher level to all creatures in the immediate area of the bounce.

If the GM wants to make the glass scorpion weaker, it can be a level 1 creature that has 3 health.

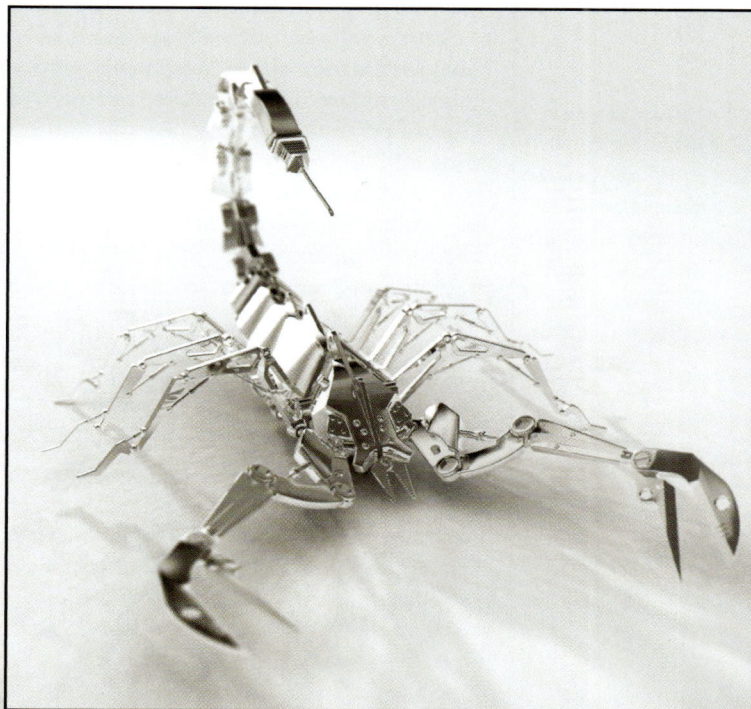

Long-term movement,
page 100

Gravity Dampener

Level: 1d6
Wearable: Medallion, ring, boots
Effect: The device automatically activates whenever its user falls 10 feet (3 m) or more. The user floats down until he lands safely, taking no damage from the fall.

Gravity Nodule

Level: 1d6
Usable: Crystal nodule affixed to a melee weapon
Effect: For the next 28 hours, the weapon the nodule is attached to seems to defy some element of gravitational pull, sliding faster through the air to seek and strike its target. The nodule essentially turns a heavy weapon into a medium weapon (usable in one hand) or a medium weapon into a light weapon (lowering the difficulty of attacks by one step). If attached to a light weapon, the nodule reduces the difficulty of attacks by another step. Damage remains unchanged in all cases.

Ground Orb

Level: 1d6
Usable: Handheld device
Effect: Unfolds into a clear, padded synth orb about 8 feet (2 m) in diameter, with a large door that swings open. Once inside, the user can strap herself in and voice-program the orb with a location. The orb will roll to said location with the user inside, increasing travel speed along a road to about 5 miles (8 km) per hour and overland travel speed to about 4 miles (6 km) per hour during long-term movement.

Unfolding the orb is an action. Getting inside and programming it is also an action.

Grow Ray

Level: 1d6 + 2
Usable: Projector ray
Effect: An inanimate object in short range grows twenty times its normal size and remains that way for 28 hours. The object's mass increases as well, but not at the same rate—only enough to keep it from collapsing in on itself.

Growth Harness

Level: 1d6 + 2
Wearable: Harness that fits around the user's torso
Effect: This device draws mass to the user from another dimension, allowing her to grow 50 percent larger for one hour. During this time, she gains 12 points to her Might Pool and deals 2 additional points of damage with all melee attacks.

Growth Serum

Level: 1d6
Internal: Liquid that is injected or swallowed
Effect: The user permanently grows a foot taller. This process is painful and takes 28 hours, during which time the affected character is impaired.

Growth Stimulator

Level: 1d10
Usable: Spray bottle, aerosol projector
Effect: One plant touched by the liquid grows to ten times its normal, full-grown size in ten minutes. If conditions can't support the plant, it soon dies.

Grub Armor

Level: 1d6 + 1
Usable: Canister of dried worms
Effect: This cypher requires a bit of water to activate the dried worms in the can. Once activated, the grubs grow to enormous size in 1d6 rounds and swarm over the user's body, providing +2 to Armor for one hour. Further, if the user is targeted by an effect that specifically affects a single creature, such as something that controls or reads her mind, one of the grubs is affected instead, effectively rendering the user immune to such things for the duration. This does not apply to straightforward physical attacks of any kind.

Gyre Loop

Level: 1d6 + 2
Usable: Complex device, handheld device
Effect: Generates a strong wind that blows in a path 5 feet (2 m) wide and 500 feet (152 m) long. The wind blows for one hour. The wind is strong enough to scatter papers and loose, lightweight objects, cause flames to gutter out, and drive back tiny creatures. The wind can also fill a sail to propel a wind-powered vehicle. The user can change the direction of the wind by simply moving the device so it faces a different way.

Habiliment Mirage

Level: 1d6
Wearable: Lapel pin, bracelet, ring
Effect: The user activates the device and scans the resulting small beam of light over a piece of clothing, armor, or other accoutrement within long range. The device then creates a hologram of that outfit over and around the user, making it seem as if he is wearing it, right down to the details. The illusion lasts for one hour or until the device is removed from the user's person.

Hand of the Conqueror

Level: 1d6 + 3
Wearable: Thin glove
Effect: When activated, this thin glove becomes as tough as the hardest metal. Punch attacks made by the wearer inflict 1 additional point of damage. Further, the wearer's hand can't be harmed. He can handle hot lava or stick his hand into a grinder and suffer no ill effects (though the grinder might be wrecked). The effect lasts for 28 hours.

Hanging Cocoon

Level: 1d6
Usable: Handheld device
Effect: After being given a firm shake, this device expands into a tapered, hanging, semienclosed tent large enough for one person. It can easily be hung from anything that will support the weight of a human. Opening and hanging the cocoon is a single action. Climbing into it is also an action. It lasts for one day before it begins to dissolve.

Harassing Companion

Level: 1d6 + 2
Usable: Metal cube
Effect: When activated, this cube becomes a small flying automaton that harasses a target for one minute. It flies at the target, getting in

Head Transference Collar GM Intrusion: An intelligent creature that remains fully aware when its head is detached from its body may go mad for a time or suffer permanent mental damage.

the way of his eyes, his movements, and so on. The difficulty of the target's actions is increased by one step. At any time, the user can take an action to command the automaton to bother a different target within short range.

Head Transference Collar

Level: 8
Usable: Adjustable metal ring
Effect: This collar fits around the neck of most creatures the size of a human or so. When activated, it slices the head cleanly from the body and preserves the head (and mind) of the creature for up to ten minutes, during which time the creature is fully conscious. If the headless body of another creature that has been dead for less than one hour is available, the head preserved by the collar can be grafted onto that body. Henceforth, the head now controls its new body as if it had always been its own. This is very likely to alter Might and Speed Pools (but not Intellect Pool) and possibly other qualities as well.

Healing Nodule

Level: 1d6 + 1
Usable: Crystal nodule affixed to a melee weapon
Effect: Once activated, this nodule functions for ten minutes. Whenever the weapon that the nodule is affixed to strikes a foe (or any hard surface), 1 point is restored to the wielder's Might Pool. The nodule cannot restore more than 1 point per round.

Health Symbiote

Level: 1d6
Internal: Inhalable powder
Usable: Injector
Effect: Activation inflicts 1 point of ambient damage as the symbiote becomes established in the user's system. For the next 28 hours, the user is immune to diseases, poisons, and other toxins.

Health Viewer

Level: 1d6
Wearable: Contact lenses, monocle, goggles
Usable: Small transparent panel
Effect: Allows the user to see through clothing and skin to view a creature's insides. Lead

blocks the special vision. The user can use this ability as an asset for any healing-related tasks. Once activated, the cypher functions for ten minutes.

Heartbeat Lock
Level: 1d6
Usable: A 3-foot (1 m) coil of thin copper wire with a flat round disk on each end
Effect: By placing the disks against the user's chest for one minute, the device becomes synchronized with her heartbeat. After this, if the disks are pushed together, they form a seal that can be broken only when the device is exposed to the original heartbeat. Opening the lock destroys the locking mechanism.

Heartburst
Level: 1d6 + 4
Internal: Pill, implant
Wearable: Ring, bracelet, pendant
Effect: This device is keyed to the heartbeat of the user. If he dies, the device explodes, inflicting damage equal to the cypher level to all within immediate range.

Heartlink
Level: 1d6 + 1
Internal: Pill, implant
Wearable: Ring, bracelet, pendant
Effect: This device is keyed to the heartbeat of the user, so that if he dies, a designated intelligent creature will be informed telepathically.

Heat Sensor
Level: 1d6
Internal: Pill, injector
Wearable: Goggles, spectacles, contact lenses
Usable: Handheld device with a screen
Effect: For one hour, the user can perceive objects and creatures based on the heat they emit. This may allow him to see otherwise invisible or hidden targets, or even certain objects inside other objects if their temperatures are vastly different.

Heat Sheath
Level: 1d6 + 1
Usable: Spray canister
Effect: This spray can coat up to one melee weapon per cypher level, but all of the

canister's contents must be sprayed at once. Coated weapons inflict 1 additional point of damage from the heat they now generate. The coating wears off after 28 hours.

Heat Stone
Level: 1d6
Wearable: Lump of rock hanging from a necklace or set in a ring
Effect: The device activates when the user would take damage from heat or fire. The device reduces the damage to 0 and makes the user immune to heat and fire for one hour.

Heatvision Lenses
Level: 1d6
Internal: Eye drops
Wearable: Eyeglasses, goggles, contact lenses
Effect: Allows the user to see infrared light for one hour. Warm creatures and objects register as bright reds, oranges, and yellows, while cool areas appear blue, purple, or black. The device allows the wearer to see in total darkness, though fine detail is impossible. A hot light source (such as the sun) effectively blinds the user while the source is in his field of view.

Heliolithic Halo
Level: 1d6
Wearable: Metallic ring 6 inches (15 cm) in diameter
Effect: When activated, the ring hovers about 3 inches (8 cm) over a living creature and creates a psychic shield of white light to protect that creature. For the protected creature, the difficulty of all Intellect defense tasks is decreased by one step for one hour. Requires a sun prayer to activate (activation is an action).

Helping Hand
Level: 1d6 + 1
Usable: A metallic, seven-fingered hand
Effect: When activated, the hand hovers near the user for 28 hours. During that time, it acts as the user's third hand—holding objects, opening doors, turning dials, and so on. The helping hand can also make attacks as the user might, with weapons provided to it, but all such attacks are modified by two steps to the user's detriment.

Some heartbeat locks are designed to work not just with an individual's unique heart rhythm, but with her exact rhythm at the time of synchronization. That means that someone attempting to force the owner to open a heartbeat lock will likely fail—the stress of the situation will cause the owner's pulse to race too hard to open the lock.

Rhythm forgers— typically called rhythmers—are thieves who train extensively in biofeedback techniques to break into devices that rely on pulse rhythms and other physiological elements.

Many numenera devices require the user to speak words to activate them. In the case of the heliolithic halo, those words must include something to do with the sun and the worship of it in the language of the Truth.

Hidden Reviver

Level: 1d6
Wearable: Elaborate hair pin, locket necklace, double bracelet
Effect: This device is always disguised as a wearable object. When worn, the device does not count against your cypher limit. To use the device, you must first dismantle the disguised object and then rebuild it into its proper form as a handheld device. Then it can revive a depleted artifact for a single additional use.

One action to build the reviver from the parts, and one action to attempt to use it.

History Tap

Level: 1d6
Wearable: Small disk that attaches to forehead, electronic bracelet, thick collar, stretchy gloves
Effect: As soon as you put on the device, it begins to pulse with a heat that runs along your skin and directly to your brain. If you think of a human or visitant that you've heard of but never met, the device grants you access to one random moment in that individual's life. You see the moment as if in a dream and may remember only parts of it once the experience is over.

Homunculus

Level: 1d6 + 2
Internal: Pill, ingestible liquid
Usable: Injector
Effect: Causes a small blister to appear somewhere on the user's body 1d6 days after activation. Every day thereafter for six days, the blister grows. After six days, the blister becomes so large that the difficulty of all the user's rolls increases by one step. On day twelve, the blister reaches its ultimate size: a massive, fluid-filled sac that leaves the user incapacitated for a full 28 hours. When the last hour ends, the blister splits open and leaks a yellow slick of phlegmy substance. In the midst of the mess is a level 1 creature about 18 inches (46 cm) tall. The creature can talk in any language the user knows and accompanies him wherever he goes, following his instructions. It vaguely resembles the user but is ugly and misshapen. It knows everything the user knows, and when it helps him perform a task other than attack or defend, the difficulty of the task is decreased by one step.

Hover Disk

Level: 1d6 + 1
Usable: A metal disk about 2 feet (0.6 m) across
Effect: The user can stand on the disk, and for ten minutes it moves as she desires, up to a long distance each round. In a combat situation, she can take an action (other than moving) and still move a long distance. Because the disk is attuned to her thoughts, falling off is possible only if she loses consciousness or is struck by a tremendous force (usually one that inflicts more than 8 points of damage in one blow).

Hover Module

Level: 1d6 + 2
Usable: Small metal and synth plate
Effect: This cypher must be attached to another cypher or artifact (a level 4 task). Once attached, it no longer counts against a character's cypher limit. The cypher or artifact it is attached to can be placed in the air and will remain there until someone grabs it and deactivates the hover property.

The module cannot be removed from the device without destroying both the module and the device.

Image Caster

Level: 1d6
Usable: Complex device, handheld device
Effect: Projects an ephemeral image within long range that looks real. The image looks like the user, speaks like the user, and moves as the user desires within long range for up to one hour. Physical interaction with the image shows it to be without substance.

Indestructible Oil

Level: 1d6
Usable: A small amount of oil, likely in a jar or flask
Effect: If a character coats an inanimate object with this oil, the object becomes almost indestructible (treat as level 10 for durability). One dose is enough for a single object about the size of a sword, a shield, or a small case.

Inertia Shield

Level: 1d6 + 4
Wearable: Belt, body harness
Effect: An energy field surrounds the user for ten minutes. No physical object can penetrate the shield if that object is moving with any force that could be constituted as an attack. The field would deflect a strike from a broadsword or a bolt fired from a crossbow. Attacks using physical objects inflict no damage on the user until the effect ends.

Inflatable Companion

Level: 1d6 + 2
Usable: Self-inflating blow-up companion
Effect: Small device self-inflates into a companion that is roughly 4 feet (1 m) tall. It is a creature of a level equal to the cypher level and can understand verbal commands of the character who activates it. Once the companion has been activated, commanding it is not an action. It can make attacks or perform actions as ordered to the best of its abilities, but it cannot speak.

The companion has short-range movement but never goes farther than long range away from the character who activated it. The companion is not artificially intelligent or capable of initiating action other than performing its purpose, as designated by its form.

The GM should roll d100 ahead of time to decide what form the companion takes.

01–50	*Attack creature*: Takes the form of an aggressive creature in the Ninth World that does damage equal to the cypher level. The creature lasts for ten minutes.
51–75	*Protective automaton*: Takes the form of a sentient defense system (such as a floating shield) that absorbs 1 point of damage that would normally be taken by the user each round. The system lasts for one hour.
76–00	*Distracting humanoid*: Takes the form of a humanoid figure that attempts to create a distraction. This causes the foe to become dazed, increasing the difficulty of all its tasks by one step. The humanoid lasts for three rounds.

Inflatable Suit

Level: 1d6
Internal: Pill, ingestible liquid
Wearable: Full bodysuit
Effect: Causes a number of bags to suddenly inflate all over the user's body. The inflated bags protect him from damage sustained

To determine the specific form of an inflatable attack creature, GMs can choose at their discretion from the creatures on page 228 in the Numenera corebook.

If an echo crystal is affixed to an instant guardian before it is grown (task difficulty 5), two guardians are created by the pod.

Echo crystal, page 49

Using insanity masks to gain Intellect points always involves a risk because a bad roll can decrease your other Pools. Damage is typically applied to Pools in this order:
1. Might (unless the Pool is 0)
2. Speed (unless the Pool is 0)
3. Intellect
Thus, if someone's Intellect Pool is at 0 when she uses the mask, any damage comes out of her Might Pool.

from impacts, such as one resulting from a fall or a great concussive force. The bags remain inflated for one minute and then deflate with a tremendous noise. While the bags are inflated, the difficulty of the user's Might rolls and Speed rolls is increased by one step.

Insanity Mask
Level: 1d6
Wearable: A metal mask with tiny holes in odd places and a locking mechanism in the back
Effect: Anyone wearing the mask begins to slowly lose her mind. The mask causes 1d6 + 2 points of Intellect damage each round for a number of rounds equal to the cypher level. Alternatively, if someone's Intellect Pool is already at 0, she can attempt to gain Intellect points by wearing the mask. Wearers who start with 0 in their Intellect Pool gain 1d6 − 2 Intellect points each round for a number of rounds equal to the cypher level. If the resulting number is negative, the wearer takes those points out of the next Pool in succession. For example, if the wearer is at 0 Intellect points and rolls a natural 1, she loses 1 point from her Might Pool. If her Might Pool is already at 0, the point of damage comes out of her Speed Pool instead.

Instant Boat
Level: 1d6 + 3
Usable: Handheld device
Effect: With the addition of water and air, this small device expands into a simple boat. The boat is 10 feet long by 4 feet wide (3 m by 1 m) and is made from a type of lightweight molded foam that begins to disintegrate after a day.

Instant Companion
Level: 1d6 + 1
Usable: Fist-sized organic pod
Effect: If submerged in water, the pod grows quickly. In one minute, it grows into a houndlike beast of a level equal to the cypher level, with appropriate health, damage inflicted, and so on, plus 1 point of Armor. The hound obeys the user's commands (as best as it can, with only animal-level intelligence) for 28 hours or until it is slain, whichever comes first, at which point it dissolves into thick liquid.

Instant Guardian
Level: 1d6
Usable: Fist-sized organic pod
Effect: If submerged in water, the pod grows quickly. In one minute, it grows into a batlike creature of a level equal to the cypher level. The creature sits on the user's shoulder for 28 hours or until the user is attacked. The guardian moves to intercept the attack in its entirety. That is the only action it will take.

Instant Shield
Level: 1d6
Wearable: Ring, earring, hair pin, wristband, lapel pin
Usable: Spray canister
Effect: When activated by a simple voice command, the device instantly sends out a spray of molecules that harden into a protective wall in the air. The wall is 4 feet by 4 feet (1 m by 1 m). It provides Armor equal to the cypher level for two rounds.
Activation is an action.

Instant Weapon
Level: 1d6 + 2
Wearable: Ring, earring, hair pin, wristband, lapel pin
Usable: Spray canister
Effect: When activated by a simple voice command, the device instantly emits a temporary light beam. For one round, the beam does damage equal to the cypher level to a foe in close range. The weapon must be activated and used as a single combined action.

Instant Wings
Level: 1d6
Wearable: Backpack
Effect: When activated, silken wings pop out of this backpack, allowing the wearer to glide (if falling or leaping from a height) for great distances, moving a long distance each round, and landing safely on the ground. The wings last until the wearer lands or for one hour, whichever comes first.

Interaction Advisor
Level: 1d6 + 2
Internal: Pill, ingestible liquid
Wearable: Temporary tattoo, amulet,

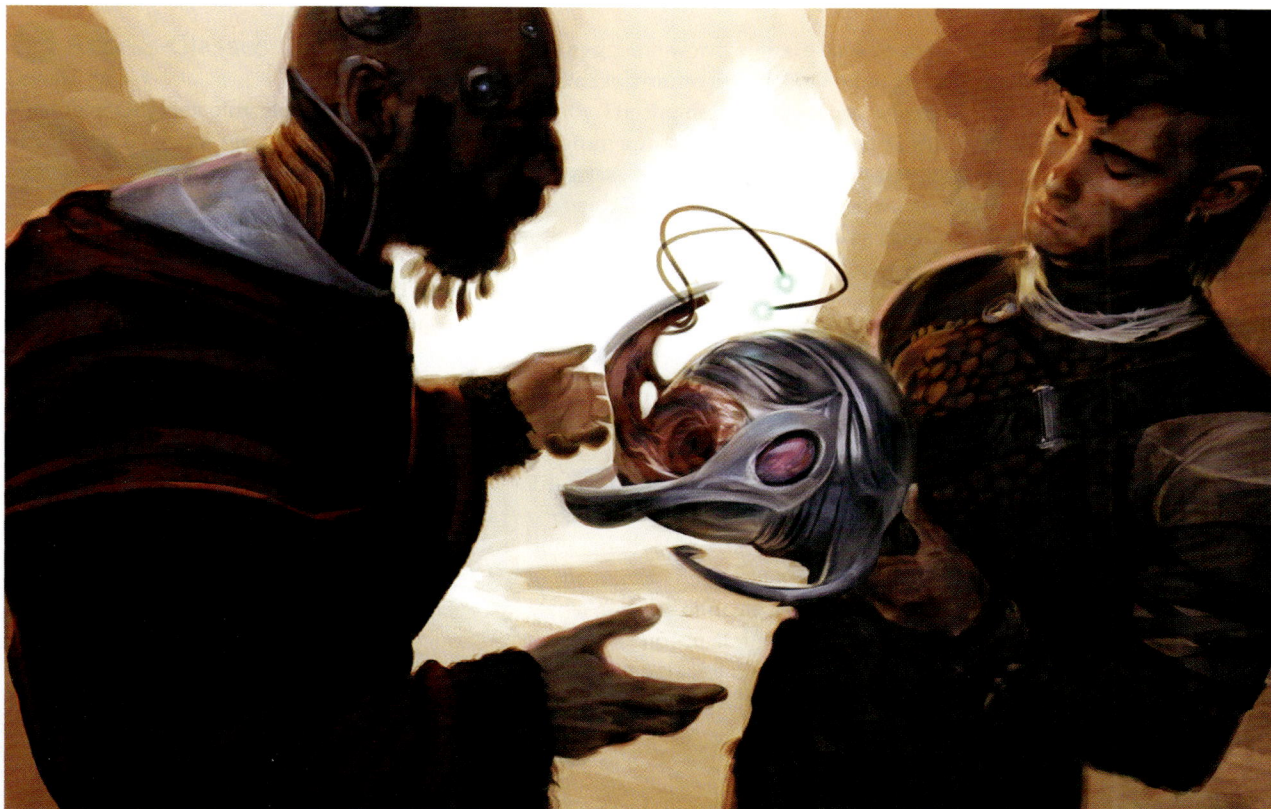

headband, crystal worn on temple
Effect: The device allows the user to access the datasphere to analyze other sentient creatures and anticipate their needs, motives, emotions, and so on. Wording, gestures, and even body language suggestions are offered. For one hour, the user has an asset for all interaction tasks.

Internal Detector
Level: 1d6
Internal: Syringe, pill, ingestible liquid
Effect: Injects a fluorescent protein gene into the user, causing her skin to glow with a bioluminescent color that reflects the conditions in the surrounding environment (within long range). Works in both air and water. Lasts for one hour.
   Blue: poison or other dangerous gasses
   Green: dangerous levels of radiation or chemical compound
   Yellow: unknown dangerous compound
   Orange: unknown safe or beneficial compound
   Purple: hallucinogenic compound
   No glow: nothing detected

Invulnerable Mesh
Level: 10
Wearable: Bodysuit
Usable: Spray canister
Effect: Grants +10 to Armor for one hour.

Jolter
Level: 1d6 + 2
Wearable: Harness with wires connecting to a metal rod that can be held or affixed to the forearm
Effect: When activated, this cypher generates a bolt of wild electricity that extends to short range before arcing into the ground or a target on the ground chosen by the user. The bolt inflicts damage equal to the cypher level, but the jolter is difficult to aim or control. The difficulty for any attack with the device is increased by one step, and a roll of 1 or 2 on the die suggests that a different target (if any) was struck. The jolter emits the bolt for four rounds, each round inflicting the same damage, but using it each round is an action and requires a new roll. There is no way to turn the jolter off once activated, so activating it is a four-round commitment. A user that does not control a jolter in a round will be struck by the bolt of electricity herself.

Jonah Ice

Level: 1d6 + 4

Usable: Liquid contained in a tiny metal canister

Effect: Adding the liquid to water raises the water's freezing point to 100 °F (38 °C). The water, as well as any other water in contact with it, freezes solid unless temperatures exceed the new freezing point. Anything in the water freezes with it and suffers 6 points of damage. Affected water returns to normal 1d20 days later.

Kinetic Rod

Level: 1

Usable: A metallic rod with an insulated handle (similar to a club)

Effect: The user strikes the device against a solid surface, and the device absorbs the kinetic energy from the impact. The next time the user hits a target with an attack using the rod, the device releases the kinetic energy and inflicts 2 additional points of damage. Thereafter, this device functions as an ordinary club.

Leap Belt

Level: 1d6 + 1

Wearable: Clamps onto belt

Effect: When attached to a standard leather belt, this device allows the wearer to leap up to long range in a single bound (vertically, horizontally, or both), landing perfectly.

Lie Eater

Level: 1d6 + 3

Usable: Cone-shaped device with two tiny tendrils

Effect: This biomechanical device feeds on brain waves associated with deception. When a creature that it is pointed at lies, the tips of the tendrils light up and wave about. Once activated, the device functions for ten minutes.

Life Sensor

Level: 1d6 + 2

Wearable: Spectacles, goggles, helmet with visor

Usable: Handheld device with display

Effect: Reveals the exact locations of every living creature within long range. At the end of each minute of operation, the user rolls a d6. On a 1, the device deactivates.

Light Binder

Level: 1d6 + 4

Usable: Explosive device

Effect: Two rounds after activation, the device explodes in a short radius. All light in the area (any place in the area illuminated by light or dim light) becomes solid, trapping everything in the area in place for one minute. Nothing in the area can move, and nothing from outside the area can enter it until the effect ends.

    Rendering any area dark, such as by

blocking a source of light, frees anything in the darkness that was affected by the device.

Light Flyer

Level: 1d6 + 1
Usable: Small metal rod
Effect: Once activated, the rod creates a winged glider about 12 feet (4 m) across beneath the user's feet. The flyer can move a long distance in a round, and it moves at the whim of the rider (requiring no action). It lasts for four hours, although if the user gets off the glider before then, it disappears, the effect ended.

Light Shield

Level: 1d6 + 2
Wearable: Wristband device
Usable: Handheld device
Effect: Emits a field around the wearer for five minutes. While the wearer is in an area of light or dim light, he has additional Armor equal to the cypher level.

Light Steed

Level: 1d6 + 1
Wearable: Wristband, ring
Usable: Handheld device
Effect: Projects a holographic image of a powerful mammalian quadruped made of glowing light. For eight hours, the image takes on a solid form—still made of light—that moves as directed by the user. The steed is a level 3 creature that cannot make attacks but moves a long distance each round. It discorporates if "slain."

Light Writer

Level: 1d6
Wearable: Wristband projector
Usable: Handheld projector
Effect: Causes glowing writing to appear in the air and remain there for 28 hours. The user can use the device to write up to twenty-five words. The words emit dim light out to a short distance.

Lightning Lance

Level: 1d6 + 2
Usable: Handheld projector (long range)
Effect: Shoots a jagged bolt of lightning at one target within range that inflicts electrical damage equal to half the cypher level. The lightning then leaps to strike a different target within a short distance of the first target and inflicts the same damage.

Living Weaponmaster Nodule

Level: 10
Usable: Crystal nodule affixed to a melee weapon
Effect: When activated, this nodule allows the weapon to which it is affixed to float into the air and attack on its own. It attacks all creatures other than the user within immediate range, striking all that are lower than level 10 (it attacks PCs as a level 10 NPC) and inflicting damage appropriate to the type

of weapon. The weapon fights on its own in this manner for ten rounds (it cannot be stopped by the user).

Lobal Sheath
Level: 1d6
Internal: Pill, ingestible liquid, syringe
Effect: Coats the user's brain with a protective sheath, offering additional Armor against Intellect damage for one hour. Armor protection is equal to the cypher level.

Lotus Paste
Level: 1d6
Usable: A bottle, tube, or jar filled with hydrophobic crystal paste, enough to completely cover two items (such as a piece of armor and a weapon, or two artifacts)
Effect: Covering an object with this paste renders it completely liquid- and fireproof. In addition, the object essentially becomes self-cleaning, repelling dirt from its surface. Action to apply paste.

If someone is wearing armor or using a weapon or an artifact coated in lotus paste, he gains +2 to Armor against fire- and liquid-based attacks for 28 hours.

Lutin (Bioengineered Insects)
Level: 1d6 + 2
Wearable: Wristband projector (long range)
Usable: Handheld projector (long range). Can also be thrown against the ground or other hard object in short range.
Effect: Bursts in a cloud of small engineered insects within short distance. The cloud lingers for 1d6 rounds unless conditions indicate otherwise. Roll to determine the effect:

01–50	*Eaten alive.* Living creatures with exposed skin suffer damage equal to the cypher level from bites and stings.
51–75	*Choking.* Living creatures that breathe lose their actions to choking and coughing for a number of rounds equal to the cypher level.
76–00	*Blindness.* In the second round after the explosion, living sighted creatures are blinded by tiny webs spun across their eyes for a number of rounds equal to the cypher level.

Lutin (Combos)
Level: 1d6 + 1
Wearable: Wristband projector (long range)
Usable: Handheld projector (long range). Can also be thrown against the ground or other hard object in short range.
Effect: Bursts in a cloud within short distance. The cloud lingers for 1d6 rounds unless conditions indicate otherwise. Roll to determine the effect:

01–50	*Spores and seeds.* Explodes in a shower of green and yellow spores and seeds. Roll on the (Engineered Spores) table for effect. The seeds implant themselves in living creatures after two rounds, causing additional damage equal to the cypher level.
51–75	*Shrapnel and gel.* Roll on the Lutin (Metal Shrapnel) table for shrapnel effect. The gel causes the shrapnel to adhere to living creatures. As a result, the effect lasts for a number of additional rounds equal to the cypher level.
76–00	*Moths and light drops.* The moths hatch from stasis cocoons at the moment of the explosion. Their reflective wings enhance the light drops, focusing the light into ray beams that do 1d6 + 4 points of damage to all creatures within long range.

Lutin (Engineered Spores)
Level: 1d6 + 2
Wearable: Wristband projector (long range)
Usable: Handheld projector (long range). Can also be thrown against the ground or other hard object in short range.
Effect: Bursts in a cloud of bioengineered spores within short distance. The cloud lingers for 1d6 rounds unless conditions indicate otherwise. Roll to determine the effect:

01–50	*Amnesia.* Living creatures that breathe and think permanently lose all memory of the last minute.
51–75	*Choking.* Living creatures that breathe lose their actions to choking and coughing for a number of rounds equal to the cypher level.
76–00	*Hallucinogenic.* Living creatures that breathe lose their actions to hallucinations and visions for a number of rounds equal to the cypher level.

Lutins are particulate matter devices that are grown or synthesized by using one or more elements of the numenera. Typically, a stretchy cellular material is placed around the desired particulate matter. Over time, the cells grow together to form an ever-shrinking skin around the matter, compressing it into a tightly bound ball. Once the cellular skin is fully synthesized, it hardens and becomes breakable. It is the tight compression of the numenera elements inside the skin that gives lutins their incredible range and velocity when they burst open.

Particulate matter inside a lutin may be as small as bioengineered spores, nanites, or living dust and as large as pieces of shrapnel created from broken bits of technological devices. The particulate matter may even be biochemical creations, captured bits of weather, or organic creatures temporarily put into stasis.

Some fashioned lutins may have more than one type of numenera inside them, causing a single explosion to have multiple effects.

Not all lutins have negative effects.

Lutin (Light Drops)

Level: 1d6 + 2
Wearable: Wristband projector (long range)
Usable: Handheld projector (long range). Can also be thrown against the ground or other hard object in short range.
Effect: Bursts in a cloud of contained light drops within short distance. The cloud lingers for 1d6 rounds unless conditions indicate otherwise. Roll to determine the effect:

01–50	*Blindness.* Living sighted creatures are blinded by the refractions of light for a number of rounds equal to the cypher level.
51–75	*Sleep.* Living sighted creatures are soothed by the warm glow of the light and fall asleep for a number of rounds equal to the cypher level or until woken by a violent action or an extremely loud noise.
76–00	*Dazzle.* Living sighted creatures are distracted by the dazzling array of lights and colors, and they become dazed for a number of rounds equal to the cypher level. During this time, the difficulty of all tasks they perform is modified by one step to their detriment.

Lutin (Metal Shrapnel)

Level: 1d6 + 2
Wearable: Wristband projector (long range)
Usable: Handheld projector (long range). Can also be thrown against the ground or other hard object in short range.
Effect: Bursts in a cloud of metal shrapnel within short distance. Roll to determine the effect:

01–50	*Sharp.* Living creatures with exposed skin suffer damage equal to the cypher level from the sharp edges of the shrapnel.
51–75	*Corrosive.* Living creatures with exposed skin suffer damage equal to the cypher level from corrosive-laden shrapnel.
76–00	*Electrical.* The shrapnel contains small amounts of electric charge. Living creatures with exposed skin suffer electrical damage equal to the cypher level.

Lutin (Nanites)

Level: 1d6 + 2
Wearable: Wristband projector (long range)
Usable: Handheld projector (long range). Can also be thrown against the ground or other hard object in short range.
Effect: Bursts in a cloud of nanites within short distance. The cloud lingers for 1d6 rounds unless conditions indicate otherwise. Roll to determine the effect:

01–50	*Absorb.* Nanites absorb all physical damage dealt by creatures within the explosive range for one round. This has no effect on Intellect damage.
51–75	*Power up.* Nanites enhance all numenera devices within range, adding 1d6 to their damage (or level) if used in the next two rounds.
76–00	*Brain buster.* Nanites do Intellect damage equal to the cypher level to all thinking creatures in range, ignoring Armor.

Magnetic Boots

Level: 1d6
Wearable: Magnets fit onto boots
Effect: These extraordinarily powerful

If a light drops lutin is combined with a metal shrapnel lutin (task difficulty 9), the resulting cypher creates a swirling vortex of energized metal shards in an immediate area. The vortex lasts for one minute and inflicts 10 points of damage each round to anyone within it.

electromagnets affix to the soles of standard leather boots.

With subtle toe movements, the wearer can activate or deactivate the magnets (no action required), allowing him to climb up a metal wall or remain, unmoved, while standing on a metal surface. The magnets' power lasts for one hour.

Magnetic Ink

Level: 1d6
Usable: Small container of ink
Effect: When used to tattoo flesh, this ink embeds powerful magnets in the subject's skin. The

magnets are powerful enough to hold up to 5 pounds (2 kg) of metal. The ink can be applied only once, and there's only enough to make a tattoo about 3 inches (8 cm) across, but once applied, it is permanent.

Magnetic Winch

Level: 1d6 + 3
Usable: Small metal box
Effect: When activated, this metal box breaks into two halves joined by a very strong and thin metal cable, which can be extended up to 120 feet (37 m). When a second switch is pressed, the boxes each become very strong magnets. When a third switch is pressed, the cable is retracted by a motor that is powerful enough to pull 5,000 pounds (2,268 kg) of dead weight until the two boxes are joined again.

Malady Maker

Level: 1d6 + 1
Usable: Short metal baton
Effect: When a living creature of a level lower than the cypher is struck by this baton (a medium weapon), it is also afflicted by a sudden and powerful nausea, making it lose its action for the next three rounds. Even after the malady maker ability is used, the baton remains an effective medium weapon.

Mass Destructor

Level: 1d6 + 4
Usable: Solid black cube about the size of a human fist encased in a larger clear cube
Effect: When activated, the clear cube begins to dissolve, which takes ten minutes. After the outer cube dissolves fully, the black cube causes all eligible victims (living creatures the size of a small dog or larger) in long range to belch forth a cloud of black vapor. This vapor fills the immediate area around the victim, inflicting damage equal to the cypher level on the victim and all other living creatures within the cloud. One round later, all eligible victims within long range of every affected victim belch forth the same cloud (even if they already did so before). This continues until no creatures are affected. The cypher is a horrific doomsday device that could easily destroy an entire city or wipe out an army.

Mass Nodule

Level: 1d6 + 1
Usable: Crystal nodule affixed to an object or a creature
Effect: If attached to an object or an unresisting creature, the nodule adheres for one hour. The object or creature's weight increases by a factor of ten, rendering most creatures unable to move, and rendering most objects unmovable by creatures whose level is less than the cypher level.

Matter Converter

Level: 1d6 + 2
Internal: Pill
Usable: Complex device
Effect: Converts material that can fit inside a 5-foot (2 m) cube into different material of the user's choice. If this is an internal cypher, the user must consume the material and then excrete or surgically remove the new material in whatever manner the GM deems appropriate.

Memory Cube

Level: 1
Usable: Small cube made of glass or crystal
Effect: Removes one memory from the user's mind and stores it inside the device, where it remains forever. Anyone holding the device can see a replay of the memory as the user experienced it. The user has no recollection of the memory, though she can become familiar with it through repeated viewings.

Memory Dust

Level: 1d6
Usable: Capsule containing nanites and visible dust particles
Effect: Opening the capsule and sprinkling its contents in an area about 10 feet by 10 feet (3 m by 3 m) causes the nanites to loosely create a projection of the events that recently occurred in that area, essentially re-enacting the previous ten minutes. The rendering is mostly created from large shapes and big movements. Smaller details are more difficult to make out.

Memory Gel

Level: 1d6 + 2
Usable: Gel contained in metal or plastic tube with a screw cap
Effect: Pouring out the tube's contents activates the device. The gel spreads over any object within immediate range that can fit inside a 10-foot (3 m) cube. Once the gel covers the object, it stays put for one minute, and then it withdraws and forms into a tiny, hard ball. At any time thereafter, a character can throw the ball a short distance. If it strikes a hard surface, the ball expands and takes the shape of the thing it covered. The material is as hard as metal and lasts until destroyed.

Mental Coupling

Level: 1d6 + 3
Wearable: Headband, glove
Usable: 2-foot-long (0.6 m) synth cable
Effect: Allows one thinking creature to speak telepathically with another creature that it touches. Although the connection lasts for only one minute, vast amounts of data can be exchanged if both creatures are willing.

Mental Director

Level: 1d6
Wearable: Needled patch that adheres to flat, hairless skin
Effect: Once applied, the patch "reads" the user's muscle action, allowing her to remotely (within long range) take a single action with another object that is her size or smaller as though she were touching it. For example, she could detonate a device or push open a door. She must actually perform the desired action in order for the cypher to read her muscle movement.

Mental Thieves

Level: 1d6 + 4
Internal: Subdermal injection
Effect: The user exhales a cloud of spores as he puts a question to a creature within immediate range. The spores infiltrate the target's body, find the answer in its thoughts, and forcefully eject themselves from the body, inflicting 2 points of damage to the target. The spores fly through the air and reenter the user's body, at which point he immediately learns the answer to the question, subject to the limits of the target's knowledge.

If you cobble together a memory cube and a rejuvenation field, you create a cypher that allows a single creature to recover one lost or erased memory permanently.

Rejuvenation field, page 83

If you cobble together a message capsule with any detonation (task difficulty 6), you create a message detonation.

Message Capsule

Level: 1d6
Usable: Synth cylinder about 1 foot (0.3 m) in length
Effect: Upon activation, a message of up to one minute in length can be recited to the cylinder. When the message is complete and the user provides a detailed description of the intended recipient (signifying title and/or name), the cylinder fades from view. Within the next 100 hours, the cylinder appears to the recipient, broadcasts the message, and crumbles into dust.

Message Detonation

Level: 1d6
Usable: Synth cylinder about 1 foot (0.3 m) in length
Effect: It takes an action to encode the cylinder with a detailed description of the intended recipient, signifying his title and/or name. Then the cylinder fades from view. Within the next 100 hours, it appears to the recipient and explodes as a detonation in an immediate radius, inflicting damage equal to the cypher level. Roll d100 for the type of damage:

01–10	Cell-disrupting (harms only flesh)
11–30	Corrosive
31–40	Electrical discharge
41–50	Heat drain (cold)
51–75	Fire
76–00	Shrapnel

Metal Patch

Level: 1d6
Usable: Small metal plate
Effect: When placed on a flat surface, the device affixes itself and rapidly expands until it becomes a plate that is 6 inches (15 cm) thick with a radius of up to 10 feet (3 m). Once in place, the device cannot be removed without destroying it.

Metamagnetizer

Level: 1d6
Usable: Handheld device
Wearable: Glove, wristband
Effect: The device creates a sudden increase in the magnetic field of a random nonliving substance that isn't usually magnetized, causing it to become drawn toward the cypher in one round. The device exerts a strong pull (holding or moving up to 10 pounds [5 kg]) within short range and a weaker pull (holding or moving up to 5 pounds [2 kg]) within long range. Roll d100 for the substance that it attracts:

01–10	Synth
11–30	Stronglass
31–40	Wood
41–50	Stone
51–75	Fabric
76–00	Leather

Mind Control Implant

Level: 1d6 + 4
Internal: Pill
Wearable: Disk that adheres to forehead, temporary tattoo
Usable: Injector
Effect: This cypher consists of two devices—an injection or pill, and a control disk or temporary tattoo. They are usually found together. For ten minutes, the disk or tattoo enables long-range mental communication with—and control of—anyone who took the injection or pill. The controller can bid the target creature to do anything it could do normally.

Mind Killer

Level: 1d6 + 3
Usable: 2-inch (5 cm) crystal dodecahedron
Effect: When activated, this crystal flies into the air and seeks the most intelligent creature in long range, which takes one round. After finding its target, the crystal fires a bolt of energy similar to lightning at the creature that inflicts 10 points of Intellect damage (ignores Armor).

Mind Module

Level: 1d6 + 2
Usable: Small metal and synth plate
Effect: This cypher must be attached to another cypher or artifact (a level 6 task). Once attached, it no longer counts against a character's cypher limit. The cypher or artifact it is attached to is now possessed of its own telepathic machine intelligence and can function on its own, obeying verbal or telepathic commands. For example, a detonation can be told to explode whenever someone in a particular uniform comes near. A windrider can be commanded to fly to a location on its own. The module cannot be removed from the device without destroying both the module and the device.

Detonation cypher, page 284

Windrider, page 313

Mind Oculus

Level: 1d6
Wearable: Glass contact lens, monocle, spectacles
Effect: Allows the wearer to create a mental connection to any living, sentient creature whose eyes they can look into for at least thirty seconds. Removing all language barriers, the mind oculus allows the wearer to ask a question that the creature should know the answer to, and get a truthful answer. If the creature is disagreeable to the exchange, the device allows only one question and answer. If the creature is agreeable, the device allows up to five questions within a ten-minute period.

Mind Sled

Level: 1d6 + 2
Internal: Pill, ingestible liquid
Usable: Injector
Effect: The user falls unconscious, and one round later, a luminous crystal bloodlessly emerges from her head (the crystal is not considered a cypher). When the crystal is touched by another creature, the consciousness of the user wakes in the body of that creature (and the host's consciousness is temporarily submerged). For all intents and purposes, the user is the creature in all ways except personality. The user transfers back into her own body 28 hours later. If her body died in the meantime, there's a chance that her consciousness will remain in the host body, but most often, her personality merely burns out.

Mini Gate

Level: 1d6 + 2
Usable: Metal sphere
Effect: When activated, this device creates a tiny portal at the user's wrist and another at a spot within long range that she can see. Her hand emerges from the second gate, allowing her to manipulate objects, attack with a light weapon, or pull a small object through the gate. The gate lasts for one round per cypher level.

Miniaturized Weapon

Level: 1
Usable: A miniature weapon (usually a sword or dagger)
Effect: When activated, the device instantly grows into the full-sized weapon that it resembles.

Mist Animator

Level: 1d6 + 3
Wearable: Synth glove
Usable: Handheld device
Effect: Allows the user to control the movement and shape of a gaseous substance. The amount of gas cannot be increased or decreased, but it can be moved a short distance in a single round, be reshaped so that the mist envelops selected targets, or be dispersed harmlessly. The animator functions for one minute.

Using a mist animator with a mist energizer or mist producer is a dangerous combination.

Mist Energizer

Level: 1d6 + 3
Wearable: Headband, ring
Usable: Handheld device
Effect: Alters the composition of a gaseous cloud no larger than 10 feet by 10 feet by 10 feet (3 m by 3 m by 3 m) so that it inflicts damage equal to the cypher level to anyone that enters it. Damage continues every round that a creature is within the energized mist, which lasts for ten minutes.

The gaseous cloud can simply be the normal air, but it could also be an already poisonous vapor or some other gas.

Mist Producer

Level: 1d6 + 1
Usable: Handheld device
Effect: Emits a cloud of poisonous gas that inflicts damage equal to the cypher level on anyone within immediate radius. The mist remains for two rounds.

Momentum Dampener

Level: 1d6
Usable: Small mechanical device
Effect: Projects an immobile field out to a short distance from the device that lasts for one minute. Any creature or object that comes into the edge of the field immediately stops moving without harm. Projectiles simply fall to the ground. Creatures stop moving. Until the effect ends, it is not possible to physically move through the field.

Mood Patch

Level: 1d6 + 2
Wearable: Adhesive patch that activates when slapped

Effect: Once activated, the patch transfers a substance that makes the wearer feel an emotion, enter a particular state of mind, or forget something unpleasant. Roll d100:

01–25	Moods ranging from tranquil to ecstatic for one hour
26–50	Moods ranging from melancholy to suicidal for one hour
51–75	Completely truthful (1–3 on d6) or pathological liar (4–6 on d6) for one hour
76–00	Permanently erases one memory chosen by the wearer

Motion Activator

Level: 1d6 + 1
Usable: Small synth nodule
Effect: When attached to another cypher or artifact, the motion activator causes it to activate if anything larger than a small dog moves within immediate range. Once activated, it cannot be deactivated.

Muscle Cart

Level: 1d6 + 3
Usable: Small metal box with wheels
Effect: When activated, this small cart vastly increases its mass and begins to move forward. It can pull up to 10,000 pounds (4,536 kg) for one hour, moving about 10 feet (3 m) per round regardless of terrain (within reason), but only in its original direction.

Mystery Box

Level: 10
Usable: Mechanical object fitted with red button
Effect: The device disappears when activated, and the GM secretly rolls 2d20 to see what happens.

2	*Vanish.* A singularity appears in the space left by the cypher and drags everything within immediate range into another reality or dimension.
3	*Storm.* A violent storm gathers in the sky over the area where the cypher was used and rages for one week before dissipating.
4	*Glow.* Everything within immediate range emits faint light for one hour.
5	*Starfall.* A meteorite falls from the sky and strikes a spot within 10 miles (16 km), destroying everything within 1 mile (2 km) of where it lands.

6   *Weird Death.* Roll 2d6 to determine an age. The first roll is the first digit of the age, and the second roll is the second digit. Every living thing of that age within 1 mile (2 km) immediately dies.

7   *Death Proof.* No living thing within 1 mile (2 km) can die for the next 28 hours.

8   *Petrifaction.* All plant matter within 1 mile (2 km) turns to stone.

9   *Drought.* All water within 1 mile (2 km) is instantly destroyed.

10 *Rust.* All ferrous objects within 1 mile (2 km) turn to rust.

11 *Warping Energy.* All characters within long range gain a harmful mutation or a beneficial mutation (50% chance of either).

12 *Temporal Distortion.* Every living thing within short range is flung 1d20 months into the future.

13 *Revision.* One NPC ceases to exist.

14 *Transmute Gender.* The user's gender changes or is removed altogether (50% chance of either).

15 *Weakness.* The user's Might Pool is permanently reduced by 1.

16 *Rigidity.* The user's Speed Pool is permanently reduced by 1.

17 *Forgetfulness.* The user's Intellect Pool is permanently reduced by 1.

18 *Blindness.* Each sighted creature within short range cannot see for 28 hours.

19 *Horrible Summons.* A level 10 creature from another dimension appears and attacks.

20 *Radiation.* A burst of radiation spreads out from the spot where the device disappeared and inflicts 6 points of ambient damage to all creatures within short range. For any creature that takes this damage, the difficulty of all tasks is increased by one step for 28 hours.

21 *Wretched Mutants.* Each creature within short range gains a harmful mutation.

22 *Antigravity.* Gravity ceases to function everywhere within long range. Anything that is not rooted to the ground flies upward a short distance per round for three rounds. After this time, gravity is restored, and everything that went up comes back down, probably taking falling damage.

23 *Dreadful Summons.* Three level 3 creatures from another dimension appear and attack.

24 *Deafness.* Each creature that can hear and is within a short distance cannot hear for 28 hours.

25 *Catatonic.* The user enters a catatonic state that persists for 1d20 hours.

26 *Mutation.* The user gains two harmful mutations.

27 *Befuddled.* For the user, the difficulty of all tasks is increased by three steps for one hour.

28 *Unexpected Development.* The user gains two cosmetic mutations.

29 *Mind Transfer.* The user swaps minds with the nearest character. The players swap characters.

30 *Psychic Connection.* All characters within immediate range can communicate telepathically regardless of distance for the next 1d20 days.

31 *Foliage.* Plants sprout from the ground and spread out to a distance of 1 mile (2 km).

32 *Awakening of the Flesh.* The user gains a beneficial mutation.

33 *Strength.* The user's Might Pool is permanently increased by 1.

34 *Quickness.* The user's Speed Pool is permanently increased by 1.

35 *Brilliance.* The user's Intellect Pool is permanently increased by 1.

36 *Fold Space.* The user and everyone within short range teleport to a destination of the user's choice anywhere in the world.

37 *Cypher Spawn.* 1d6 randomly determined cyphers appear on the ground in a pile.

38 *Artifact.* A randomly determined artifact appears on the ground.

39 *Vitality Surge.* All characters within immediate range increase their stat Pools by 1 for 28 hours.

40 *Cosmic Awareness.* For the user, the difficulty of all tasks is reduced by three steps for one hour.

Navigator Daemon

Level: 1d6 + 2
Usable: Small handheld device
Effect: The user names a location or the coordinates of a location. The device projects a beam of light that creates a tiny, flying level 1 creature. It takes a minute for the creature to form, and then it wings off to lead the user to the stated destination. After 28 hours, the creature dissipates into motes of light that fade away, whether or not the user has reached the destination.

Mutations, page 123

When characters who fall hit the ground, they suffer 1 point of damage for every 10 feet (3 m) fallen.

Nectar Dispenser

Level: 1d6
Usable: Small canister
Effect: This device produces a thick, delicious liquid that provides nutrition and sustains up to three people for one day (or one person for three days) if there is a container to hold the nectar.

Needle Sphere

Level: 1d6 + 1
Usable: Metal and synth sphere
Effect: Upon activation, the sphere floats in the air next to the user for one round per cypher level. Each round, it fires a large needle (more like a dart) that inflicts 3 points of damage at a target designated by the user within long range. (This occurs on the user's action in addition to her normal actions.) The player makes the attack rolls, and although she cannot use Effort or skills to modify her rolls, the difficulty of each attack is decreased by two steps.

Needleburst

Level: 1d6 + 4
Usable: A crystal with many jagged protrusions
Effect: This device is activated when the user plays a certain high-pitched note within long range of it. (This may require the user to have a pitch-pipe, flute, or other such instrument, but it's possible to sing the note as well if one is talented.) When activated, the device explodes in a short radius with needlelike crystal shards, inflicting damage equal to the cypher level.

Neuron Disruptor

Level: 1d6 + 4
Usable: A metal cylinder with several buttons and dials
Effect: When activated, the device releases a pulse that travels out to a 1-mile (2 km) radius. All living things in the area whose level is lower than the cypher level become catatonic for 28 hours.

Nevermind

Level: 1d6 + 2
Internal: Pill, ingestible or injectable liquid
Wearable: Earring, ring, circlet

Effect: The wearer's mind can't be telepathically sensed or contacted for 28 hours. If the wearer has telepathic abilities or psychic attacks, they're inaccessible. On the other hand, during this period, defense rolls against all kinds of psychic and mental attacks are modified by two steps to the wearer's benefit.

Numbing Oil

Level: 1d6
Wearable: Gloves that secrete oil
Usable: Small flask of oil
Effect: Skin touched by this oil instantly loses almost all sensitivity for one round. This makes things like pickpocketing or surreptitious injections far easier (provides two assets to such actions).

Once used, the oil remains active on the glove or applicator for ten minutes.

Numenera Analyzer

Level: 1d6
Internal: Brain implant
Wearable: Eyeglasses, goggles, helmet
Usable: Small mechanical device
Effect: Automatically identifies all cyphers and artifacts within immediate range.

Numenera Net

Level: 1d6 + 2
Usable: A square of fine mesh
Effect: Before this device can be activated, at least three cyphers must be activated within a short distance of it. Once this occurs, the net becomes charged for 28 hours. The next time the user uses an occultic cypher while in possession of the net, he can transfer energy from the net to the cypher so that the cypher can be used one additional time.

One Perfect Cut

Level: 1d6 + 4
Usable: Knife, dagger, or similar blade
Effect: A user can use the blade to cut through 5 feet (2 m) of any material it touches one time. If used as a weapon, the cypher deals damage equal to the cypher level and ignores Armor.

Orbital Armor

Level: 1d6
Usable: Three small clear balls attached to each other with stretchy synth. One ball has a simple push button.
Effect: When activated and thrown into the air, the balls set up an orbit around the user, protecting her from incoming piercing, striking, or other physical damage for ten minutes. The device provides Armor equal to the cypher level, but it doesn't protect against Intellect damage. Activation is an action.

Orbital Launcher

Level: 1d6 + 4
Wearable: Glove of synth
Usable: Small handheld device
Effect: One unanchored item within immediate range that weighs no more than 50 pounds (23 kg) is launched upward at a chosen angle with a steady, sustained velocity that sends the object into the void over the course of several hours. If the cypher is used underground or directed to launch the item toward some sort of barrier, the cypher doesn't activate.

Organ Patch

Level: 1d6
Usable: Complicated handheld device with control panel
Effect: The device is used to take a sample of the user's skin. The user can set the control panel to choose a single organ he would like to regrow (typically something the size of an ear, a finger, a toe, or an eyeball). Shortly thereafter, the device produces a strip about 4 inches by 2 inches (10 cm by 5 cm) of a sticky, fleshlike substance that the user places on his arm or leg. In 28 hours, he has a newly grown organ. Once the organ is fully grown and properly placed, it self-sticks and begins to grow connections to the user's body. If allowed to attach for 28 hours without taking damage, the new organ becomes permanent.

Ostracized Vapor

Level: 1d6
Wearable: Smoking mask
Usable: Electronic smoking implement
Effect: Allows the user to inhale a potent chemical that changes his body chemistry for ten minutes, causing him to give off pheromones that have a variety of effects.

The GM should roll d100 ahead of time to determine the effect:

01–50	Makes the user smell like prey to the closest nonhuman creature (within long range)
51–75	Makes the user smell like a predator to the closest nonhuman creature (within long range)
76–00	Makes the user smell exactly like the closest nonhuman creature (within long range)

Overwatch Defender

Level: 1d6 + 4
Usable: Sphere on a tripod
Effect: Once activated, this device functions for 28 hours. If a creature with hostile intent comes within long range, the device creates a force field around itself (and anything nearby) that encapsulates an immediate radius. This force field has 100 health; anyone wishing to get in or out of the field must batter their way through. It lasts until destroyed or for one hour, whichever comes first. Once the force field is down, the device is no longer active.

Overwatch Slayer

Level: 1d6 + 3
Usable: Sphere on a tripod
Effect: Once activated, this device functions for 28 hours. If a creature with hostile intent comes within long range, the device immediately fires a blast of energy that inflicts damage equal to the cypher level. It continues to fire, once per round, for a number of rounds equal to the cypher level. Once the device is done firing, it is no longer active.

Pain Inverter

Level: 1d6
Internal: Pill, ingestible liquid, inhalable powder
Usable: Injector
Effect: For one hour after activation, whenever the user takes damage, she has an asset for her next roll made before the next round ends.

Panoramic Capture Ball

Level: 1d6
Usable: Synth ball about 6 inches (15 cm) in diameter, with an electronic device inside and a series of glass lenses

"I once took parts from an overwatch defender and an overwatch slayer and attempted to make something that performed both functions and worked permanently, rather than just over the course of a day. The resulting device ran off and terrorizes the countryside in Milave to this day."
~Sir Arthour

Effect: When the user throws the ball into the air and it reaches its peak, it records a picture through each of its 1d20 + 5 lenses, capturing them all on a screen in a single panoramic image.

Parous Cypher Ball

Level: 1d6
Usable: Synth ball about 6 inches (15 cm) in diameter, with a large, sealable slit in the side
Effect: The parous ball can hold one cypher (as long as it is no larger than a typical handheld device). Once the cypher is sealed in the ball, it must remain there for 28 hours. At that point, the cypher is released. Thereafter, for a number of hours equal to the cypher level, the ball releases exact duplicates of the cypher, one per hour.

While the original cypher is in the ball, it doesn't count against the character's cypher limit. The duplicates do not count against the character's limit until all duplicates are expelled.

Parous Oddity Box

Level: 1d6
Usable: Synth box about 6 inches (15 cm) square, with a large, sealable seam along one side
Effect: The parous box can hold one oddity (as long as it is no larger than a typical handheld device). Once the oddity is sealed in the box, it must remain there for 28 hours. At that point, the oddity is released. Thereafter, for a number of hours equal to the cypher level, the box releases a random oddity, one per hour. Each new oddity is different from the one that was originally put in the box.

Perma-Damp

Level: 1d6 + 4
Usable: Spray canister
Effect: Coats something that can fit within a 5-foot (2 m) cube with gel. The gel remains damp for 1d6 hours. Anything covered by the gel has Armor equal to the cypher level against corrosive, electrical, and fire damage. When the effect ends, the gel grows and becomes spongy, like cake. It provides bland nourishment for up three human-sized characters for one day.

Permanent Handle

Level: 1d6
Usable: Handle-shaped metal and synth piece
Effect: When activated, this device permanently bonds (on a molecular level) to whatever it touches, giving that object a handle. It inflicts damage equal to the cypher level to any living creature it bonds to.

Photon Igniter

Level: 1d6 + 4
Wearable: Wristband
Usable: Handheld device
Effect: Emits a beam at one target within long range. If the beam strikes the target, it changes how the target interacts with light energy for one minute. Until the effect wears off, it inflicts damage based on the level of light to which the target is exposed at the start of each round. Light inflicts 3 points of damage, dim light inflicts 2 points of damage, and very dim light inflicts 1 point of damage.

Photonic Fabricator

Level: 1d6 + 2
Usable: Complex handheld device
Effect: Creates one item of solidified light (user's choice) anywhere within immediate range. The item cannot have moving pieces and must normally be made from a rigid material. For example, a user could create a broadsword, ladder, or shield, but not a backpack, buzzer, or bow. The item emits dim light in a short radius and lasts for 28 days before fading away.

Photonic Hand

Level: 1d6 + 2
Wearable: Wristband projector (long range)
Usable: Handheld projector (long range)
Effect: Creates a glowing copy of the user's hand at a spot within range. The hand is 10 feet (3 m) tall and made from solid light. When activated, the hand attacks a target within immediate range of it. The hand inflicts 4 points of damage and prevents the target from moving for one minute. While held in this way, the target has +2 to Armor.

Photonic Smasher

Level: 1d10
Wearable: Wristband projector (short range)

If you cobble together a photon igniter with a mini gate (task difficulty 7), you create a cypher that emits a beam at one target within long range that inflicts 8 points of damage and teleports the target in a random direction up to 20 feet (6 m) away.

Mini gate, page 73

Buzzer, page 79

Usable: Handheld projector (short range)

Effect: Creates a glowing bludgeon about 5 feet (2 m) tall that floats in the air in an open space within range. When the bludgeon appears, it immediately attacks a target within short range of it and, if it hits, inflicts 4 points of damage. The bludgeon remains for one minute, and whenever the user takes an action, he can move the bludgeon a short distance and attack with it.

Piezoelectric Engine

Level: 1d6 + 2

Wearable: Medallion, headband with small mechanical disc

Usable: Handheld device

Effect: Creates an invisible energy barrier in a short radius from the device that lasts for one hour. The barrier moves with the device. The barrier converts any sound that reaches it into light. Soft noises cause the barrier to emit very dim light out to a short distance, normal conversation produces dim light out to a short distance, and loud noises produce light out to a long distance.

Pleasure Center

Level: 1d6 + 1

Usable: Small metallic disk

Effect: When applied to a creature's head, the disk immediately unleashes microfilaments that enter the brain. Within five minutes, the microfilaments release a chemical compound that provides an increased sensation of pleasure and a decreased sensation of pain or displeasure. Adds 1 to the creature's Might Pool for one hour.

Portable Biolab

Level: 1d6

Usable: Glass orb

Effect: Inside the orb is a complex, self-sustaining ecosystem that creates a useful compound, plant, or creature. When the glass is broken, the lab-produced item becomes available to the user. Although the creation inside could be almost anything, common options include:

01–10	Inhalable gas that allows the user to see in complete darkness as if it were daylight for one hour
11–30	Bioluminescent grubs that, when eaten, cause the user's skin to glow green for one hour
31–40	Drinkable purple liquid that adds 5 to the Pool of the user's choice for one hour
41–50	Orange-petaled flower that increases stamina when eaten, adding 1 to the user's Might Edge for one hour
51–75	Red speckled mushroom that, when licked, causes the user's mind to open, decreasing the difficulty of all skills related to perception, telepathy, and telekinetics by one step for 28 hours.
76–00	Blue-green moss that, when rubbed on skin, makes the skin tacky and sticky. The difficulty of all tasks elated to keeping a good grip (including climbing, balancing, and lockpicking) is decreased by one step for 28 hours.

direction away from the user, traveling a long distance before it dissipates. As it moves, the vortex inflicts damage equal to half its level to anything it touches. The vortex is strong enough to pick up creatures and objects not anchored in place that weigh up to 500 pounds (227 kg) and throw them a long distance away, which inflicts damage equal to half the vortex level when the target lands.

Portal Ring
Level: 1d6 + 4
Usable: Small metallic ring
Effect: The cypher automatically affixes itself to any flat surface on which it is placed. It instantly widens until it reaches 5 feet (2 m) in diameter or until the ring reaches an edge, at which point it stops expanding. The surface inside the ring vanishes, opening a hole through the material or to a depth of 5 feet (2 m).

Power Siphon
Level: 1d6 + 1
Usable: Handheld device
Effect: Transfers power from one device to another. This device can drain power from one cypher to fuel another that has been used but is still intact, or from one artifact to recharge another that has been depleted.

Prismatic Field Projector
Level: 1d6 + 3
Usable: Large device
Effect: To be activated, this device must be placed on level ground. It creates a field of scintillating force around the user that provides Armor equal to the cypher level. However, the device can't be moved once activated, which means the user can't move from where she stands.

The force field lasts for ten minutes.

Portable Steed
Level: 1d6 + 2
Usable: Complex device
Effect: The box unfolds into a mechanical steed. The steed is a level 3 creature that is large enough to carry two human-sized riders. The steed serves for seven hours and then shatters into 1d6 oddities.

Portable Vortex
Level: 1d6 + 4
Usable: Small, disk-shaped device
Effect: One round after activation, the device breaks apart and creates a cyclone. The cyclone is 30 feet (9 m) across at its base, 90 feet (27 m) tall, and 60 feet (18 m) across at the top. When it forms, it sets off in a

Projectile Module (Homing)
Level: 1d6 + 1
Usable: Small metal and synth plate
Effect: This cypher must be attached to another cypher or artifact (a level 4 task) that fires solid projectiles, like a slugspitter or a compactor. Once attached, it no longer counts against a character's cypher limit. The projectile(s) of the cypher or artifact it is attached to now hone in on the desired target,

Slugspitter, page 311

Compactor, page 106

reducing the difficulty of the attack roll by one step.

The module cannot be removed from the device without destroying both the module and the device.

Projectile Module (Mind-Blasting)
Level: 1d6 + 1
Usable: Small metal and synth plate
Effect: This cypher must be attached to another cypher or artifact (a level 4 task) that fires solid projectiles, like a slugspitter or a compactor. Once attached, it no longer counts against a character's cypher limit. The projectile(s) of the cypher or artifact it is attached to now are ghostly psychic missiles that inflict Intellect damage rather than normal damage, and they ignore Armor.

The module cannot be removed from the device without destroying both the module and the device.

Projectile Module (Poison)
Level: 1d6 + 1
Usable: Small metal and synth plate
Effect: This cypher must be attached to another cypher or artifact (a level 4 task) that fires solid projectiles, like a slugspitter or a compactor. Once attached, it no longer counts against a character's cypher limit. The projectile(s) of the cypher or artifact it is attached to now also carry a poison that inflicts 4 points of Speed damage that ignores Armor.

The module cannot be removed from the device without destroying both the module and the device.

Projectile Module (Teleport)
Level: 1d6 + 1
Usable: Small metal and synth plate
Effect: This cypher must be attached to another cypher or artifact (a level 4 task) that fires solid projectiles, like a slugspitter or a compactor. Once attached, it no longer counts against a character's cypher limit. The projectile(s) of the cypher or artifact it is attached to now teleport through barriers to get to the target, but the target must be seen. The attack ignores Armor and can even pass through solid barriers.

The module cannot be removed from the device without destroying both the module and the device.

Psychic Focus
Level: 1d6
Internal: Pill, injection
Wearable: Headband, crystal placed on temple or forehead
Usable: Handheld device
Effect: Increases the intensity of the user's next mental ability, such as a mental Onslaught esotery or the use of psychokinesis. Damaging attacks inflict 2 additional points of damage, and other abilities have double the normal range or duration (user's choice).

Purgspitter
Level: 1d6 + 2
Usable: Handheld device
Effect: This device spits out a tentacled creature called a purg up to long range. The purg is a level 2 creature that adheres to whatever it strikes, producing a keening screech and a strong odor for 28 hours. Grasping with powerful tentacles and an even more powerful natural adhesive, the purg is difficult to remove. To do so, the purg must be slain and scraped away, a task with a difficulty equal to the level of the device. If the purg is slain but not removed, the screech ends, but the stench remains.

Purity
Level: 1d6
Usable: Liquid in a metal or glass canister
Effect: Pouring the canister's contents into another liquid or onto solid material instantly eradicates any toxins, poisons, diseases, or other contaminants in that liquid or material. The purity liquid also prevents the target from being contaminated by such things for 28 hours.

Pushpull Beam
Level: 1d6 + 3
Usable: Handheld device
Effect: This device emits a beam up to long range. The user chooses whether the beam will push or pull. Either way, an unsecured object or creature will be moved a long distance toward or away from the device with the strength of ten humans. The beam lasts for one round.

The purgspitter can be used as a nuisance or as a warning or crude tracking device. A creature or an object with a purg attached can always be found easily.

Pyrolytic Pulser

Level: 1d6 + 2
Wearable: Wristband projector, headband projector, shoulder- or arm-mounted launcher (long range)
Usable: Handheld projector
Effect: Sends out a series of rapid-fire encapsulated heat pellets up to 200 feet (61 m). The pellets burst into flame upon contact, causing disintegration damage equal to the cypher level to all creatures within immediate range of the explosion.

Quadraturin

Level: 1d6
Usable: Gel in a tube
Effect: This substance warps space, expanding it. When applied to a surface, it expands the space around that surface—for example, making an interior room larger. The tube has enough gel to cover an area of about 10 feet by 10 feet by 10 feet (3 m by 3 m by 3 m), expanding it into an area of about 50 feet by 50 feet by 50 feet (15 m by 15 m by 15 m).

Quadraturin GM Intrusion: *Imprecise application can bend space, making an area that expands in one dimension more than the others, or perhaps an area that never stops expanding.*

Radiant Web

Level: 1d10
Usable: Handheld projector (short range)
Effect: Creates a mesh of invisible light across a plane up to 10 feet (3 m) wide and tall. The paper-thin mesh inflicts damage equal to the cypher level to any creature that passes through it. (A target can take this damage only once per round regardless of how many times it passes through the mesh.)

Anything reduced to 0 health by the mesh is sliced into pieces that are 1 inch (3 cm) wide and tall.

Ranged Protector

Level: 1d6
Wearable: Two rings, circlets, bracelets, or belts
Effect: This cypher comes as a pair of items, but one is the master of the other. When the master item is activated, the creature wearing the other item is surrounded by a force shield that provides Armor equal to the cypher level for ten minutes.

While one character could wear both items, many people use ranged protectors to put a shield around a pet, a child, or a defenseless charge who cannot normally activate a cypher.

The master item can be activated from any range to surround its counterpart with the protective shield.

Ranged Retaliator

Level: 1d6 + 2
Wearable: Two rings, circlets, bracelets, or belts
Effect: This cypher comes as a pair of items, but one is the master of the other. When the master item is activated, the other item pulses with electricity that inflicts damage equal to the cypher level. The master item can be activated from any range to damage the wearer of the other item.

Ray Emitter (Molecular Rearrangement)

Level: 1d6 + 3
Wearable: Wristband projector, shoulder- or arm-mounted launcher (long range)
Effect: Emits a ray that causes random molecular rearrangement on a small scale. The ray inflicts damage equal to the cypher level at a range of 200 feet (61 m). Wounds inflicted on living creatures are twisted and bizarre, with tissue literally turned into another substance, another state (liquid or gas), or even energy. Damage to inorganic objects is similarly strange.

Reanimator

Level: 1d6 + 4
Internal: Injectable liquid
Wearable: Disk with a strap to be fastened to the head
Usable: Metal bolt injected into the head
Effect: If a mammalian or reptilian creature has not been dead for more than 28 hours, this device restores a basic semblance of life by reactivating its nervous system. The creature does not have the knowledge, skills, personality, or memories of its former self. It's just a mindless shell that can perform basic motor functions: walk, run, or otherwise move; pick up and hold objects; and make crude attacks. The reanimated creature obeys the verbal commands of the user and operates for one hour before collapsing. Although the GM makes the final call, small creatures are typically level 1, and others are level 2.

Regrow

Level: 1d6
Usable: A metal canister filled with bright blue ointment
Effect: When the entire contents of the canister are smeared on the stump of a missing limb or another body part, the ointment causes the body to regrow the missing part. The user must roll a d6: on a 1 or 2, the body part is half the normal size; on a 3 or 4, it's normal size; on a 5 or 6, it's twice the normal size. Regardless of the result, the body part is the same color as the ointment.

Rejuvenating Shield

Level: 1d6 + 2
Internal: Injector
Wearable: Ring, bracelet
Usable: Small handheld device
Effect: When activated, the device surrounds the user with a field of white energy that remains for ten minutes. During this time, the user gains +2 to Armor. Further, during each of the first ten rounds, she regains 1 point to one of her stat Pools (her choice each round; cannot exceed normal Pool maximums).

Rejuvenation Field

Level: 1d6 + 2
Usable: Handheld device
Effect: This device projects a nimbus of energy that fills the immediate area. All characters within the area regain a number of points equal to the cypher level in one Pool.

Roll a d100:

01–50	Might Pool
51–75	Speed Pool
76–00	Intellect Pool

Creatures and NPCs in the area regain the points to their health.

Remake

Level: 1d6 + 2
Internal: Pill, injectable liquid, inhalable powder
Wearable: Dermal patch
Usable: Injector
Effect: The user can permanently move up to 4 points from one stat Pool to another.

Remote Scarificator

Level: 1d6 + 2
Wearable: Wristband projector, shoulder- or arm-mounted launcher (long range)
Effect: Shoots out a device that extends twelve blades upon hitting its target. If the scarificator hits a living creature, it does damage equal to the cypher level and causes the creature to bleed slowly for up to one hour. If it hits nonliving material, it shaves off strips of the material and creates a permanent mark.

Remote Sensorium

Level: 1d6
Usable: Moldable synth
Effect: Allows the user to create a replica of one of her sensory organs and place it in a remote location up to 1 mile (1.6 km) away, thus enhancing that particular sense. She can see, hear, touch, taste, or smell things that are within short range of the replicated organ as if she were also within short range.

Reproductive Bud

Level: 1d6 + 1
Usable: An expandable organic sac
Effect: This organic device allows a character to reproduce asexually. First the sac is grafted onto a character for 28 hours. Then it is removed and placed in a warm, moist environment. Half a year later, it bursts open and reveals a living, infant clone of the character.

Repulsion Field

Level: 1d6 + 2
Wearable: Belt, harness, amulet
Effect: Emits a field around the user that lasts for one minute. Whenever he would take damage from a physical object such as a weapon or an arrow, the field emits a pulse of energy that inflicts 2 points of ambient damage to everything within immediate range, and then the user moves an immediate distance away from the source of the damage.

Reset

Level: 10
Wearable: Amulet, headband, helmet
Usable: Small handheld device
Effect: Utterly erases the last five minutes of time. Everything goes back to the way it was

Hunters and trackers employ remote scarificators to tag their prey from a distance and follow it back to its nest or lair.

and no one except the user remembers what happened during the lost five minutes.

Revealer Dart

Level: 1d6
Wearable: Wristband projector (short range)
Usable: Handheld projector (long range)
Effect: The device fires a metal dart at a single target within range. Upon striking the target, the device flashes bright red and issues a soft ringing that lasts for one hour. If the target tries to remove the dart, it delivers a current of electricity that inflicts 3 points of damage that ignores Armor. Until the effect ends, the user has an asset on all attack rolls against the target.

Reviver

Level: 1d6
Internal: Injectable liquid, pill
Effect: The device causes an unconscious, sleeping, or comatose character to wake up immediately, completely alert. This treatment does not repair damage or cure illness.

Root Spike

Level: 1d6
Wearable: Wristband or headband projector (short range)
Usable: Handheld projector (long range)
Effect: Shoots a single thorn at a target within range. The thorn inflicts 2 points of damage and wraps the target in a mesh of roots and vines that anchor it in place for one minute or until it or another creature uses an action to free it.

Rynrad Skin

Level: 1d6
Wearable: Full-body skinsuit designed to be worn over armor, complete with hood, mask, and chemical bladder
Effect: When fully enclosed in a rynrad skin, the wearer pushes the release button on the chemical bladder, and the suit begins to seep invisible streams of rynrad poison into the surrounding area. Rynrad poison does nerve damage (equal to the cypher level) to all living creatures in long range for two rounds.

The suit protects the wearer from the effects of all poisons and grants +1 to Armor against piercing attacks for one hour.

Rynrad poison is a concoction that is easy to find ingredients for but incredibly difficult to manufacture. The mixture of plants and chemicals must be wrapped in a synth balloon and fed to a dossi (a domesticated creature raised for its meat and scales). The concoction must churn in one of the creature's stomach sections for at least two days and then get passed without breaking open and killing the animal.

Sanity Assassin

Level: 1d6 + 1
Internal: Pill, ingestible or injectable liquid
Wearable: Lipstick, false fingertip, ring with needle
Usable: Injector
Effect: This is a poison or drug that drives the affected target mad for 28 hours. The madness can take many forms (usually at least somewhat dependent upon the individual), but it can include hallucinations, paranoia, hearing voices, or simply a skewed outlook on reality. The madness is very strong and affects most or all of the target's actions, but it is not entirely debilitating.

Screaming Madness

Level: 1d6 + 2
Usable: Small red polygon
Effect: One round after activation, this device emits a loud, piercing noise. Living creatures within immediate range suffer 2 points of Intellect damage (ignores Armor), and for all those affected, the user makes a second roll. Those affected by the second roll are driven mad temporarily. Roll d100 to determine the expression of this insanity, which lasts for one minute.

01–20	Run off in a random direction for a short distance and then attempt to hide
21–30	Attack the nearest creature with whatever means is closest at hand
31–60	Do nothing but cover ears and scream
61–80	Fall down and roll on the ground
81–90	Drop whatever is held and cover eyes and face with hands
91–00	Activate most powerful available ability, cypher, or artifact that is not an attack (if none, roll again) and then hide

The noise continues for five rounds, and the damage and madness continue each round, affecting those that remain in or enter the area.

Second Sight Symbiote

Level: 1d6
Internal: Inhalable powder
Usable: Injector
Effect: Activation inflicts 1 point of damage as the symbiote establishes itself in the user's system. For the next hour, the user has an asset for all perception-based tasks.

Secret Finder

Level: 1d6 + 4
Internal: Pill, ingestible liquid
Wearable: Temporary tattoo, amulet, headband, crystal worn on temple
Usable: Small handheld device, crystal
Effect: Tapping into the datasphere, the user names one place, creature, or object and immediately learns his distance from the thing named and the direction he must travel to reach it.

Secret Pocket

Level: 1d6
Wearable: Shirt, jacket, pants
Effect: The article of clothing has a special pocket. The pocket's opening connects to an extradimensional space that's about the size of a 3-foot (1 m) cube. The opening appears to be a normal pocket, but it can stretch to permit entry by an object capable of fitting into the extradimensional space. Placing an object in the space causes the pocket to shut until the user takes an action to open it. While the pocket holds an object, it cannot be opened by anyone except the person who placed the object inside it. Anyone inspecting the clothing finds no sign that the pocket or object exists. Furthermore, the clothing's weight is unchanged regardless of the weight of the object placed in the pocket. When the user removes the object from the pocket, the pocket closes behind it and the space collapses.

Security Clamp

Level: 1d6 + 2
Usable: Mechanical device
Effect: When activated and placed on an object that can be opened or closed, the device prevents the object from opening by normal means. The only way to open the object is to destroy it.

See You Goggles

Level: 1d6
Wearable: A near-matching set of goggles or glasses, each with a tiny mechanical viewer on the side
Effect: When two people wear these goggles at the same time and activate the viewers, each can see what the other person sees. There is no range restriction, as the devices seem to connect to each other via some lingering element of the datasphere. The goggles work for a number of hours equal to the cypher level.

Seed Boat

Level: 1d6
Usable: A small seed or pellet
Effect: Dropping the cypher into a pool of water at least 10 feet (3 m) in diameter causes the device to absorb the water and instantly grow into a flat-bottomed boat. The boat is large enough to hold ten human-sized creatures.

Seed of Knowledge

Level: 1d10
Usable: Large organic seed
Effect: If planted, this seed blooms into a full-grown plant in about a year, at which point it is about as tall as a human. At this time, it bears 1d6 pieces of fruit, all of which are telepathic, thinking creatures that know one fact keyed to the being that planted the seed. This fact might be some truth or bit of knowledge the planter seeks, the answer to a question he has, or something that will come in handy in the future, whether he knows it or not.

Sense Record

Level: 1d6 + 2

Wearable: Helmet, goggles

Usable: Small metal and glass device

Effect: The device emits a bright flash and then records ten seconds of images, sounds, and smells of everything within short range. At any time thereafter, the user can activate the device again to replay the recording. The device overlays its surroundings with a hologram of what it recorded. The device can replay the recording only once.

Sensory Disruptor

Level: 1d6 + 2

Wearable: Wristband projector (close range)

Usable: Handheld projector (close range)

Effect: Shoots out a single projectile that contains a bundle of nanowires. Upon contact with a living creature, the nanowires unfold and inject themselves into the skin, causing an instant sensory response within the target. Roll d100 for the effect:

01–10	*Synesthesia*: The target senses sound as light and color as taste, causing disorientation. The target loses his next two actions.
11–30	*Perceptual deprivation*: The target's visual senses are overwhelmed, causing temporary blindness. The difficulty of all tasks attempted by the target is increased by one step. The effect lasts for ten minutes.
31–40	*Ultrasensation*: The target's senses overload, causing a heightened response to stimuli. On his next round, he attempts to flee.
41–50	*Fear override*: The target's senses are dulled, causing him to ignore pain and fear. He rushes in, increasing the difficulty of all actions by one step. The effect lasts for ten minutes.
51–75	*Off balance*: The target's sense of balance is disrupted, causing him to fall prone for one round.
76–00	*Hallucinations*: The target experiences an auditory or visual hallucination, causing him to lash out at nothing and miss all attacks during his next action.

Sexual Alteration Device

Level: 1d6

Wearable: Belt, bracelet

Usable: Handheld device

Effect: Alters some element of the user's sexuality for one day. Roll d100 for the effect:

01–10	Allows user to tweak his gender in any way he sees fit
11–30	Allows user to change his sexual orientation or interests
31–40	Removes all sexual drive
41–50	Doubles all sexual drive
51–75	Causes the user to produce a pheromone that sexually attracts anyone within close range
76–00	Causes the user to produce a pheromone that sexually repels anyone within close range

Shadow Net

Level: 1d6 + 2

Wearable: Wristband projector (long range)

Usable: Square of dark cloth

Effect: Causes the area within short range to become darkness for one hour. The darkness negates any light that is brought into the area or that would otherwise shine into the area.

Shrink Ray

Level: 1d6 + 2

Usable: Ray projector (short range)

Effect: Shrinks one human-sized or smaller creature or object within range to one-twentieth of its normal size. It remains at this size for 1d20 hours. For an affected creature, the difficulty of all Might-related tasks is increased by two steps.

Shudder Stones

Level: 1

Usable: Smooth piece of brittle stone

Effect: Breaking the device activates it. The two halves vibrate when they are separated by more than 10 feet (3 m) and continue to vibrate until they are brought back to within this distance or for 28 hours, after which time the device ceases to function.

Sidestep Portal

Level: 1d6

Wearable: Cloak, cape, bodysuit

Usable: Piece of cloth

Effect: The user steps sideways and disappears into an extradimensional space, where she can remain for as long as she wishes. The space is an empty void of pale

If you cobble together a shrink ray with a device that produces any kind of force field or solid light (task difficulty 9), the resulting cypher creates a portal to another universe known to the activator that remains open for 28 hours.

grey light in which the user floats. She can perceive nothing outside this space, and nothing outside it can perceive her. She experiences the passage of time and may act normally while in the space, though it cannot connect to the datasphere or interact with the world outside in any way.

When the user emerges from the space, she returns to the spot she left or an open space nearest to that spot, and the extradimensional space vanishes. Anything left in the space is lost.

Signal Detector
Level: 1d6
Wearable: Monocle, spectacles, helmet with visor
Usable: Small handheld device
Effect: Grants the user an asset on his Intellect roll to find cyphers and, on a success, allows him to roll a d6 and add the number to the total number of cyphers found.

Sleep Watch
Level: 1d6
Wearable: A flat insect with seven legs that must be fitted onto the user's face
Effect: The insect sinks a dozen threads into the user's skull until they reach his brain. The device remains active for 28 hours. During this time, the user perceives through the bug and has an asset for any task to perceive. If he sleeps during this time, he can wake up whenever he chooses.

Sleeper Spray
Level: 1d6
Wearable: Wrist-mounted sprayer (immediate range)
Usable: Spray canister
Effect: This aerosol compound causes any living creatures that breathe it in to fall asleep instantly. The effect lasts for ten minutes.

Smart Bugs
Level: 1d6
Internal: Pill or tablet (dissolved in liquid) that releases genetically designed microbes
Effect: Upon ingestion, the microbes enter the body and begin to do the task they were created for: targeting and enhancing a specific part of the body. The GM should roll d100 ahead of time to determine the effect:

01–50	*Brain bugs:* The user experiences a heightened mental acuity that makes it feel like her brain is tingling. Grants +2 to her Intellect Edge for one hour.
51–75	*Fast-twitch bugs:* The user's muscles begin to quickly tighten and release, creating the sensation that her muscles are jumping beneath her skin. Grants +2 to her Speed Edge for one hour.
76–00	*Meat bugs:* A few seconds after ingesting the microbes, any lingering sense of exhaustion or pain slips away from the user's muscles. Grants +2 to her Might Edge for one hour.

Snake Eye
Level: 1d6
Usable: A synth cable 50 feet (15 m) long
Effect: The eyelike sensor on one end of this cable allows anyone holding the other end to see what it sees. Lasts for one hour.

Snake in the Grass
Level: 1d6
Usable: Mechanical homing automaton about 3 feet (1 m) long and 6 inches (15 cm) in diameter
Effect: The device can safely and secretly carry messages or other small objects across long distances and then return home undetected.

Snow Lens
Level: 1d6
Internal: Eye drops, eye injector, eye smear
Wearable: Disposable goggles, glasses, glass contact lenses, full face mask with special lenses
Effect: Protects wearer from snowblindness, extremely bright light, and other light- or vision-based damage. User gains +1 to Armor against these types of attacks for 28 hours.

Solar Reviver
Level: 1d6
Usable: Sticky, bendable patch
Effect: When applied to a device such as a cypher or an artifact during daylight hours, the patch increases the effect of the next use of the device (such as providing additional damage or healing equal to the patch's level, increasing the distance from close range to long range,

Because snakes in the grass—typically known as sigs—are trained to return home no matter what, some armies use that to their advantage, trapping an enemy's sigs and filling them with detonations or poisons before sending them back to their owners.

and so on). When applied to an expired device, the patch repowers it once, allowing it a single additional use.

🔘 Solid Light Gloves

Level: 1d6
Wearable: Ring, bracelet
Effect: The user's hands are sheathed in gloves made of solid light for one hour. The user can touch or handle dangerous substances as though he had 12 Armor. This protection does not apply to combat situations.

🔘 Solid Light Retribution

Level: 1d6 + 1
Wearable: Bracelet, ring
Usable: Handful of metal spheres
Effect: When activated, metal spheres fly into the air and project a large shield of solid light that protects the user as a normal shield (reducing the difficulty of Speed defense rolls by one step). Anyone who attacks the user and misses strikes the shield instead, creating a backlash of energy that inflicts 4 points of Intellect damage (ignores Armor). It lasts for one hour.

A solid light retribution doesn't need to be wielded; it protects the user while leaving both hands free.

🔘 Sound Amplifier

Level: 1d6
Wearable: Full bodysuit, headband, metallic disk that hangs from a chain
Usable: Small handheld device
Effect: Amplifies sounds within immediate range so they can be heard up to 1 mile (2 km) away. The amplified noise lasts for a few minutes. Until the effect ends, everyone within immediate range of the device becomes deafened while it emits sounds.

🔘 Sparkle

Level: 1d6 + 4
Usable: Handheld device
Effect: Causes 1d6 glowing lights to shoot from the end of the device, travel a long distance, and explode in a flash of brilliant colors that blinds anyone in an immediate radius for one minute.

🔘 Spatial Distorter

Level: 1d6
Wearable: Harness, necklace, helmet
Usable: Handheld device
Effect: Emits a field around the user that lasts for

one minute. The field makes her appear to be far away to creatures that are more than an immediate distance from her. This distortion decreases the difficulty of her Speed defense rolls by one step when she is attacked by creatures at that distance.

Speed Heal
Level: 1d6 + 2
Internal: Pill, ingestible liquid
Usable: Injector
Effect: At the end of each minute for the next hour, the user adds 1 point to his Might Pool, up to the Pool's maximum. This is especially useful for someone who is taking frequent or long-term damage.

Spike Balls
Level: 1d6 + 2
Usable: A bag or other container filled with 100 black marbles
Effect: Pouring the balls from the container causes them to roll across the ground to a point you choose within short range. The balls then spread an immediate distance from that point, sprout spikes, and disappear. The balls inflict 1 point of damage to anything that moves across the ground they cover. They last for a number of hours equal to the cypher level.

Spine Spheres
Level: 1d6
Usable: Clear synth tube filled with living, spiny spheres
Effect: Each of these bioengineered, poisonous devices is about the size of a thumbnail. Once activated, they scatter across the floor, covering an area of immediate radius, and then become invisible. Anything passing through the area steps on at least one sphere, and those who are affected by the poison suffer Speed damage equal to the cypher level, fall prone, and cannot stand for one round.

Standstill
Level: 1d6
Wearable: Wristband projector (close range)
Usable: Handheld projector (close range)
Effect: This device projects an electric shock that causes a living target's muscles to seize up, rendering him immobile for one round.

Stasis Field Emitter
Level: 1d6 + 2
Wearable: Wristband
Usable: Flat, round synth device
Effect: Emits a wave of energy at a target within short range. The energy inflicts 4 points of radiation damage and, if the target's level is equal to or lower than the cypher level, the target cannot take actions for one round.

Stealthy Serpent
Level: 1d6 + 2
Usable: Metal disk that is actually a tightly coiled strand
Effect: When activated, this cypher uncoils to form a small metal serpent about 2 feet (0.6 m) long. It remains animate for one round per cypher level. It can be given a single command that must be something it can accomplish within its allotted time. Once the command is carried out, the serpent deactivates, even if its time is not yet up. It is a level 2 creature, but it moves with stealth as level 5. It can bite once for 2 points of damage and inject a poison that inflicts 4 points of Speed damage (ignoring Armor) if the victim fails a Might defense roll.

Steel Sentinel
Level: 1d6 + 4
Usable: A 10-foot (3 m) tall featureless humanoid assembled from metal components
Effect: The device activates and becomes a level 5 creature for one hour or until destroyed. The device accompanies you and follows your instructions until the effect ends. As a level 5 creature, it has a target number of 15 and a health of 15, and it inflicts 5 points of damage. If the device is reduced to 0 health, it is destroyed and the effect ends.

Still Field
Level: 1d6 + 2
Wearable: Vest, belt, bracelet, jumpsuit
Usable: Handheld device
Effect: For 28 hours, the user does not register on any device that senses or tracks movement or uses sonar or similar means. A creature that relies on sonar or similar methods of sensing cannot perceive the user.

If a speed heal is combined with any pill, liquid, or injector cypher (task difficulty 9), the resulting cypher is a level 9 poison that inflicts 8 points of damage every minute over the course of five minutes.

Stone Form

Level: 1d6 + 2
Internal: Pill, ingestible liquid
Wearable: Gel
Usable: Injector
Effect: Causes the user's body to become a stone statue for 28 hours. While in this form, he is immune to damage inflicted by energy and has 4 Armor. He is in a catatonic state until the effect wears off.

Stone Guts

Level: 1d6
Internal: Pill, ingestible liquid
Usable: Injector
Effect: Any time within 1d6 hours after activating the device, the user can vomit the contents of his stomach anywhere within immediate range. The liquid hardens to the consistency of concrete within a few seconds of being exposed to air. The amount of vomit is enough to cover a human-sized creature. A covered target cannot move until it breaks free or someone else frees it by shattering the rocklike shell. The difficulty of this task is equal to the cypher level.

Stone Melt

Level: 1d6 + 2
Usable: Spray canister
Effect: A quantity of stone that can fit inside a 5-foot (2 m) cube becomes sand when sprayed by this cypher.

Store-all

Level: 1d6
Usable: Small box-shaped container with hinged lid
Effect: A user can pull and stretch the box, increasing its dimensions to a maximum size of a 50-foot (15 m) cube. The container's size can only be increased, not decreased, and once stretched out, it can never be restored to its original size. When the lid is closed, the box is watertight.

Stronghold

Level: 1d6
Wearable: Unfolding synth harness
Effect: Allows the user to lift and carry twice as much weight as normal with minimal exertion for one hour.

Summoning Staff

Level: 1d6 + 3
Usable: Metallic staff with a small attached cylinder
Effect: This device requires two separate actions to fully activate. The first action involves the small cylinder, which has a glass lens on one end. With the cylinder, the user locates a random ultraterrestrial being (whose level is equal to or less than the cypher level) dwelling somewhere other than the Ninth World. The being becomes visible in the lens. On the next action, the user can use the staff to open a portal and pull the ultraterrestrial into this world.

The ultraterrestrial cannot resist, but once

it arrives, it is not automatically compelled to do anything. Unless it can return under its own power or through some other means, it is in this world to stay. When the user finds an ultraterrestrial in the first step of this process, he can choose not to bring it into this world, but he cannot use the device to find another being.

Swarm Herder

Level: 1d6
Wearable: Adheres to temple and launches projectile
Usable: Handheld device that launches projectile
Effect: The device launches a tiny pointed capsule that moves at great speed. If it hits a living creature, it punctures the skin or exoskeleton and explodes, instantly releasing a compound of pheromones and impulse-controlling nanites. In response, the creature attempts to round up other members of its herd or group and move them away from combat to an area of perceived safety. If the creature is solitary, the cypher has no effect (or may cause it to attempt to round up whatever other creatures are nearby, including the PCs, as though they were part of its herd). The effect lasts for ten minutes.

Sweeping Glove

Level: 1d6 + 3
Wearable: Synth glove
Effect: With a gesture (an action), the wearer can make any creatures or objects within immediate range fly backward up to 20 feet (6 m), essentially putting them in short range. Creatures affected suffer 2 points of ambient damage and are prone. The wearer can select which targets to affect. This glove functions for three rounds, during which time the wearer can perform this action each round.

Synth Corroder

Level: 1d6 + 3
Wearable: Glove
Usable: Wandlike device
Effect: This device can be used in two ways. Either it can destroy a touched object made of synth that is small enough to be held in a human's hands, or it can destroy a 4-foot-by-4-foot-by-4-foot (1 m by 1 m by 1 m) area of a larger object made of synth. The object must have a level lower than the cypher level.

Talio's compass is named after Sybil Talio, who is rumored to have created the first device of its kind. She died shortly after attempting to use it on herself, only to accidentally pull out one of her vital organs. Her grandsons continue her work to this day.

Talio's Compass

Level: 1d6
Usable: Handheld device
Effect: Pinpoints a source of metal within living tissue and can draw it out. If used to remove a dangerous object (such as a projectile) from a living creature, the device restores a number of points equal to the cypher level to the creature's Might Pool.

If used to discover and remove a beneficial or benign object (such as an implant) from a living creature, the device does 2 points of damage.

Targeting Oculus

Level: 1d6 + 1
Wearable: Mask with single glass lens
Effect: When applied to a creature's head, the mask completely envelops the head for one hour. During this time, the creature can breathe and sense normally, and all of its ranged attacks are modified by one step to its benefit.

If any two teleporter cyphers are combined into a single device (task difficulty 6), the resulting device works as one of the original cyphers (user's choice) but affects twice as many targets.

Task Drone

Level: 1d6
Usable: Small winged device with a tendril ending in an hand
Effect: When activated, this drone flies up to a long distance and performs one simple task with its tendril arm, such as pull a lever, open a door, lift an object, or push an object. Returning to the user can be a part of the task (so the drone can go get something and return with it). The drone has the strength of a normal human and is a creature of a level equal to the cypher level, with 1 Armor. It cannot make attacks and ceases to function after it performs its single task.

Teleport Seal

Level: 1d6 + 3
Usable: Handheld device or crystal shard
Effect: When activated, this device prevents all teleportation within 1 mile (2 km). No extradimensional gates function, and no phasing is possible in this area. The seal lasts for 28 hours.

Teleport Trap

Level: 1d6 + 2
Usable: Paper-thin, flexible synth disk the size of a plate
Effect: When the device is activated, the next person to touch the disk is teleported to a spot designated by the user, up to a long distance away. The destination must be a place known to be open (the target cannot teleport into solid matter), but it could be 100 feet (30 m) in the air, at the bottom of a deep pool, or a similarly inhospitable place.

Teleporter (Mass)

Level: 1d6 + 4
Wearable: Belt, wristband, ring
Usable: Complex device, handheld device
Effect: The user teleports herself and a number of other creatures equal to the cypher level. They can travel up to 100 × the cypher level in miles to a location she has previously visited. The group arrives safely with anything that they can carry, either individually or as a group.

Temporal Sheath

Level: 1d6 + 4
Wearable: Belt, headband, bracelet
Usable: Handheld device
Effect: The user is enveloped by invisible energy for six hours. During this time, she has +1 to Armor against any type of energy attack (including those that normally ignore Armor) and is immune to any effect that would alter time, hold her in stasis, or do anything similar.

Tendril Gloves

Level: 1d6 + 2
Wearable: Synth gloves that glow with traceries of light
Effect: When the device is activated, the wearer can produce a 10-foot (3 m) tendril of solid light from each of his palms. These

tendrils are prehensile and dexterous and as strong as the wearer. They can manipulate objects; wrap around, lift, and move objects; or be used as medium weapons. The tendrils remain for ten minutes.

Tether
Level: 1d6
Usable: Handheld projector (short range)
Effect: Fires a metal spike at a target within range that inflicts 2 points of damage. Then, as part of the same action, the spike shoots a second metal spike at a different target within immediate range of it that inflicts the same damage. The spikes are connected by a tether. Until either target uses an action to remove the spike, neither target can move away from the other.

Third Man
Level: 1d6
Usable: Handheld device
Effect: When activated, the device creates the perception of an unseen presence among the party. This presence provides a sense of comfort and support to all members of the group (except the one who activated the device), giving them each an asset to a task of their choosing for one hour.

Three-Part Alarm
Level: 1d6
Usable: Handheld device
Effect: When activated, three sensor pieces detach from the main device. Each piece can be placed anywhere within a half mile (1 km) of the main device. For 28 hours, if anything larger than a small dog moves within an immediate distance of one of the sensors, the main device indicates this fact and tells the user which sensor was activated.

Time Auger
Level: 1d6
Usable: Handheld drill-like device
Effect: Allows the user to "drill" through time the way that one might drill through wood. The user doesn't move through time, nor is he able to affect the past or the future. Instead, he creates a timehole that allows him to see thirty seconds into the future for the next ten minutes.

As soon as he moves his eye away from the timehole, it collapses.

Time Capsule
Level: 1d6
Usable: A metallic container large enough to hold a human-sized creature
Effect: Anything placed inside the container does not experience time's passage for 1d20 years. At the end of this period, or if the contents are removed before then, the cypher becomes inert.

Time Delay
Level: 1d6
Usable: Very small nodule
Effect: This device can be affixed to any other cypher and activate it by timer. The user can set the timer for up to one week.

Tranquility Pod
Level: 1d6
Wearable: Submersion hood
Effect: This device wraps around the user's head to provide a unique sensory experience, eliminating all external sounds, smells, and sights. Instead, the wearer experiences soothing sounds, soft light, and gentle vibrations. If he wears the pod for ten minutes, the experience restores a number of points equal to the cypher level to a single Pool of his choosing.

Transdimensional Gate
Level: 1d6 + 4
Wearable: Belt with device, amulet, or ring
Usable: Small handheld device
Effect: This device creates a portal that leads to a different dimension, level of existence, or reality. It is automatically keyed to a specific destination determined by the GM, but a character can attempt to reorient it to another extradimensional destination that she is aware of (task difficulty equal to the cypher level). The portal is about 5 feet (2 m) in diameter and remains open for one minute, unless the user wishes it to close earlier (closing the portal is an action).

"The one time that I created a device to travel into the past, I encountered my younger self and inadvertently sent him into the future. I have yet to encounter the full ramifications of this, I believe."
– Sir Arthour

Transference Beam

Level: 1d6 + 3
Usable: Large handheld device
Effect: This device turns the user and up to six other individuals within immediate range into energy, which is then projected (at the speed of light) as a beam to a target destination that is in line of sight.

When the beam reaches its destination, the travelers are turned back into matter along with their equipment, and their Might and Speed Pools are at maximum.

Transformation Torque

Level: 1d6
Usable: Necklace made of malleable metal and biotech elements
Effect: Placing the necklace around your neck activates the device, which then sends small projections (similar to cilia) beneath the skin. These projections release a genetic compound that causes a mutation in the wearer for one hour.

Additionally, the necklace houses a visage changer, which allows the wearer to hide his mutation if desired. If that's the case, the wearer gets the effects of the mutation but others cannot see, hear, or otherwise sense the mutation. Different necklaces have different effects. Roll d100:

01–50	Causes a beneficial mutation
51–80	Causes a powerful mutation
81–90	Causes a harmful mutation
91–95	Causes a distinctive mutation
96–00	Causes a cosmetic mutation

To determine the specific mutation caused by the device, GMs can choose or roll randomly on the mutation tables on page 124 in the Numenera corebook.

Transient Inscriber

Level: 1d6
Usable: Handheld spray device or bottle and liquid brush, filled with a swarm of tiny bioluminescent, hydroponic creatures
Effect: The device allows the user to write or draw a message on any living or nonliving object, covering up to 3 feet by 3 feet (1 m by 1 m). After a few minutes, the hydroponic creatures begin to dry out and their glow fades, rending the image invisible.

The message or image can be seen again by adding a drop of liquid to the general surface area. This causes the creatures to glow again for about one minute before they extinguish fully.

Transposer

Level: 1d6 + 2
Wearable: Belt with device, amulet, or ring
Usable: Handheld device
Effect: The user swaps positions with a creature of roughly similar size that it can see within long range.

True Speak

Level: 1d6 + 2
Usable: Injector
Effect: When the solution is injected into a creature, that creature cannot knowingly speak a lie for one hour.

Truth Inducer

Level: 1d6 + 2
Wearable: Glove, synth finger overlay, temporary fingertip tattoo
Effect: One creature touched by the device answers questions truthfully for one minute.

Variable Tool

Level: 1d6
Usable: Small handheld device
Effect: The device becomes a mundane weapon, adventuring item, or common or rare special item for one hour.

Verdant Nectar

Level: 1d6
Internal: Ingestible liquid
Usable: Injector
Effect: Causes the user's skin to turn green for ten days. Until the effect wears off, the user does not need to eat during a day provided that he spends at least four hours in sunlight during that day. The hours need not be consecutive.

Vision Subjugator

Level: 1d6 + 1
Usable: Handheld device
Effect: Inhibits brain function in a target within short range for one hour so that the target's vision is affected. The user can specify one category of creatures, objects, substances, and so on that the victim cannot see. The effect is extremely specific, so that if "humans" are selected, the victim cannot see people but would still see clothing worn, objects carried, and so on. Possible categories might include (but are not limited to): metal, vapor, water, mammals, synth, weapons, numenera, the color blue, and plants. It's worth noting that this does not grant the victim X-ray vision. If he cannot see stone and he stands next to a stone wall, his brain creates what he sees instead out of whole cloth based on the context of what he can see. This can lead to seriously delusional behavior.

Vocal Changer

Level: 1d6
Internal: Pill, injection
Wearable: Choker collar
Effect: Changes the pitch, timbre, pronunciation, and other audio characteristics of one creature to match those of another (or as desired). The change lasts for 28 hours.

Volcanic Heart

Level: 10
Usable: Handheld device
Effect: This device does nothing upon activation or in the next two rounds. In the fourth round, it begins to create intense heat. This heat does 12 points of damage to all creatures within immediate range, 6 points of damage to all within short range, and 3 points of damage to all within long range. This effect lasts for three rounds. After that, damage within all ranges starts to fade at a rate of 1 point of damage per round.

It is likely that after a volcanic heart is depleted, the surrounding area is a small wasteland of burning slag.

War Mites

Level: 1d6 + 1
Usable: Spray canister
Effect: A stream of tiny mites sprays out of the canister when this cypher is activated. They strike a single target in immediate range. The target is covered by these bioengineered mites, which immediately begin biting and stinging the target. The target takes 1 point of damage each round for a number of rounds equal to the cypher level. Further, during each of these rounds, the target is distracted, and the difficulty of all tasks it undertakes is increased by one step.

Warming Pouch

Level: 1d6
Usable: Cloth bag
Effect: When you put an object into the cloth bag and activate the string closure, the object heats to human body temperature within one minute. If the object isn't removed, the pouch will keep it at body temperature for 28 hours.

Water Repellant Plates

Level: 1d6 + 1
Wearable: Boots, shoes
Usable: Metal plate
Effect: When activated, this device repels water so strongly for one hour that it can force up to 200 pounds (91 kg) of pressure away from the user. If the plates were in a pair of shoes, a character could appear to walk on water. The plates could also be used to allow an object to float across the surface of the water.

Water Weapon

Level: 1d6 + 2
Wearable: Wrist-mounted device
Usable: Handheld device
Effect: Fires a bolt of energy through water at a target within long range, inflicting damage equal to the cypher level. The energy must have water to conduct it or the device will not function, so both weapon and target must be at least partially submerged.

Way Back

Level: 1d6
Wearable: Belt bag
Effect: When activated and hung from the user's belt, bag, or similar gear, the device releases contained droplets of radioluminescent light every 50 feet (15 m). The droplets stay dark for one day, then crack with light and become visible for five days.

Weaver Drone

Level: 1d6
Usable: A spiderlike automaton equipped with a 50-foot (15 m) spool of strong synth cable
Effect: Responding to simple voice commands, the weaver drone can climb almost any surface, releasing the strong synth cable out behind it as it travels in a simple or complex pattern. Once the cable runs out, the drone anchors itself (and the

end of the cable) to a designated place and shuts down permanently. As long as the cable is anchored by the drone, it can sustain the weight of up to two average-sized people at a time.

Wing Symbiote
Level: 1d6 + 2
Wearable: A large winged insect that attaches to the user's spine
Effect: The device inflicts 2 points of damage to the user as it digs its claws into her spine and uses a tendril to burrow into her brain stem. For the next 28 hours, the user can fly by making a Speed roll (level 1) each round. In combat, she moves a short distance each round, but on extended trips, she can move up to 40 miles (64 km) per hour.

Wish Disk
Level: 10
Usable: A set of metal disks nested within each other
Effect: The user states a change in reality that she wishes to have happen, and it—or something very like it—occurs. This warping of reality can affect matter, energy, and time. Objects can be created or destroyed, creatures can be slain, and events from the past can be undone. Reality can be altered so that dead beings are still alive (because they never died).

However, the minds of most users are insufficient to fully comprehend the vast implications of the reality they change. This means that the wish fulfillment may not be entirely what they thought it would be. The repercussions are too varied to list, but here are a few examples:
- A complex object created is brittle, of poor quality, or made of a substance that turns out to be dangerous.
- A significant change to the past results in a "bubble" of space-time in which the change occurred, trapping the user in a sort of limited closed dimension, even while normal, unchanged reality continues outside the bubble.
- Creatures altered by the change develop health issues ranging from new allergies or minor ailments to cancer or mutations.
- Minds altered by the change suffer from long-term trauma, confusion, memory loss, or brain damage.

Using a wish disk is taxing. The user moves two steps down the damage track.

Witless Powder
Level: 1d6
Usable: A thin metal tube with a fragile powder cartridge in the center
Effect: To activate the device, the user blows through one end of the tube to propel the cartridge's contents out the other at a creature within immediate range. If the creature is hit by the powder, and its level is equal to or lower than the cypher level, it becomes stunned for one minute. During this time, if the user speaks to the target in a language the target can understand, she can implant a suggestion in the target's mind. This suggestion is a course of activity the target must follow under the specific conditions the user describes. The course of activity can be anything she chooses, though it cannot be anything that poses a significant risk to the target's life, property, or loved ones. The conditions can be as general or as specific as the user decides. If the described conditions happen during the next 28 hours, the target behaves as instructed.

Wrist Launcher
Level: 1d6
Wearable: Wrist-mounted device
Effect: Launches a small object (such as a dart, a stone, or a detonation cypher) up to long range. If the object is hard (preferably pointed), it inflicts 4 points of damage. A detonation inflicts its own explosive damage.

X-ray Extractor
Level: 1d6 + 4
Usable: Glass panel with selection of dials
Effect: When held up against a solid surface, this panel allows the user to see through up to 2 feet (0.6 m) of material. The selection of dials allows him to discriminate between various items within the material, permitting him to see buried objects, supports in walls, or organs in a body. A successful difficulty 4 Intellect roll vaporizes a visualized discrete object or a portion of it. An unsuccessful roll disintegrates a random chunk of material, gouging a hole in the solid surface. The device operates for one minute, and it works only if the cypher's level is higher than the material's level.

Many people claim that wish disks don't exist and are the stuff of explorers' tales (or dreams). However, the devices do exist, and they can be as much a bane as a boon.

Sometimes, a PC's use of a wish disk should work as expected. If it is simple, straightforward, and not outlandish in power or scope, reality is changed without repercussions. Negative aftereffects, as suggested, might come as the result of a GM intrusion.

CHAPTER 3

ARTIFACTS

Artifacts, page 298

Repair rules, page 106

Rides the Lightning, page 71

Creating new artifacts, page 317

Creation lantern, page 107

Bloodblade, page 104

Vision snake, page 141

Occasionally, you may want to add a quirk to an artifact. See page 299 in the Numenera corebook for more information.

As with cyphers, artifacts are the remnants of the prior worlds that have been recovered by explorers or, more rarely, crafted by artificers using secrets discovered by studying the distant past.

Artifacts are numenera objects with effects that usually have more than one use. This distinguishes them from cyphers. Artifacts are not more powerful than cyphers. Instead, they have a very different effect on the character as a whole. While cypher abilities are fleeting, artifacts are somewhat more dependable. If a character finds a creation lantern, she can reliably make copies of other items, at least for a while. A character with a bloodblade can turn his blood into poison for his weapon. These things change the character and likely change the way the player plays that character.

Unlike the dozens of cyphers a typical character might possess over the course of her career, most characters will only ever find and use a handful of artifacts. That makes them even more special.

All artifacts have a level. Unlike cyphers, each also has a unique form, and most have a rate of power depletion. When an artifact is used or activated, the player rolls the designated die (1d6, 1d10, 1d20, or 1d100). If the die shows the depletion number(s), the item works, but that is its last use. A depletion

entry of "—" means that the artifact never depletes, and an entry of "automatic" means that it can be used only once.

Depowered artifacts can sometimes be recharged using the repair rules. The focus Rides the Lightning and other special abilities can also repower an expended item, but probably for only one use.

For more information on finding, identifying, and using artifacts, see chapter 19 in the Numenera corebook.

In this chapter, you will find 225 new artifacts. Added to the 75 in the Numenera corebook, that gives you 300 artifacts to choose from. Variety and weirdness are the spice of Numenera life, and you'll find both amid these selections.

UNIQUE VERSUS UBIQUITOUS

When a PC scavenges through an ancient ruin and finds a vision snake, is he the first person in his world to come upon such a thing, or are they common enough that he's already heard of them? No rarity is provided for numenera devices, and that's intentional, because it's up to the individual GM.

A device might be unique, it might be one of a few such things cataloged by learned scholars and explorers, or it might be ubiquitous, at least in a particular region. Glowglobes, for example, are objects from the past, but they're so common that they aren't even treated as cyphers or artifacts—they're just equipment. (It's also likely, given their ubiquity, that more than one Ninth World source has discovered how to produce them and manufactures new glowglobes.) Perhaps in the area around a particular ruin, vision snakes, indestructible oil, or instant ladders are found with enough regularity that locals can identify them on sight. Maybe they're even available from a vendor in a marketplace. Interestingly, a traveler might go 30 miles (48 km) south, and the people in that area have never heard of those items.

Ultimately, then, when a PC discovers and identifies a new device, the GM determines whether she figures out what it likely does, whether she's heard of such things in past studies, or whether she recognizes it because she's seen things like that before.

MIXING THE OLD AND THE NEW: AMALGAM ITEMS

A great deal of the numenera devices in the Ninth World aren't being used the way that the original creators intended. There's no better example of that than the devices that are a strange amalgam of both old and new. A numenera device that is extremely cold to the touch makes a fine cattle prod when affixed to a wooden shaft. Likewise, a high-pressure air compressor filled with iron nails makes an excellent nail-driving tool. These combination devices truly convey the odd nature of the Ninth World setting, as they are a mixture of very high and very low tech. Lots of devices—both cyphers and artifacts—are assumed to be amalgam items. As a general rule, if it's an item that can be easily identified as something one might find in a Ninth World community, like a piece of clothing or a weapon like a sword or a mace, it's probably an amalgam item, with ancient parts affixed to or worked into the more recent portion.

Some specific examples of amalgam devices might include the adhesion clamps, bounding boots, or healing sword from the Numenera corebook, or the domination rod, flicker cloak, or thunder vocalizer in this tome. And, of course, devices like the box of embers or any weapon or armor nodule are designed to become amalgam items. A few more are described below.

Arc Maul: This is a wooden shaft about 3 feet (1 m) long with a numenera object affixed to the end. Scavengers have found that many numenera devices, when struck, produce a burst of energy of some kind—a flare of heat, an arc of electricity, or something weirder. In general, an arc maul is a heavy weapon that inflicts 2 additional points of damage with each hit. A depletion roll sometimes indicates that the artifact has run out of power, as normal, but sometimes it indicates that the device is too battered to continue serving as an effective weapon.
Depletion: 1 in 1d20

Glidon: This artifact vehicle looks much like a circular covered wagon, except that it has no wheels. Instead, it hovers about 2 feet (0.6 m) above the ground thanks to a powerful repulsor field beneath it. The wagon part built atop the floating platform is entirely of Ninth World make. What's more, the disk-shaped platform can't move on its own, so people typically hitch it to a beast of burden that can pull it along. A glidon can carry far more weight than a typical wagon can (ten times as much, in fact) and offers a perfectly smooth ride.
Depletion: —

Light Suit: Many numenera devices give off light via small synth bulbs, glowing screens, or glowing bits of metal. A light suit is a simple manufactured artifact that stitches a number of these devices into clothing. The wearer is constantly surrounded by a nimbus of faint light out to immediate range, but her hands are always free.
Depletion: —

When amalgam items are found via scavenging, only the ancient numenera parts are found. The newer parts must be added by the scavenger or by crafters employed for such a purpose.

ARTIFACT LISTS

To choose artifacts at random, first roll a d6 to figure out which table you should roll on.

01–02   Artifact List A
03–04   Artifact List B
05–06   Artifact List C

* Items marked with an asterisk are from the Numenera corebook.

ARTIFACT LIST A

01	Adamantine cable	35	Concussion mace
02	Agony scarab	36	Control spike
03	Aim true goggles	37	Coolclothes
04	Amber casement*	38	Crawler tank
05	Amulet of safety*	39	Creation lantern
06	Analyzing shield*	40	Crimson polyhedron
07	Annihilation chamber	41	Crown of eyes
08	Armored flesh*	42	Cryogen box
09	Armoring cloth	43	Cryogen rod
10	Augmenter harness	44	Crystal armor
11	Automapper	45	Crystal helmet
12	Automated cook*	46	Cthonic bore
13	Autoscribe	47	Cyclops helm
14	Battle armor*	48	Cypher bag*
15	Battlesuit*	49	Data armor
16	Beam lance	50	Data imager
17	Biometric patch	51	Demonflesh
18	Bloodblade	52	Destabilizer
19	Bone garden	53	Detachable eye
20	Bounding boots*	54	Detonation catalyst
21	Box of embers	55	Digestion parasite
22	Brain bud*	56	Dimensional armor*
23	Burning egg	57	Disruption blade*
24	Cacophony blade	58	Disruptive sword
25	Calridian proboscis	59	Distance imager
26	Carryall*	60	Domination rod
27	Cellular disruptor*	61	Doroa of the Silent Song
28	Chameleon cloak*	62	Drill spear*
29	Chiurgeon sphere*	63	Earth caller
30	Chronometer	64	Ebon eyes
31	Clawed gauntlets	65	Ecstasy paralyzer*
32	Cohesion stabilizer*	66	Electromagnetic projector
33	Communication beads	67	Emitter enhancer
34	Compactor	68	Energy converter

69	Environment suit
70	Ephemeral garb
71	Eternal journal
72	Ever-write
73	Everyoung choker
74	Exploding arrow*
75	Extraneous arm
76	Extraneous leg
77	Extreme lenses
78	Exuvia
79	Eye of the sky
80	Eye spy
81	Fabricator
82	Fearmaker*
83	Feather cloak
84	Fiber optic sleeves
85	Fiery hellmaker*
86	Filtration straw*
87	Finger talkers
88	Flame caster
89	Flaming torrent
90	Flesh-render wand
91	Flexsteel weapon
92	Flicker cloak
93	Flight pack
94	Foldable coach
95	Food scanner*
96	Food tube*
97	Force dome*
98	Force shield
99	Globe projector
00	Glow boots

ARTIFACT LIST B

01	Glowglobe nest	42	Living tentacle	83	Phasing piton*
02	Graviton emitter	43	Living wall	84	Photon transporter
03	Graviton suppressor	44	Logic spike	85	Pincer arm
04	Gravity suit	45	Machine's heart	86	Plant jar*
05	Greenstone adaptor	46	Manybag	87	Point clamp
06	Guardian sphere	47	Matter separator	88	Poison brain implant*
07	Gut worm	48	Mechanical arm	89	Poisoner's touch
08	Hand of annihilation	49	Mechanical leg	90	Portable lavation
09	Handy hollow	50	Memory shard	91	Power glove
10	Hard light cutter	51	Mental storage	92	Printing stylus
11	Hard light goggles	52	Mephitic staff*	93	Probability engine
12	Healing sword*	53	Mesmerizing flame	94	Probability mantle
13	Homing volt projector	54	Mesoglea gloss	95	Projectile drone
14	Hoop staff*	55	Metabolism bud*	96	Protection amulet
15	Hot-cold stone	56	Mind blade	97	Psycap
16	Hover belt*	57	Mind displacer	98	Psychic helmet*
17	Hover square*	58	Mind imager*	99	Psychic whistle*
18	Husk	59	Minute lenses	00	Pulse staff
19	Hypno-lenses	60	Mirage generator		
20	Hypnotic nanny	61	Mobile arm		
21	Imager*	62	Molecular bonder*		
22	Impossible blade	63	Monitor bracelet		
23	Impulse collar	64	Monowhip		
24	Instant bridge*	65	Mother parasite		
25	Instant ladder	66	Multidimensional blade*		
26	Interceptor	67	Multiphasic ray		
27	Kill dart projector	68	Murder globe*		
28	Kinetic shield*	69	Music makers		
29	Launcher*	70	Mutation mask		
30	Leap boots	71	Nano-needler*		
31	Light discus	72	Needler*		
32	Light spike*	73	Neural disruptor		
33	Light tendril	74	Nightvision goggles*		
34	Lightning whip	75	Null blade		
35	Lightwings	76	Obedient rope		
36	Likeness thief	77	Ocular graft		
37	Liminal scanner	78	Ocular helm		
38	Liquid armor*	79	Oubliette		
39	Liquid sword*	80	Periscopic eye		
40	Living armor sheath*	81	Personality adjuster		
41	Living cable	82	Phase axe		

ARTIFACT LIST C

01	Punishment tick	22	Skin of water breathing	61	Thought storage
02	Pyroclastic staff	23	Skull blaster*	62	Thoughtlight
03	Quickice axe	24	Sky chariot	63	Thunder boots
04	Recorder headband*	25	Slave cap	64	Thunder cannon*
05	Redlight clip*	26	Slugspitter (heat)	65	Thunder vocalizer
06	Remnant reader	27	Slugspitter (inorganic phasing)	66	Time machine
07	Remote clamp*	28	Slugspitter (mass increasing)	67	Tongue snake
08	Repair sphere*	29	Slugspitter*	68	Torment wand
09	Replacement hand	30	Smart boots	69	Tracer nodule
10	Restoration pod	31	Smart cape	70	Transdimensional blade
11	Ring of Iron Wind	32	Smart gloves	71	Transdimensional ray projector*
12	Roving eyes	33	Smart helm	72	Transformation chamber
13	Safe corridor*	34	Smoke helm	73	Traveling coiffeur
14	Seated lift	35	Snail shell	74	Trigger trap*
15	Second hand	36	Snipewand*	75	Trio
16	Second skin*	37	Snuffler	76	Truth seeker
17	Shatter wand*	38	Solid light bindings	77	Tunneling gauntlets
18	Shock manacles*	39	Solid light helm	78	Twin mirrors
19	Silver ichor	40	Sonic blade	79	Ultimate grapnel
20	Skill bud*	41	Sphere thrower	80	Ultra armor
21	Skin of fire sloughing	42	Spider harness	81	Urchalis mask
		43	Spine armor	82	Usurper
		44	Spinneret ring	83	Vision snake
		45	Spirit call	84	Void clamp
		46	Stasis projector	85	Void knife
		47	Stimulation stem	86	Vox scrambler
		48	Strangelight torch	87	Vuechi*
		49	Stunner*	88	Water finder
		50	Suspensor belt*	89	Water skimmers
		51	Synthsteel shield	90	Wavespliter
		52	Telescopic beast	91	Weapon graft*
		53	Telltale glass*	92	Weapon mount
		54	Temporal armor	93	Wheeled porter
		55	Temporal maul	94	Whisperer in the Ether
		56	Tendril graft*	95	Windrider*
		57	Tentacle harness (bladed)	96	Windslice blade*
		58	Tentacle harness (clawed)	97	Wing blade
		59	Tentacle helmet	98	Woodwind of the broken
		60	The Death by Angles	99	Yarrin
				00	Yesterglass

Adamantine Cable

Level: 1
Form: A 50-foot (15 m) length of black rope
Effect: This length of rope has the flexibility
of ordinary rope but a hardness greater than
steel. The rope is impervious to all damage
and cannot be cut.
Depletion: —

Agony Scarab

Level: 1d6 + 2
Form: A small beetle-shaped device
Effect: To activate the device, a user must place
the beetle on the bare skin of a living creature.
The beetle immediately burrows into the flesh,
inflicting 1 point of damage, and travels just
under the skin until it lodges at the base of the
creature's spine. Once there, the beetle drills
into the creature's spine to control its nervous
system. At the user's spoken command, the
beetle sends horrific pain shooting through
the target's body, and the target becomes
stunned and loses his next action. The beetle
then releases its hold on the target and tears
free, inflicting 1 point of damage as it emerges
through the skin and returns to the user, at
which point it becomes dormant once more.
Depletion: 1 in 1d6

Aim True Goggles

Level: 1d6
Form: A pair of goggles, a pair of glasses, a full
or half mask that covers the eyes with lenses
Effect: By pressing small buttons on both
sides of the device, the user activates the
lenses. These special lenses block blue and
violet rays, which can impair vision, thus
enhancing the wearer's sight. The difficulty
of all ranged attacks is decreased by one step
when wearing the goggles. Lasts for one hour.
Depletion: 1 in 1d20 for lens activation (after
depletion, the goggles can still be worn as
normal goggles)

Annihilation Chamber

Level: 1d6
Form: A metal canister 3 feet (1 m) tall and 1
foot (0.3 m) in diameter, with a flip-up lid
Effect: Anything placed inside the canister is
instantly and permanently destroyed.
Depletion: 1 in 1d100

Armoring Cloth

Level: 1d6
Form: Typical clothing
Effect: If this clothing is struck, it hardens
upon impact, providing +1 to Armor. It then

*If a singularity
detonation is placed
in an annihilation
chamber, the resulting
explosion utterly
destroys everything
within long range.*

*Singularity detonation
page 285*

immediately returns to its normal state (which is in no way encumbering).

This clothing cannot be worn with armor of any kind.

Depletion: —

Augmenter Harness

Level: 1d6

Form: A thick, wide belt with a mechanical device as a buckle and two bands that extend from the belt up and over the wearer's shoulders

Effect: The device enhances the wearer's physical strength and power. She inflicts 1 additional point of damage with weapon attacks, and the difficulty of carrying or lifting tasks is reduced by one step.

Depletion: 1 in 1d10 (check once each day while worn)

Automapper

Level: 1d6

Form: Thin metallic slab with lights and a toggle

Effect: This slab tracks its own progression through the world, creating a virtual light map on its surface for about a month. At the end of that time, it resets itself and begins again.

Depletion: —

Autoscribe

Level: 1

Form: A severed hand fitted with a metal plate on the stump that holds a writing implement

Effect: Speaking the command causes the hand to animate, rise up, and ready the writing implement to record whatever you say on whatever surface the implement touches. The hand deactivates when you speak the command again.

Depletion: 1 in 1d100

Beam Lance

Level: 1d6 + 3

Form: Forearm bracer

Effect: When mounted on a creature's forearm, this weapon fires a beam of concentrated green light up to 200 feet (61 m), inflicting 6 points of damage. Alternatively, the beam can be shortened to 6 feet (2 m) in length and used as a melee weapon for one minute, inflicting 6 points of damage.

Depletion: 1–3 in 1d100

Biometric Patch

Level: 1d6

Form: A patch of skin that must be grafted onto another artifact

Effect: The patch bonds to whatever it touches and prevents creatures other than the user from using the artifact. To use the artifact, the user must place his lips on the patch, which reads the biometric signature and activates the artifact.

Depletion: —

Bloodblade

Level: 1d6 + 1

Form: A metal blade with spikes that must be inserted into the flesh of the wielder's forearm

Effect: When inserted into the wielder's arm, this device inflicts 3 points of damage (ignores Armor). Thereafter, the wielder can use this weapon as a light weapon that inflicts 3 points of damage. Further, when the wielder wishes it (requiring no action), the blade can

Numenera Device Names

Some numenera have Ninth World colloquial names, such as "obedient rope," while others sound more scientific, such as "neural disruptor." This is intentional and reflects both halves of the science fantasy nature of Numenera. The idea is that while everything was named by Ninth Worlders, some things were named by average explorers, and some by nanos, Aeon Priests, or others with at least a small amount of experience and knowledge. Of course, while this book is written in English, in the Truth—the predominant language of much of the Ninth World—the names would be similar in nature. Thus, a less educated person might call the neural disruptor a "mind whip," while the more educated nano who named it would use more precise and loftier terms from her language.

Of course, in many, many cases, items found by player characters in the course of a game should be named by those characters, because they will not have the context of someone else having already provided a name.

absorb 3 points from his Might Pool and turn them into a powerful poison. The poison coats the blade so that a victim suffers 5 additional points of damage if affected.
Depletion: —

Bone Garden
Level: 1d6 + 2
Form: Long-needled injector filled with liquefied calcium
Effect: The liquefied bone is injected directly into the bone marrow of the user. Within ten minutes, the user's bones are fortified by the calcium injection, and his Might Pool is permanently increased by 2.
Depletion: —

Box of Embers
Level: 1d6
Form: Very small synth panel or patch affixed to a melee weapon or other tool
Effect: Once attached, this nodule causes the hilt of the weapon or tool to glow with a pulsing reddish-black light. The patch has no effect on the item during combat, but three small buttons on the side allow the user to control the other effects: light (a red glow that allows the user to see at night as if it were daylight), heat (enough to melt ice or keep one person warm even in freezing temperatures), and firestarting (while in this mode, blowing on the hilt will release enough embers from the weapon to start a fire).
Depletion: —

Burning Egg
Level: 1d6
Form: A small metal, egg-shaped object with a button on top
Effect: Pressing the button causes the device to flash once each round for three rounds.

After this time, it emits a loud buzzing noise and releases a wave of invisible energy. The wave inflicts ambient heat damage equal to the artifact level on every living thing within a short distance.
Depletion: 1 in 1d6

Cacophony Blade
Level: 1d6
Form: A dull, heavy, medium-length sword, dripping oil, with a fine spiked chain running along the edge
Effect: This sword is unwieldy and heavy. The difficulty of attacks made with this weapon is increased by one step. However, if the user activates the artifact, the spiked chain begins to rock back and forth, creating an awful shrieking noise. When the weapon hits a target, the chain catches and rips through the target, inflicting 4 additional points of damage. The damage penetrates (ignores) 2 Armor.
Depletion: 1 in 1d20

Calridian Proboscis
Level: 1d6 + 2
Form: Prehensile, biomechanical proboscis about 3 inches (8 cm) long that can be surgically grafted anywhere on a person's body
Effect: Once grafted, the proboscis sniffs the air constantly, attempting to detect nanites. It provides the host with an asset on all tasks related to discovering (within long range) and identifying the numenera. The proboscis must be surgically and permanently grafted (a task with a difficulty equal to the artifact level). In skilled hands, the procedure takes about one hour. It works best if grafted in an area that is typically free of clothing or hair.
Depletion: —

Obedient rope, page 126

Neural disruptor, page 126

"Completed a grafting procedure today with an entirely unknown piece of the numenera. [NAME REDACTED] called it a calridian proboscis. Its wrappings had the mark of the alizarin market. This would lead one to believe that calridian proboscides are neither crafted nor found elements of the numenera, but rather organs from living, breathing creatures. If there is such a thing as a calridian out there, I for one have certainly never seen it. The operation itself was not a success, per se. But I would surely like to get my hands on another one of those devices." ~notes from Tireso Hinyer, Draolis chiurgeon

Chronometer
Level: 1
Form: A wristband with a mechanical display in the middle
Effect: The device keeps perfect time. The device also has a stopwatch and timer function.
Depletion: —

Clawed Gauntlets
Level: 1d6
Form: Metal gauntlets
Effect: With a flick of one's hands (not an action), these gauntlets produce long steel claws that are medium weapons, inflicting 1 additional point of damage on each attack.
Depletion: —

Communication Beads
Level: 1
Form: A pair of tiny insects with strange sucker heads
Effect: To activate this item, each insect must be placed inside an ear canal. If placed in the ears of two different creatures, each creature can hear the other speak regardless of the distance between them or the volume at which they speak.

Depletion: 1 in 1d100 (checked each hour the devices are used)

Compactor
Level: 1d6 + 2
Form: A tube that is 24 inches (61 cm) long and 5 inches (13 cm) wide
Effect: When the tube is pointed at an inanimate, unsecured, solid object that is 10 to 30 inches (25 to 76 cm) across within immediate range, that object implodes, compacts into a ball no more than 4 inches (10 cm) across, and is drawn into the tube. Using another action, the user can project the ball up to long range with incredible force, inflicting 10 points of damage. Only one object can be compacted and loaded at a time.
Depletion: 1 in 1d10

Concussion Mace
Level: 1d6 + 2
Form: A metal baton that emits a soft blue light when gripped
Effect: The baton functions as a club (a light weapon). However, if the wielder uses an action to activate it, the weapon hums with crackling energy for one round. During that round, the foe is stunned.
Depletion: 1 in 1d6

Control Spike

Level: 1d6 + 4

Form: A long metal spike and separate viewscreen

Effect: The device activates when the user hammers the spike into the head of a creature, which inflicts no damage. Upon doing so, the user can use the viewscreen to control the creature. The user decides what the creature says and does each round provided that they remain within long distance of each other. Removing the spike ends the effect. No hole or injury remains from the spike once it's withdrawn.

Depletion: 1 in 1d10 (checked each round the device is used)

Coolclothes

Level: 1d6

Form: Full body jumpsuit

Effect: These clothes keep the wearer's body temperature at the same level as her surroundings. Not only do they keep her comfortable, they also make her invisible to creatures or automatons that use heat sources to sense (such as infrared vision).

Depletion: —

Crawler Tank

Level: 9

Form: A vehicle 12 feet (4 m) long, 6 feet (2 m) wide, and 6 feet (2 m) high

Effect: This biomechanical vehicle pulls itself along with living tendrils and motorized treads, moving a short distance each round.

The tank has two different weapons built into it. The main weapon is a twinned set of ray projectors that can fire up to a range of 500 feet (152 m) and inflict 8 points of damage. The secondary weapon is an emitter that releases a cloud of poisonous gas in an immediate radius. Anyone in the cloud suffers 4 points of damage (ignores Armor).

The tank can move and activate one (but not both) of its weapons as a single action.

In order to function, the tank must have an occupant, and there is room for only one human inside. The vehicle obeys thought commands from this occupant, who uses her action to give the tank new orders. If no new order is given, the tank continues to obey the previous order.

Depletion: 1–4 in 1d100 (check once each day used)

Creation Lantern

Level: 1d6

Form: Egg-shaped synth device with a hollowed center containing a metal orb

Effect: When activated, the device scans a 5-foot (2 m) cube of material within a short distance and then creates a physical copy from solidified light in an open space within a short distance. The copy lasts for a number of hours equal to the artifact level.

Depletion: 1 in 1d10

Crimson Polyhedron

Level: 10

Form: Small red crystal

Effect: This device must be embedded into the user's body through a surgical procedure. The procedure takes about an hour in a skilled chiurgeon's hands.

If successful, the polyhedron ties itself to the user's vital functions. The user can designate a cypher or artifact to be activated if she is ever rendered unconscious (as opposed to just asleep), impaired, or debilitated. A different device can be tied to each of these three states, but only one per state. The user can also designate one, some, or all of her cyphers and artifacts to activate in the event of her death.

Depletion: —

Crown of Eyes

Level: 1d6

Form: Metallic circlet set with several crystal spheres

Effect: It takes one round to activate the crown. When activated, the crystal spheres separate from the crown and fly around the wearer at immediate range for an hour. He can see anything the crystal spheres can see. This allows him to peek around corners without being exposed to danger. This gives the wearer an asset in initiative and all perception tasks.

Depletion: 1 in 1d100

Cryogen Box

Level: 1

Form: A 5-foot (2 m) cube made of metal with a door on the front

Effect: The box's interior is 34° F (1° C) and stays at that temperature indefinitely. Anything placed inside the box cools until it reaches this temperature.

Depletion: —

Cryogen Rod

Level: 1d6
Form: A smooth length of metal that has a bronze cube at one end
Effect: When activated, the cube at the end of the device rapidly cools until it reaches absolute zero (approximately −460° F, or −273° C) and remains at that temperature for about one minute before warming back up to local temperature. The rod can be used as a club (a light weapon) that inflicts additional ambient damage equal to the artifact level.

If the frozen tip is placed in any liquid, it causes all the liquid within a 50-foot (15 m) radius to solidify. The rod cannot be removed from the solid until it melts.
Depletion: 1 in 1d6

Crystal Armor

Level: 1d6 + 1
Form: Suit of armor made of crystal
Effect: This appears to be a harness of highly articulated plate armor, but the pieces are made of very thin crystal rather than metal. This is heavy armor. Any ray or beam attacks that strike the wearer are reflected back at the attacker. When the armor depletes, it turns to powder.
Depletion: 1–2 in 1d100 (check once each day)

Crystal Helmet

Level: 1d6
Form: A glass globe with a hole on the bottom. The hole is large enough for a human to place the globe over his head, and a soft band around the opening cushions its weight.
Effect: When a user activates the device while wearing it, the band surrounding the hole fuses with his skin to make the globe airtight. The globe creates a breathable atmosphere for him that lasts for up to four hours or until he deactivates it (not an action). In addition, the globe allows him to perceive his surroundings clearly to a distance of 500 feet (152 km). However, the device interferes with his ability to hear and increases the difficulty of any task that involves hearing by one step.
Depletion: 1 in 1d20

Cthonic Bore

Level: 1d6 + 4
Form: A 10-foot long (3 m), 5-foot wide (2 m), and 7-foot tall (2 m) tracked vehicle made from steel equipped with an enormous drill on the front and a door on the back
Effect: This vehicle can be piloted by someone who makes Intellect rolls (level 1) each round. Inside, there's a seat for the pilot and two benches that run along either side for up to four people to sit comfortably.

When activated, the device moves a short distance each round or up to 10 miles (16 km) per hour on extended trips. The device can also be used to tunnel through 10 feet (3 m) of earth or 5 feet (2 m) of stone each round.
Depletion: 1–4 in 1d100

Cyclops Helm

Level: 1d6
Form: A metal helmet that fits over the wearer's entire head and has a single lensed eye in the front
Effect: The wearer sees through the lens on the front of the helm via screens inside the

helmet. It gives her an asset on all visual perception tasks.
Depletion: —

Data Armor
Level: 1d6
Form: A tiny metal disk with a glowing crystal in the center
Effect: When placed just under the ear, tiny prongs sprout from the disk to anchor it in the flesh. The device reinforces the user's mind with an information stream from the datasphere. The device adds 1 to her Intellect Edge.
Depletion: —

Data Imager
Level: 1d6
Form: A small handheld device
Effect: When the device is activated, the user names one type of creature or object, and the device draws information about the subject from the datasphere, creating an image of it anywhere the user chooses within immediate range. The image is visual only, and any physical object that touches it passes right through it. The image remains for one minute.
Depletion: 1 in 1d10

Demonflesh
Level: 1d6 + 1
Form: A ball of dark blue synth
Effect: When activated, this ball liquefies and coats the body of the user for one hour, appearing to be a dark blue bodysuit veined with pathways of soft light. Demonflesh confers two abilities. First, the wearer can become invisible. While invisible, she is specialized in stealth and Speed defense tasks. This effect ends if she does something to reveal her presence or position—attacking, performing an esotery, using an ability, moving a large object, and so on. If this occurs, she can regain the remaining invisibility effect by taking an action to focus on hiding his position.

Second, the demonflesh wearer can inflict 3 points of damage with a touch. This attack ignores Armor as it breaks down molecular bonds, disintegrating anything that comes in contact with it.
Depletion: 1 in 1d20

Destabilizer
Level: 1d6
Form: A synth cube made of smaller cubes
Effect: The user activates the device and

points it at a small stone or piece of metal within immediate range. The device causes the target to become unstable for one hour. If the target is thrown while unstable, it explodes in an immediate radius on impact, inflicting shrapnel damage equal to the artifact level.
Depletion: 1 in 1d6

Detachable Eye
Level: 1d6
Form: Synthetic eyeball
Effect: To use this device, the user must press it into an empty eye socket and hold it there for at least one minute while filaments plug into the brain. Once it's properly installed, she can see through it as if it were a normal eye, and she can also see in areas of darkness as if they were lit.

At any point, the user can use an action to pluck the device from her head. She can continue to see through the device while she is within 1 mile (2 km) of it.
Depletion: —

Detonation Catalyst
Level: 1d6
Form: Small handheld device with clips on wires
Effect: When the device is affixed to a detonation cypher for one hour, the detonation is enhanced, inflicting 2 additional points of damage. If the detonation does not normally inflict damage, it now inflicts 2 points in addition to whatever effect it normally has.
Depletion: 1 in 1d10

Demonflesh was so named long ago because those who discovered it believed that it was the creation of evil gods and was itself inherently evil. A few people still believe this.

Digestion Parasite
Level: 1d6
Form: A living grey worm with a mouth at either end
Effect: The worm functions only if it is swallowed whole. Once ingested, it grows until it completely replaces the user's digestive tract. Henceforth, the user receives sustenance from anything he ingests, even if that substance is poisonous, contaminated, or something that cannot normally be digested. The worm breaks down the substance and passes it while supplying the host with life-sustaining nutrients.
Depletion: —

Disruptive Sword
Level: 1d6 + 1
Form: An energy-entwined broadsword
Effect: This broadsword inflicts 1 additional point of damage from the disruptive energy projected around the blade. This energy cannot be turned on or off, and it eats through sheaths at a rate of about one a week.
Depletion: 1 in 1d20 (check once each week)

Distance Imager
Level: 1d6 + 1
Form: Synth cube with a screen and a number of controls
Effect: When pointed at an enclosed structure within 1 mile (2 km), the screen shows the interior of that structure, room by room. The user can "move" through the structure (even through walls or other barriers) at a speed of 10 feet (3 m) per round. One use of the item lasts for ten rounds.
Depletion: 1 in 1d10

Domination Rod
Level: 1d6 + 2
Form: A short wooden haft with a crystalline tip
Effect: This device saps the will of a creature touched by the rod. The affected creature makes all Intellect defense rolls with the difficulty increased by one step. Actions involving seeing through deceptions, resisting urges, and other similar tasks are likewise affected. Creatures are affected for 28 hours.
Depletion: 1 in 1d20

Doroa of the Silent Song
Level: 1d6
Form: Complex standalone device carved of soapstone in the rough shape of a woman, about 4 feet (1 m) high, with two bright green gems lodged into the face
Effect: When activated, the device begins to recount the Sacred Chronicle of High Father Calaval in a soft, slightly metallic voice. The entire tale takes about 28 hours from start to finish. If the tale is interrupted during the telling for any reason, the device starts again at the beginning.
Depletion: —

Earth Caller
Level: 10
Form: A metal staff about 5 feet (2 m) long that tapers down to a rounded point at one end
Effect: When the narrow end is pushed into the ground and activated, the top half repeatedly lifts up and slams back into place. This action sends a tremor through the ground. It continues for ten minutes and then stops. If the device operates for the full time, a violent earthquake tears through the area in a 1-mile (2 km) radius. The quake persists for five minutes and causes widespread damage. Buildings made of wood, stone, or brick collapse; walls topple; cliffs crumble; ceilings cave in; some areas of ground rise up; and other areas sink. Characters inside collapsed buildings or beneath a crumbling cliff or falling wall are subject to a crush or huge crush, and they may have to dig themselves free as the GM decides. A crush inflicts 3 points of damage, and a huge crush deals 6. Furthermore, the force of the quake knocks creatures to the ground and prevents them from standing until the shaking stops.
Depletion: Automatic

Ebon Eyes
Level: 1d6
Form: A small bottle of black liquid with a dropper
Effect: Placing a droplet in each eye turns the user's eyes solid black. For the next 28 hours, he can see in areas of dim light or very dim light as if they were illuminated with bright light. The user's eyes adjust to protect him from sudden light changes, and he can't be blinded by light effects.
Depletion: 1 in 1d10

The Sacred Chronicle of High Father Calaval, page 6

If a single drop of ebon eyes is carefully mixed with any liquid cypher with a beneficial effect (task difficulty 4), the resulting cypher enhances the user's eyes so that the difficulty of all ranged attacks is reduced by one step.

Electromagnetic Projector

Level: 1d6 + 4

Form: A large, heavy, handheld device that has two long metal rods protruding from a cushioned metal stock. A small metal sphere floats between the rods near the base of the weapon.

Effect: The device propels the sphere with incredible speed up to 10 miles (16 km). The sphere inflicts damage equal to the artifact level to whatever it strikes. Once used, the device must cool down for one minute before it can be used again.

Each time the weapon is used, the user and everyone within an immediate distance becomes deafened for one hour unless they took precautions to protect their hearing—earplugs, for example.

Depletion: 1 in 1d6

Emitter Enhancer

Level: 1d6

Form: Complex set of tubes and hinged rods

Effect: When the device is fit over and around any kind of ray emitter cypher, the emitter inflicts 2 additional points of damage. If the emitter does not normally inflict damage, it now inflicts 2 points in addition to whatever effect it normally has.

Depletion: 1 in 1d20

Energy Converter

Level: 1d6

Form: A mechanical plug that must be installed somewhere in the user's body

Effect: The device transforms physical energy into mental energy. Whenever the user would apply Effort on an Intellect roll, she may spend the points from her Might Pool instead.

Depletion: 1 in 1d100 (check once each day)

Environment Suit

Level: 1d6 + 1

Form: A full bodysuit made from synthetic material that's covered with tubes and wires

Effect: When worn, the suit protects the wearer from extreme temperatures and transforms her excretions into a foul-tasting but edible substance that can be retrieved from pouches in the legs. In addition, she suffers no ill effects from temperatures as cold as −58° F (−50° C) or as hot as 212° F (100° C). In addition, she takes no damage from extreme cold or heat.

Depletion: 1 in d100 (check each day while the suit is worn)

Ephemeral Garb

Level: 1d6

Form: A suit of transparent clothing

Effect: The clothing has no appearance. The wearer looks like he is not wearing any clothing at all. However, the suit gives him +1 to Armor.

Depletion: —

Eternal Journal

Level: 1d6

Form: Leather- and metallic-bound book that is housed inside a stronglass case

Effect: The pages of this book are designed to be written on with a finger, rather than a

Extraneous limbs are often found in groups. Thus, a creature that would normally have two arms might have four or six. In addition, they often have mechanical arms or legs, so a creature that normally has two legs might have six, and all of them are cybernetic (and just as often, inappropriate in size, shape, and configuration for that creature).

traditional writing utensil. The pages pick up the oils and skin cells shed from the writer's finger, turning them into a soft grey ink. Whenever the book is returned to the stronglass case for more than 28 hours at a time, another blank page is created from the skin cells and added to the back.
Depletion: —

Ever-Write
Level: 1
Form: A slender metal tube that ends in a point
Effect: Someone can use the device to write on any surface, even liquid. The writing cannot be erased.
Depletion: —

Everyoung Choker
Level: 1d6
Form: A metal choker with a glowing crystal set on the clasp
Effect: While wearing the device, the user shows no physical effects of aging and remains at the same age he was when he put on the device. If the device is removed, he ages normally.
Depletion: 1 in 1d100 (check once each year)

Extraneous Arm
Level: 1d6
Form: A metal arm
Effect: Unlike a mechanical arm, this cybernetic limb is meant to be affixed to a position on a host body that would not normally have such a limb. This, then, could be seen as an additional arm.

The arm must be surgically and permanently attached (a task equal to the artifact level). The procedure takes about an hour in a skilled chiurgeon's hands.

Once the arm is attached, the user has complete control over the limb and uses it naturally, which might end up allowing her to hold an additional object. She is granted an asset for all lifting tasks, but the extra arm does not confer additional actions.
Depletion: —

Extraneous Leg
Level: 1d6
Form: A metal leg
Effect: Unlike a mechanical leg, this cybernetic limb is meant to be affixed to a position on a host body that would not normally have such a limb. This, then, could be seen as an additional leg.

The leg must be surgically and permanently attached (a task equal to the artifact level). The procedure takes about an hour in a skilled chiurgeon's hands.

Once the leg is attached, the user has complete control over the limb and uses it naturally. He is granted an asset for running tasks.
Depletion: —

Extreme Lenses
Level: 1d6
Form: Synth eye cups
Effect: The wearer can refocus her eyes to see up to one hundred times farther than normal.
Depletion: 1 in 1d20

Exuvia

Level: 1d6 + 1

Form: Armor made of what appears to be large animal shells (or rather, what the shell of a human might look like, if humans had shells)

Effect: This form-fitting biological armor can be donned very quickly and is very light and unencumbering. It is treated in all ways like light armor but offers +2 to Armor.

Depletion: —

Eye of the Sky

Level: 1d6

Form: A large tube mounted on a flat platform with a viewscreen

Effect: Inside the tube is a fist-sized orb with a dozen or so lenses positioned across its surface. When activated, the tube fires the orb to a distance of 1 mile (2 km) in whatever direction it is facing. Provided the orb does not encounter a solid surface en route to its destination, once it moves the full distance, it stops and captures a perfect image of everything it can see within 5 miles (8 km). It then slowly floats to the ground, where it can be retrieved.

Placing the orb into the tube after it has been retrieved allows a user to see the image on the viewscreen. The device is typically used to create a detailed map of the surrounding environment.

When fired, if the orb strikes a solid object in its path, it inflicts damage equal to the artifact level and immediately shatters, rendering the artifact worthless.

Depletion: 1 in 1d100

Eye Spy

Level: 1d6 + 1

Form: Large synth sphere

Effect: When activated, the sphere stores up to 28 hours of visual and audio information around it. The sphere can "see" and "hear" as far as an average human, and information is recorded from a 360-degree perspective around it. The information can be replayed on the sphere itself when it is activated again.

Depletion: 1 in 1d20

Fabricator

Level: 1d6 + 2

Form: A bulky metal frame with glass plates on each side and a metal compartment at the top

Effect: Causes raw materials placed in the compartment to transform into a finished item, which appears inside the frame. The process of fabrication takes one minute. The device can be used to create just about any sort of item provided that it has a supply of raw materials needed to make the item.

Depletion: 1 in 1d20

Feather Cloak

Level: 1d6

Form: A cloak made from golden feathers

Effect: The feathers stiffen when struck to protect the wearer from injury. The user gains +1 to Armor while wearing the cloak.

Depletion: —

Fiber Optic Sleeves

Level: 1d6 + 4

Form: Flexible, lightweight sleeves with integrated fiber optic wires, designed to go over existing armor

Effect: These armor sleeves grant +1 to Armor in addition to whatever armor the user is currently wearing. Further, when active, the sleeves light up in a random, pulsing pattern for ten minutes. When used with melee attacks, this pattern confuses the target during that attack, modifying all defense actions by one step to its detriment.

Depletion: 1 in 1d20 for the confusion ability (after depletion, the sleeves still function as armor)

Finger Talkers

Level: 1d6

Form: Six adjustable black rings and one black bracelet (which stores the rings when they are not in use)

Effect: When worn on the thumb, pointer, and middle finger of both hands, the rings translate the wearer's hand gestures into spoken words that are emitted by the bracelet. The bracelet also converts other people's spoken words into text, which the wearer can read on a small screen on the side of the bracelet. While converting hand gestures into speech and speech into written language, the device also does any necessary translating. The device works automatically for most commonly used sign languages of the Ninth World, but if a user wishes to "train" the device to a new hand language, she must use it simultaneously with speaking for about an hour.

Depletion: —

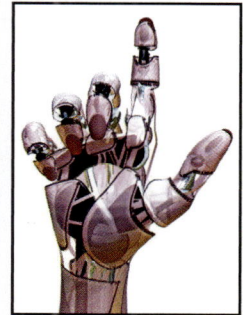

The trick to using a fabricator is knowing what raw materials are needed. Something as complex as a cypher or an artifact requires a task involving knowledge of the numenera with a difficulty of the device level + 4. If the result is above 10, it's impossible for anyone to get the fabricator to make that device. All powered devices successfully created by a fabricator start off depowered.

Flame Caster

Level: 1d6 + 2

Form: A metal canister with a flexible hose emerging from the top and ending at a nozzle

Effect: The device has two settings. The user chooses which setting to use when he activates it.

The first setting causes the nozzle to emit a short beam of white-hot flames. The flames are hot enough to cut through 6 inches (15 cm) of steel each minute the device is used. It can also be used as a melee weapon that inflicts damage equal to the artifact level. The device burns for ten minutes and then deactivates.

The second setting releases a ball of flame that travels a long distance and detonates at the end of this point or when it comes into contact with a solid object. When the ball explodes, it throws fire a short distance that inflicts 4 points of ambient damage.

Depletion: 1 in 1d6

Flaming Torrent

Level: 1d6 + 1

Form: Short synth wand with a small synth globe at the back end

Effect: This sprays a gout of flame out to short range in a cone that is 30 feet (9 m) wide at the terminus, potentially affecting multiple targets that are close together. The flames inflict damage equal to the artifact level.

Depletion: 1 in 1d20

Flesh-Render Wand

Level: 1d6 + 4

Form: A small handheld device fitted with a tiny tube

Effect: This device projects a wide spray of sharp fragments that inflicts 2 points of damage to everyone within an immediate area, and 1 point of damage to everyone within a short area. The fragments also penetrate (ignore) up to 4 Armor. In other words, targets in range who have 4 Armor (or less) take 2 points of damage, targets with 5 Armor take 1 point of damage, and targets with 6 Armor (or more) take no damage.

Depletion: 1 in 1d6

Flexsteel Weapon

Level: 1d6

Form: A weapon normally made from hard material such as a greatsword or battleaxe

Effect: The weapon looks like it is made of steel, but when it is swung with force, it stretches. A wielder can stretch the weapon in his hands as if it were made of elastic material. When stretched in this way, it always snaps back to its original shape.

The difficulty of attack rolls made using this weapon is increased by one step. However, if the attack misses, the user can repeat the attack roll once. If the second roll succeeds, the weapon inflicts half its normal damage.

Depletion: —

Flicker Cloak

Level: 1d6 + 2

Form: A long cloak made from material woven with circuitry

Effect: Causes the user to flicker in and out of existence for ten minutes. At the end of each of her turns while wearing the cloak, she must roll a d6. On an odd number, nothing happens. On an even number, she disappears, ceasing to exist. At the start of her next turn, she reappears in the space she left (or an open space nearest to that space). She has no idea what happened during the time she ceased to exist.

Depletion: 1 in 1d10

Flight Pack

Level: 1d6 + 1

Form: A metal device worn on one's back

Effect: The wearer can move in the air for one hour, moving an immediate distance per turn in any direction. If desired, this speed can be increased to almost 100 miles (161 km) per hour for that hour, but doing so automatically depletes the artifact.

Depletion: 1 in 1d20

Foldable Coach

Level: 1d6 + 3

Form: A chest that folds out into a self-powered coach

Effect: It takes two rounds to fold the coach out of its chest, whereupon it becomes a vehicle able to seat up to five humans. The vehicle has six hard synth wheels. When sealed inside, characters are not visible to external creatures, but they can see outside. Furthermore, characters inside gain +5 to Armor against all attacks made from outside the coach. Each time the coach is set up, it responds to audible voice commands from passengers and can travel for up to one hour per artifact level, with long movement on roads and short movement on rough or difficult terrain. It's possible for up to four additional human-sized creatures to ride on top of the coach while it travels. When exhausted, the vehicle folds back into its compact form, ejecting any passengers still within, and can't be used again for several hours.

Depletion: 1 in 1d20

Force Shield
Level: 1
Form: A wristband with a round device attached in the middle
Effect: When activated, an energy field expands out from the device until it attains the size of a shield. The energy field functions as a shield for one hour.
Depletion: 1 in 1d20

Globe Projector
Level: 1d6 + 2
Form: A short device with a narrow synth tube that flares at the end
Effect: When activated, the device shoots a glittering orb at a target within short range. Upon striking the target, the orb expands into an opaque white bubble that completely envelops the target and then floats away at a rate of 10 feet (3 m) per round for ten minutes. It then pops and drops the target to the ground. Until the effect ends, nothing can pass through the bubble.
Depletion: 1 in 1d6

Glow Boots
Level: 1d6
Form: A pair of leather boots
Effect: The boots cause the wearer to leave behind faint footprints that reveal themselves in very dim light or darkness. The prints glow with faint light that is strong enough to be followed, but not strong enough to illuminate the area. The prints last for 28 hours before fading away.
Depletion: —

Glowglobe Nest
Level: 1d6
Form: Either a small synth bowl or a synth object with two or three round receptacles
Effect: This device holds one to three glowglobes. After ten minutes of sitting in the nest, the globes are fully recharged and ready for use again. Some people speculate that these devices were once far more common. In particular, the nests must have been used heavily by whatever prior civilization used glowglobes so much that they are still ubiquitous.
Depletion: —

Graviton Emitter
Level: 1d6 + 2
Form: A handheld device with a dial and several buttons
Effect: This long-range weapon fires a beam of gravitons that inflicts no damage. Whatever object or creature the beam hits emits a powerful gravity field that extends out to 30 feet (9 m) in all directions. Anything in the area "falls" toward the target unless it is fixed in place. A falling creature or object takes damage based on the distance it fell as normal when it strikes the target or another solid object in the way. Each creature or object struck by a falling object takes half the

damage sustained from the fall.

A creature flying through the area is unaffected provided that it continues flying. For attacks using projectile weapons in which the projectile passes through the affected area, the GM may increase the difficulty of the attack by one step.

The weird gravity lasts until the end of the next round. Until then, any creature in the affected area functions as if gravity pointed to the target. The target cannot move until this effect ends.

Depletion: 1 in 1d6

Graviton Suppressor

Level: 1d6 + 4
Form: A flat metal disk with a display and several buttons
Effect: Once activated, it takes two rounds for the device to take effect. The device shuts off gravity within a short distance. Anything not bolted down or anchored in some way floats up 30 feet (9 m) and hangs there until the effect ends, one minute later. Anyone pulled outside of the area or still in the area when the effect ends falls to the ground.
Depletion: 1 in 1d10

Gravity Suit

Level: 1d6 + 1
Form: A light but tough full-body leather suit
Effect: This light armor not only provides +1 to Armor as expected, but it also allows the wearer to reverse gravity for herself. In other words, she can choose to "fall" upward, walk across the ceiling as if it were the floor, and so on. This change in gravity orientation is true of everything she carries, but if she lets go of an object or drops something, normal gravity takes over for that object.

It is an action to change the gravity orientation.

Depletion: 1–2 in 1d100 (remains light armor even when depleted)

Greenstone Adaptor

Level: 1d6
Form: A glowing stone laced with wires
Effect: The device bonds to any artifact to which it is touched. The wires plug into the artifact and embed themselves in it. Henceforth, whenever a user rolls for depletion of that artifact, he can roll twice and use either result.

This device is radioactive. At the end of each day during which a user spent any time around the device, he must make a Might roll with a difficulty equal to the artifact level. On a failure, the device inflicts radiation damage equal to half the artifact level (minimum 1 point). This damage ignores Armor.

Depletion: —

Guardian Sphere

Level: 1d6

Form: A black metal sphere fitted with a glowing red disk made of glass that moves across its surface

Effect: The sphere follows whoever activated it around for one hour by rolling across the ground to stay within an immediate distance of the user. The sphere jumps over obstacles that are 3 feet (1 m) tall or less. Otherwise, it maneuvers around them if possible or stays put if not. Once per round, whenever the user is attacked by a foe that is within an immediate distance, the ball leaps toward the foe and sprouts long spikes from its body that inflict damage equal to the artifact level on a hit. After making this attack, the spikes retract and the sphere falls to the ground.

Depletion: 1 in 1d20

Gut Worm

Level: 1d6 + 2

Form: A 6-inch (15 cm) fleshy worm

Effect: A user must swallow the worm whole to activate it. Until the worm is expelled two days later, the user must consume twice as much food as normal each day.

Activating the device causes a fleshy tendril to burst from the user's body, inflicting 1 point of damage that cannot be reduced in any way. The tendril is a level 2 creature under the user's control. As a level 2 creature, it has a target number of 6, inflicts 2 points of damage, and has 6 health. The tendril cannot leave the user's body. It can attack targets at a short distance from the user.

Depletion: —

Hand of Annihilation

Level: 1d6 + 3

Form: A metallic pincer that fits over the wrist

Effect: When activated, this device creates a small orb of light that can be wielded as a medium weapon that annihilates the matter it touches, disintegrating it. This inflicts 10 points of damage, but it is very difficult and dangerous to use. The difficulty of attacks is increased by two steps, and a roll of 1 or 2 results in GM intrusion.

The orb can be dispelled with an action.

Having the orb in the pincer for an extended period of time (walking around outside of combat, for example) is dangerous, and GM intrusions should be common.

Depletion: 1 in 1d10

Handy Hollow

Level: 1d6 + 2

Form: A square piece of black cloth

Effect: It takes one round to fold the black cloth across a flat surface such as on the ground, draped down a wall, and so on, to cover an area 5 feet by 5 feet (2 m by 2 m). The cloth becomes a permeable passage through the surface reaching up to 10 feet (3 m) through solid material. The permeability lasts for one hour and creates no instability in the surrounding structure.

Depletion: 1 in 1d10

Hand of Annihilation GM Intrusion: *The character drops or otherwise inadvertently looses the orb. This could mean that the damage is inflicted upon the user or another target within immediate range, or that the orb falls at the user's feet, making a hole that he likely falls into.*

When the wielder gets a major effect on an attack using a hard light cutter, the blade can lop off one of the target's limbs, with consequences determined by the GM.

Hard Light Cutter

Level: 1d6 + 2

Form: A short metal baton with a crystal mounted at the top and buttons along one side

Effect: Activating this device causes a 3-foot (1 m) blade of solid light to extend from the baton's tip and remain until deactivated (not an action). The blade inflicts damage equal to the artifact level.

Depletion: 1 in 1d100

Hard Light Goggles

Level: 1d6 + 2

Form: A metal visor with a lens that, when looked through, tints everything red

Effect: A wearer can tap the side of the goggles and cause them to emit a pulse of solidified light that travels a long distance. The light inflicts 4 points of damage.

If the user gets a major effect on an attack roll using this device, the light inflicts 12 points of damage to the target, and it inflicts 4 points of damage to everything within a short distance of the target. After resolving this effect, roll for depletion again.

Depletion: 1 in 1d10

Homing Volt Projector

Level: 1d6

Form: Small handheld device

Effect: Fires tiny pellets that veer toward organic targets and burst with a jolt of electricity that deals 5 points of damage (ignores Armor). Attacking inorganic targets increases the difficulty by two steps, but attacking an organic target decreases the difficulty by one step. Hiding behind inorganic cover provides no protection, but hiding behind organic cover (like a tree) increases the difficulty of attacking the target by one step.

Depletion: 1 in 1d20

Hot-Cold Stone

Level: 1

Form: A small, round, flat mechanical device with four vents at the top

Effect: When activated, the device changes the temperature in the area within a short distance. It can increase or decrease the temperature by up to 68° F (20° C), as the user decides. The effect lasts for up to seven hours.

Depletion: 1 in 1d20

Husk

Level: 1d6 + 2

Form: A featureless, hairless humanoid creature

Effect: Activating the device causes it to become a level 1 creature. The creature follows the user wherever it goes, but otherwise does nothing. As a level 1 creature, it has a target number of 3 and has 3 health. If reduced to 0 health, the device is destroyed.

The first time a human or humanoid within short range of the creature dies, the creature absorbs the target's personality, memories, and identity, and transforms to assume the target's appearance in the prime of its life. In effect, the device becomes the creature. After nine years, the body dissolves into a slick of foul-smelling slime.

Depletion: —

Hypno-Lenses

Level: 1d6 + 2

Form: A pair of pink lenses held in a silver frame

Effect: The wearer has an asset on any task that involves deceiving or persuading a creature that meets his gaze.

Depletion: 1 in 1d20

Hypnotic Nanny

Level: 1d6

Form: Fur-covered, squishy oval device about 3 feet by 1 foot (1 m by 0.3 m)

Effect: When activated, the device croons and hums various songs and tunes, flashes in a series of calming, mesmerizing lights, and begins to vibrate softly. Creatures that listen for more than one minute are calmed and compelled to remain listening for as long as the effect lasts (one hour). During that hour, creatures of a lower level than the artifact fall asleep for 2d6 hours.

Depletion: —

Impossible Blade

Level: 1d6 + 4

Form: A small, extremely thin blade with a short handle

Effect: This tool can be used for very fine work, cutting or carving almost any (small) object with amazing precision. It allows for surgeries and crafting that would likely otherwise be impossible (it counts as two assets for such tasks).

It can also be used as a weapon. In this capacity, it is a light weapon that ignores

Armor. However, the blade is somewhat fragile, so using it as a weapon risks damaging it.
Depletion: 1 in 1d20

Impulse Collar
Level: 1d6
Form: A thick leather strap that wraps around one's throat with a pulsing light set into a metal casing on the front of it
Effect: While within short range of another living creature, the wearer can activate the device by pressing the light with his thumb and aiming it in the general direction of another person. The device picks up and broadcasts the general emotional state of that person. A blue light signifies indifference, red signifies anger, purple signifies arousal, and yellow indicates good will, friendship, or love. Activation is an action.
Depletion: 1 in 1d20

Instant Ladder
Level: 1d6
Form: Small lightweight rod
Effect: When activated, the rod extends and produces rungs so that it can be used as a ladder up to 28 feet (9 m) long.
Depletion: 1 in 1d100

Interceptor
Level: 1d6 + 2
Form: Shoulder-mounted device
Effect: When small, fast-moving physical objects (arrows, thrown rocks, or other projectiles) coming toward the device reach a distance within immediate range, it fires bursts of energy that destroy the projectiles if they are of lower level than the interceptor. Although the interceptor can fire at multiple targets at once, depletion is rolled for each use.
Depletion: 1 in 1d20

Kill Dart Projector
Level: 1d6
Form: A small handheld device with a narrow tube
Effect: This device projects a tiny dart made of glowing metal up to long range. The dart inflicts 1 point of damage and then saturates the target with radiation. The target takes 1 point of ambient damage each round, and the difficulty of all tasks it performs is modified by one step to its detriment. If the target removes the dart, the effect ends after 28 hours.

This device is a rapid-fire weapon and thus can be used with the Spray or Arc Spray abilities that some glaives and jacks have, but

"I once discovered a cache of thirty-seven glowglobe nests. I used their parts to build a glowglobe 30 feet across that lit up an entire small town in the Beyond. Sadly, I can no longer remember the location of the town."
~Sir Arthour

each round of ammo used or each additional target selected requires an additional depletion roll.
Depletion: 1 in 1d6

Leap Boots
Level: 1d6
Form: A pair of heavy boots
Effect: The user can activate these boots to jump up to a long distance and then land safely.
Depletion: 1 in 1d10

Light Discus
Level: 1d6 + 2
Form: A metal plate worn on the back and held in place by two shoulder straps
Effect: The user must be wearing the device to activate it. After doing so, he can pull a disk made of glowing, solidified light out of the plate and throw it at a target within short range. The disk inflicts damage equal to half the artifact level. After making the attack, the disk may fly to attack up to two different targets, each within a short distance of the last, and inflicting the same damage as the first attack. After the disk makes its last attack, it flies back to the user's hand and dissipates.
Depletion: 1 in 1d10

Light Tendril
Level: 1d6
Form: A metal and synth tendril with an illuminated end
Effect: This mechanical tendril grafts easily (and without surgery) onto the user's back. She controls the tendril, which always shines light on whatever she wishes.
Depletion: —

Lightning Whip
Level: 1d6
Form: A short handle with a 10-foot-long (3 m) filament extending from the end
Effect: When activated, energy crackles all along the length of the filament for one minute. While energized, the device can be used like a whip (a light weapon) that inflicts 4 points of damage. The damage ignores Armor.
Depletion: 1 in 1d10

Lightwings
Level: 1d6
Form: Set of lightweight collapsible wings and harness built of adamant silk and azure steel. The spine of the wings is actually a stronglass terrarium hosting the bioluminescent worms that power the device.

Effect: When activated, the wings light up and can carry the user and her equipment up to 50 feet (15 m) in the air. Each time the wings are used, they last a number of minutes equal to the artifact level × 10 (a new roll is required for each use). As the power gets used up, the bioluminescent light begins to wane, alerting the wearer. The worms require about a day of rest between each use of the wings. (The wings don't work as well if used more than once per day. For subsequent uses within 28 hours, they last only a number of minutes equal to the artifact level × 2).

Action to attach. Action to activate.
Depletion: 1 in 1d20

Likeness Thief
Level: 1d6 + 2
Form: A pink-hued gelatinous mass
Effect: The device activates when placed onto the face of another creature, and once activated, it cannot be removed for one minute. During this time, the mass excretes digestive enzymes that inflict 10 points of corrosive damage, destroying the face of the creature it touches. Afterward, the mass hardens into a perfect copy of the face it destroyed. When a creature wears the mask, it becomes like real tissue and moves in a lifelike and realistic manner.

If the victim survives having its face stolen, it is blind, and its facial features are almost completely erased. Nothing remains except a nub of a nose and a slit for a mouth.
Depletion: Automatic

Liminal Scanner
Level: 1d6 + 2
Form: A large device that fits over the user's hand and has a screen, an array of controls, and a long metal tendril that functions as a sensory apparatus
Effect: This device scans an object or creature within short range and determines a variety of qualities (some quite esoteric) that cannot be observed with the naked eye. This grants the user an asset in dealing with the material in some desired way, chosen by the user. For example, a scanned wall might be easier to break through, a foe might be easier to attack, a device might be easier to understand, and so on. The asset is always specific to the single object or creature and to the single task specified, but it remains indefinitely.
Depletion: 1 in 1d20

Living Cable
Level: 1d6
Form: A spool of hard, flat, segmented cable
Effect: When activated, the cable unspools and sprouts two rows of impossibly long legs from either side, one pair per segment, while a row of knobby protrusions that resemble handles rise up from it, perpendicular to the legs. The cable then slithers to the vertical surface the user indicates and climbs up or down until it reaches the top or bottom or until it has extended its body to a distance of 100 feet (30 m). It uses its legs to grip the surface and remains in place until a button is depressed near the top or bottom, which causes the thing to release, coil up, and retract all its legs and knobs.
Depletion: 1 in 1d20

Living Tentacle
Level: 1d6
Form: Thick, genetically created rope, approximately 20 feet (6 m) long, with suction disks all along its length and a bulbous opening on one end, that self-coils into a buoyant, waterproof case
Effect: The cord suctions to anything that it is pressed against, living or nonliving. When one suction disk is set, the others follow suit, always forming as straight a line as possible. Once the cord has suctioned to something, it will not release until the bulbous opening has been "fed" (usually a bit of meat, although tastes can vary from cord to cord).
Depletion: 1 in 1d100

Living Wall
Level: 1d6 + 2
Form: A 10-foot (3 m) cube of metal mounted on two wide tracks
Effect: This device functions as a level 3 creature that accompanies the user and follows his instructions. The only action the device can take is to move where the user directs it. As a level 3 creature, it has a target number of 9 and a health of 9. It has 5 Armor. The creature can move only across the ground. The device is destroyed if reduced to 0 health.
Depletion: —

Logic Spike
Level: 1d6
Form: A long metallic spike
Effect: To activate this item, the user must hammer the spike into his head, which inflicts no damage. Once installed, the device decreases

If you cobble together the internal workings of a single leap boot with any ray emitter (task difficulty 6), you create a cypher that allows the user to teleport an object within long range to a location of her choosing, up to 10 miles away.

the difficulty of any task that involves reason, logic, or recall by two steps. However, it increases the difficulty of any task that involves communication by one step.

An installed spike cannot be removed without permanently reducing the user's Intellect Pool to 0.
Depletion: —

Machine's Heart
Level: 1d6
Form: A 7-foot-tall (2 m) collapsible metal stand with a 3-foot-by-3-foot (1-m-by-1-m) empty box on top and a control panel along the side
Effect: It takes two rounds to assemble and set up this device, and then it takes an action to activate it.

The empty box can hold four depleted, broken, or otherwise unusable cyphers and artifacts. When the box is filled with the numenera and the machine's heart is activated, it combines all of the numenera items inside it and reconfigures them into a number of new cyphers or artifacts equal to the artifact level.
Depletion: 1 in 1d6

Manybag
Level: 1d6
Form: Stiff leather bag of fairly large size
Effect: This leather bag has dozens of sealed compartments of different sizes. By verbal command, portions of the bag can become selectively intangible so that anything in the bag can be accessed quickly. In effect, the user can speak a command word and draw out whatever object in the bag is desired, because all other obstructing compartments (and their contents) are rendered out of phase for a moment.
Depletion: —

Matter Separator
Level: 1d6 + 2
Form: A small handheld device equipped with prongs at one end
Effect: This device causes the atomic bonds holding together a creature or object within an immediate distance to separate, creating a cloud of dust that spreads out a short distance in all directions and remains there for one round. Unless dispersed by wind (which utterly destroys the target), the target snaps back together after the effect ends. The user then rolls a d20. On a result of 11 or higher, a part of the target, as decided by the GM, is missing. The disappearance inflicts 4 points of damage that ignores Armor.
Depletion: 1 in 1d6

Mechanical Arm
Level: 1d6 + 2
Form: Mechanical arm grafted to a stump on a person's body
Effect: The arm must be surgically and permanently attached (a task equal to the artifact level). The procedure takes about an hour in a skilled chiurgeon's hands.

Once the arm is attached, the user has complete control over the limb and uses it naturally. The arm grants an asset on any task involving carrying or lifting.
Depletion: —

Ericlofgren

Mechanical Leg

Level: 1d6 + 2
Form: Mechanical leg grafted to a stump on a person's body
Effect: The leg must be surgically and permanently attached (a task equal to the artifact level). The procedure takes about an hour in a skilled chiurgeon's hands.

Once the leg is attached, the user has complete control over the limb and uses it naturally. The leg grants an asset on any task that involves running.
Depletion: —

Memory Shard

Level: 10
Form: A sharp metal spike that must be inserted into the base of the neck at an upward angle. Installing the spike inflicts no damage, but it cannot be removed without killing the person.
Effect: The spike contains a personality fragment from a person long dead. Installing the spike floods the host's mind with shreds of memory, feelings, and sensations until he absorbs the extra personality. He can immediately choose and gain a second focus.
Depletion: —

Mental Storage

Level: 1d6 + 4
Form: Large device with multiple screens and controls as well as wires with electrodes
Effect: When used, this device records a thinking creature's knowledge, memories, and personality—basically, a copy of his consciousness. The recording process takes four hours. The device can then store this data indefinitely. It can be accessed and downloaded into another appropriate device or body (if those capabilities are available). The device can be used only once.
Depletion: Automatic

Mesmerizing Flame

Level: 1d6 + 2
Form: Large handheld device with a star-shaped wheel on the end of a long extension
Effect: When the device is activated, two things happen. First, the user is protected by a shield of force that provides +1 to Armor, and +10 to Armor against flame. Second, the star-shaped wheel begins spinning and spitting out flames. This is a heavy melee weapon that inflicts damage equal to the artifact level + 2, and all of the damage is fire and heat (ignores Armor). Once activated, the device remains active for one minute.

Moreover, when the device is activated, creatures within immediate range that can see the patterns in the spinning flames become mesmerized, losing their action in the next round. Creatures that come within immediate range once the device is active may also become mesmerized. No creature ever loses more than one action to the patterns.
Depletion: 1 in 1d10

Mesoglea Gloss

Level: 1d6
Form: A living gelatinous creature encased in a medium-sized orb
Effect: After breaking the orb and essentially killing the creature inside, the user can then slather a piece of armor with the goo. Once the goo dries into a hard shellac (about ten minutes), it provides protection against water, wind, and light. Additionally, the user can add a single drop of liquid to the gloss to activate it. When activated, the gloss becomes both hard and slippery, decreasing the difficulty of all Speed and Might defense actions by one step for one hour.

Applying the gloss is an action. Activating the gloss is also an action.
Depletion: 1 in 1d20 for the Speed and Might defense abilities (after depletion, the glossed armor retains its water-, wind-, and light-reflection properties)

Mind Blade

Level: 1d6
Form: A weapon (usually a broadsword or dagger) made from grey crystal
Effect: The material from which the weapon is made is highly receptive to thought and stores mental energy placed into it. When a user attacks with the weapon and would apply Effort, he can spend points from his Intellect Pool instead of his Might Pool.
Depletion: —

Mind Displacer

Level: 1d6 + 4
Form: A metal helmet with an opaque visor
Effect: When activated, the device blasts the user's mind with vivid colors for one minute. At the end of this time, the user sees and hears as if at a fixed point in a place that she has visited at least once before. The perception lasts until she removes the device.
Depletion: 1 in 1d6

Minute Lenses

Level: 1d6
Form: Synth eye cups
Effect: The wearer can refocus her eyes to magnify whatever she is looking at within an immediate distance by up to one hundred times.
Depletion: 1 in 1d20

Mirage Generator

Level: 1d6 + 4
Form: A complex mechanical device bristling with multicolored lenses
Effect: Activating the device takes ten minutes. At the end of this time, the device creates a complex scene of images (chosen by the user) within immediate range. The entire scene must fit inside a 100-foot (30 m) cube. The images are made from solidified light and look and feel completely real. The device also creates sounds to make the images seem real. If the images include creatures, those creatures look and act like real creatures, but when they talk, they speak in gibberish. The only quality the device cannot produce is smell—nothing created by the device has an odor. The images last for one hour or until the device is deactivated (not an action).

If the scene is something that could be harmful (such as a roaring inferno), the device inflicts ambient damage equal to half its level to all creatures within long range.

The images cannot conceal terrain features.

They can change the features' general appearance but must incorporate them into the scene. Thus, a pit in the area would still be a pit, though the color might change so that it blends in with the created scene.
Depletion: 1 in 1d6

Mobile Arm

Level: 1d6 + 1
Form: A small handheld device and a larger complex mechanical device with treads and a multijointed arm
Effect: The bigger device is about 3 feet (1 m) long, with an arm that can extend out to 7 feet (2 m). It is controlled by the smaller device. The larger device can be made to move across almost any solid surface, and the mechanical arm can manipulate objects in a crude fashion. It can open doors, pull levers, push buttons, pick up and drop objects that a human could pick up in one hand, push or pull objects about the size of a human or smaller, and so on. It is neither fast enough nor precise enough to make attacks. When activated, it operates for one hour.
Depletion: 1 in 1d20

Monitor Bracelet

Level: 1
Form: A bracelet made from a flexible, synthetic material and a viewscreen
Effect: The device activates when a creature puts on the bracelet. While the bracelet is worn, the viewscreen displays the wearer's exact position and vital signs.
Depletion: 1 in 1d100 (checked each day the bracelet is worn)

Monowhip

Level: 1d6 + 4
Form: Hilt with connected red sphere
Effect: Produces a 10-foot-long (3 m), hair-thin, glowing white cord. The whip cuts through any material of a level lower than its own. If used to attack, the whip is a light weapon that ignores Armor of a level lower than its own, but each attack requires a depletion check. Furthermore, each missed attack requires a difficulty 3 Speed defense roll to avoid accidentally taking damage from the retracting whip.
Depletion: 1 in 1d20

Multiphasic creatures look like there are dozens of versions of themselves taking up basically the same space, so there is a stuttering trail behind each movement. When a multiphasic character strikes a transdimensional foe in melee, it probably looks as though some versions strike the foe while others pass through it, all at the same time.

Mother Parasite

Level: 1d6 + 2
Form: A flat nodule of tissue equipped with a round, toothed mouth on one side and a great roaming red eye on the other
Effect: The user must position the parasite so it can bite his skin. The parasite sinks its teeth into his skin and remains there. The bite inflicts 1 point of damage. While in place, the parasite draws sustenance from its host, reducing his Might Pool by 1.

The parasite automatically activates whenever the user fails a Might or Speed defense roll. An orifice opens on the parasite and sprays corrosive slime at a target of the user's choice within immediate range. The slime inflicts damage equal to the artifact level. The damage penetrates (ignores) up to 2 Armor.
Depletion: 1 in 1d10

Multiphasic Ray

Level: 1d6
Form: Small handheld device
Effect: Emits a ray of yellow-orange light that bathes up to three human-sized targets in a burst of energy. For the next ten minutes, those affected by the ray are multiphasic, existing in multiple phases and dimensions at one time. Multiphasic characters are not subject to the special resistances of creatures that are normally difficult to touch or attack because they are out of phase or transdimensional in nature. Likewise, if the attacks of foes who are out of phase or transdimensional would normally ignore Armor, this benefit does not apply to multiphasic characters.
Depletion: 1 in 1d20

Music Makers

Level: 1d6
Form: Yellow and blue gloves with glowing fingertips
Effect: While the gloves are worn and the fingertips are pressed to the surface of any living creature, they sound off in a series of notes. The notes may be altered by the amount of applied pressure, the angle of the touch, and the movement of the living creature. The sounds can be heard by anyone within 500 feet (152 m).
Depletion: 1 in 1d20 (roll each time when putting the gloves on)

Mutation Mask

Level: 1d6 + 4
Form: A leather face mask with a variety of synth protuberances
Effect: When worn, the mask conforms to the wearer's head, enclosing it. While wearing the mask, the character can trigger a mutation by spending an action fiddling with the mask. Over the next few rounds, any previous mutations fade, and a new mutation appears. Roll on the mutation tables for a harmful mutation (1 on a 1d6), a beneficial mutation (2–5 on a 1d6), or a powerful mutation (6 on a 1d6).
Depletion: 1 in 1d100 (checked each day the mask is worn, and checked each time the mutation is changed)

Mutation tables, pages 124–128

The rope cannot move of its own volition other than to tie or untie itself.
Depletion: 1 in 1d100

Ocular Graft

Level: 1d6 + 1
Form: A fleshy mass with three eyes that fits over the head (and one eye) of a human
Effect: This living device feeds off the nutrients in the host's blood, so her total Might Pool is reduced by 1 while the graft is worn. She has an asset on perception tasks and can see in complete darkness as if it were dim light. Perhaps most impressive, the host can see creatures and objects within short range that are invisible, out of phase, or dimensionally displaced.

The graft inflicts 8 points of damage to the host if removed.
Depletion: —

Ocular Helm

Level: 1d6 + 1
Form: A synthsteel helm with seven round eyes
Effect: The wearer of this strange helm sees a variety of visual sensors, clarity enhancers, viewfinders, rangefinders, and other aids to sight. She gains an asset on perception tasks and all ranged attacks.
Depletion: 1 in 1d20 (check each day used)

Oubliette

Level: 1d6 + 2
Form: A small metal box
Effect: When thrown (short range) at a human-sized creature, the box unfolds, expands, and snaps shut around a target. The box is a 7-foot (2 m) cube. There is enough air inside to allow the target to breathe (if it needs to). If the user activates the artifact while it contains a target, the box opens, releases its contents, and returns to its normal small size. If it deactivates while holding a target, the device must be destroyed in order to free its contents.
Depletion: 1 in 1d10

Periscopic Eye

Level: 1d6
Form: Mechanical implant
Effect: This device must be surgically implanted behind the user's eyeball (a level 1d6 task that takes about one hour). Once it's placed, the user can push on the inside of his eye and extend his eyeball out a number

Neural Disruptor

Level: 1d6 + 2
Form: Small cylinder with a few studs
Effect: Fires a green neural disruption beam at long range. Those struck suffer 2 points of Intellect damage (ignores Armor) and must make an Intellect defense roll or lose their next turn, stunned.
Depletion: 1 in 1d10

Null Blade

Level: 1d6 + 4
Form: A sword whose blade is covered with circuitry
Effect: This weapon functions as a normal sword (sometimes a dagger). However, if the user kills a creature with this weapon, the creature and everything it wears and carries disappears, erased from existence.
Depletion: —

Obedient Rope

Level: 1d6 + 4
Form: A 50-foot (15 m) length of thin metallic cable
Effect: This extremely useful, semi-intelligent cable obeys the verbal commands of the user. The cable can tie itself in knots and untie those knots. It can become sticky to adhere to surfaces (selectively—parts of the cable can remain normal) or rigid (again, selectively).

of feet equal to the artifact level. Doing this allows him to see around corners, down thin tunnels, and anywhere else he is willing to risk sending his eyeball.

Depletion: —

Personality Adjuster

Level: 1d6 + 4

Form: A metal helmet trailing wires with several spikes on the inside

Effect: When placed on a creature's head, the helmet inflicts 2 points of damage. If the helmet is activated, it completely erases the creature's memories and personality, turning the creature into a blank slate, a process that takes about one hour. After this time, the user who activated the device can implant new memories that build the creature's personality. If used on a character, the character remains at his tier, but he can swap out his type, descriptor, and focus for different ones.

Depletion: Automatic

Phase Axe

Level: 1d6 + 4

Form: A battleaxe whose blade is made of an unknown translucent material

Effect: This weapon functions as a normal battleaxe except the blade can pass through anything made of rock or metal. Attacks with the weapon ignore Armor made from these materials.

Depletion: —

Photon Transporter

Level: 1d6 + 4

Form: Two metal disks, each 5 feet (2 m) in diameter

Effect: When activated, anything on one of the metal disks instantly transports to the other disk. The device accomplishes this by transforming the item or passenger into light particles and broadcasting them to the second disk. When the particles arrive, the disk reassembles them in their original form. The devices allow instant transport from one disk to the other and back again, regardless of the distance separating them.

Depletion: 1 in 1d20

Pincer Arm

Level: 1d6 + 1

Form: A metal arm with a pincer rather than a hand

Effect: The arm must be surgically and permanently attached (a task equal to the artifact level). The procedure takes about an hour in a skilled chiurgeon's hands.

Once the arm is attached, the user has complete control over the limb and uses it naturally. The arm grants an asset on grabbing, grappling, and any task involving carrying or lifting. Further, the arm is considered a medium weapon if used to attack. However, the arm allows for no delicate or fine manipulation.

Depletion: —

Point Clamp

Level: 1d6 + 3

Form: Flat metal disk 4 inches (10 cm) across

Effect: When this object touches another object, it forms a point-to-point connection that is almost unbreakable. The connection can be undone by activating a control on the side of the disk. The disk can be connected to multiple objects at once. For example, a character could attach it to a rope and then fling the disk up to the ceiling, where it would attach, allowing him to climb up.

Depletion: —

Poisoner's Touch

Level: 1d6 + 1

Form: Very thin transparent glove

Effect: When the wearer concentrates (taking an action), the glove secretes a small amount of nerve toxin. The next creature touched suffers Speed damage equal to the artifact level (ignores Armor) and must make a new defense roll each round or suffer the damage again until either she succeeds at the defense roll or five rounds pass, whichever comes first.

Depletion: 1 in 1d10

Portable Lavation

Level: 1d6

Form: Black synth cube 1 foot (0.3 m) on a side that expands to a shelter 3 feet by 3 feet by 7 feet (1 m by 1 m by 2 m)

Effect: When set up near water (or if set up prior to a rainstorm), the device cleans and heats up to 1 gallon (4 L) of liquid and then creates a pressurized shower that lasts for ten minutes. The pressurized water also contains a scented residue that stays on the skin, which produces an odor that most humans find pleasing.

Those who shower for ten minutes (and don't wipe the scented residue off their skin) find that the difficulty of all actions related to charm, charisma, and persuasion is reduced

Photon Transporter
GM Intrusion: *If a use would deplete the device, there could be a mishap. If the device transports an object, the object disappears. If it transports a creature, something goes horribly wrong and the device inflicts damage equal to the artifact level. This damage ignores Armor. If the creature survives, it gains a random harmful mutation.*

by one step for one hour, but only when they are dealing with humans.

The device takes 28 hours to recharge between uses.

When in its box form, the device is sturdy enough to use as a stool or small table.
Depletion: 1 in 1d20

Power Glove
Level: 1d6 + 1
Form: An oversized metal gauntlet with thick protrusions on the knuckles
Effect: Unarmed strikes made while wearing the glove inflict 1 additional point of damage. However, if the user takes an action to activate the glove, energy sparks between the protrusions for one round. During that round, if the attack is successful, the glove inflicts 5 additional points of damage and throws the target back a short distance.
Depletion: 1 in 1d6

Printing Stylus
Level: 1d6 + 2
Form: A thick stylus that produces quick-hardening "ink" of varying firmness and strength, as desired
Effect: The stylus can be used to draw three-dimensional objects in midair. It takes a few rounds to draw a piece of basic equipment, such as rope, a backpack, spikes, a sword, or a shield. Upon completion of the drawing, the user makes an Intellect roll against a target number determined by the GM. The roll might be modified by any skill the GM agrees is pertinent. On a success, the item drawn becomes a real piece of equipment.
Depletion: 1 in 1d10

Probability Engine
Level: 1d6 + 2
Form: A synth cube made of small white cubes and blue spheres
Effect: When the user activates the item, the GM secretly rolls a d20 and notes the result. Anytime the user chooses, she can replace the result of one roll with the number that the GM rolled. The GM rolls a new secret number each time the device is activated.
Depletion: 1 in 1d100

Probability Mantle
Level: 1d6 + 2
Form: A multicolored cloak
Effect: If the wearer fails a defense roll or an attack roll, she can call on the probability

mantle for a second chance (and another roll).
Depletion: 1 in 1d10

Projectile Drone
Level: 1d6 + 3
Form: A 3-foot-tall (1 m) collapsible tripod with a metallic projectile weapon mounted on top
Effect: It takes two rounds to assemble and set up this device. Once set up, it takes an action to activate. When activated, this device follows whoever activated it around for one hour on its tripod legs (movement: short). If the user comes under attack, the drone fires one shot per round at attackers within long range, inflicting damage equal to the artifact level.
Depletion: 1 in 1d20

Protection Amulet
Level: 1d6
Form: A stylized amulet worn on a chain
Effect: The amulet reduces one type of damage by an amount equal to the artifact level. Roll a d20 to determine the kind of damage the amulet protects against.

1–4	Cold
5–8	Electrocution and shock
9–12	Fire
13–16	Poison
17–20	Radiation

Depletion: 1 in 1d6 (check each time the amulet reduces the damage)

Psycap
Level: 1d6 + 2
Form: A weave of thin metallic wires worn on a shaved head
Effect: The weave protects the wearer's mind from mental attacks. While he wears it, he has an asset on Intellect defense rolls and cannot be contacted by telepathic means.
Depletion: 1 in 1d10 (check each time the user makes an Intellect defense roll)

Pulse Staff
Level: 1d6 + 2
Form: A short, fat tube joined with a long, thin tube
Effect: Fires pulses of energy up to 200 feet (61 m) that explode in an immediate radius for 5 points of damage. However, whenever the device is used, if the player rolls a 1 or 2, the pulse explodes early at a point determined by the GM.
Depletion: 1 in 1d20

Punishment Tick

Level: 1d6 + 2
Form: A round metal disk with an adhesive patch and a handheld device that controls it
Effect: When the disk is touched to a creature's skin, tiny metal barbs sprout from the perimeter and embed the disk in the flesh. Pressing the button on the handheld device inflicts 2 points of electrocution damage to the creature to which the disk is attached.
Depletion: 1 in 1d10

Pyroclastic Staff

Level: 1d6
Form: A long metal pole with a handle in the middle and two buttons above it
Effect: A user can wield this device as a normal quarterstaff. It also has two functions, which can be activated by pressing one of its two buttons.

The first function causes a short jet of bright blue flame to rise from one end. The flame emits bright light out to a short distance. In addition, the staff inflicts 2 additional points of fire damage that ignores Armor. The flame burns for up to one hour.

The second function causes a blast of flames to wash out from one end at up to three targets within immediate range. The flames inflict burn damage equal to the artifact level.
Depletion: 1 in 1d20

Quickice Axe

Level: 1d6 + 2
Form: A long metal pole
Effect: The end of this pole sprays out liquid that immediately freezes into an axe blade, turning the pole into a heavy weapon. Further, if the blade is touched to water or other liquid, it freezes an area approximately 6 feet (2 m) in radius around it. Using this secondary function also triggers a depletion roll. Once created, the axe head lasts for 28 hours.
Depletion: 1 in 1d100

Remnant Reader

Level: 1d6
Form: A small handheld device
Effect: When activated and slowly passed over bones, skin, or some other bit of organic tissue, the device "reads" the material and compares its composition to information stored in the datasphere. After one minute, the device emits a tiny shimmering hologram that reveals what the creature looked like when it was alive. This image lasts for about a minute and then flickers before disappearing altogether.
Depletion: 1 in 1d100

Datasphere, page 24

It is very likely that other quickice devices exist, quickly freezing liquid to create other solid objects such as walls, ladders, tools, shields, armor, or storage boxes, to name a few.

Replacement Hand

Level: 1d6 + 1
Form: A metallic hand
Effect: To use this device, a user must hold it to the stump of an arm for at least one minute. At the end of this time, filaments bind the hand to the arm and connect with the user's nerve endings so that it can be used as if it were a normal hand.

After the item has been attached, the user can take an action to detach the hand from the stump. The hand drops and moves about, scuttling like a spider. The user can control the hand and perceive through it out to a short distance. The hand is a level 1 creature under the user's control and has a target number of 3, inflicts 1 point of damage, and has 3 health. The hand can remain separated for up to one hour. At the end of this time, the device powers off and must be reattached for at least one hour before it can be separated again.
Depletion: 1 in 1d20

Restoration Pod

Level: 1d6 + 4
Form: A lidded canister made of metal and glass containing a padded bed
Effect: The artifact activates only when a creature climbs inside the device. When this happens, roll a d20. If you roll any number other than 1, the lid seals shut, the device replenishes the creature's stat Pools up to their maximum, and it also removes any poisons, diseases, and contaminants that might be affecting the creature. However, if you roll a 1, the device malfunctions and takes the creature apart piece by piece, painting the interior with gore and killing the creature almost instantly.
Depletion: 1 in 1d10

Ring of Iron Wind

Level: 1d6
Form: Freestanding device with small control panel
Effect: When activated prior to the arrival of a storm, the device implodes, creating a gravitationally null ring about 6 feet (2 m) in diameter and 8 feet (2 m) tall. The space inside the ring is protected from the majority of all external effects (including heat, cold, rain, wind, and storms) for a number of hours equal to the artifact level.
Depletion: 1 in 1d6

Roving Eyes

Level: 1d6
Form: A clear synth panel and 1d6 + 4 metal spheres with glass eyes, each about the size of a fist
Effect: The spheres float in the air, moving in designated patrol patterns assigned to them by the user, moving no more than 300 feet (91 m) before they return to their starting point. Each sphere can have its own pattern, but once set, it cannot be changed. At any time, the user can see on the synth panel what any one of the spheres sees with its eye. The glass eyes see with the same ability as a human's.
Depletion: 1 in 1d20

Seated Lift

Level: 1d6
Form: A series of fabric straps that open to form a seat like a swing
Effect: When a person sits in the device, she can use a small dial on the right side to be lifted up to 3 feet (1 m) in the air. The device holds only one person at a time. While active, it gives a few inches in any direction when pushed, but it never moves more than that.
Depletion: 1 in 1d20

Second Hand

Level: 1d6
Form: A pair of skintight gloves made from synthetic material woven with circuitry
Effect: Putting on the gloves causes them to merge with the wearer's skin, and they can never be removed. The wearer has an asset on all tasks that involve perceiving by touch.
Depletion: —

Silver Ichor

Level: 1d6 + 4
Form: An injector filled with silvery liquid
Effect: To activate this device, the user must inject the liquid into her body. An hour after activation, the liquid spreads throughout her system and links her to the datasphere, giving her complete control over her body, with several benefits.

She can control her heart rate, breathing, and any other body functions she chooses. Her Might Edge increases by 1 as the device allows her to coax more energy from her body and achieve greater control over its systems.

If she becomes diseased, poisoned, or sickened by a harmful environmental effect such as radiation, she can use an action to flush the toxin from her body.

She can use an action to adapt her body to extreme heat or cold. While adapted, she reduces damage from cold or fire by 2 points.

Finally, whenever she makes a recovery roll, she can roll twice and use the higher result.
Depletion: —

Skin of Fire Sloughing

Level: 1d6 + 1
Form: When not affixed to a creature, this looks like a mass of diaphanous fabric. On a creature, it is almost invisible.
Effect: When stretched over a creature's normal skin, this organic material adheres and conforms to its body shape. While wearing the skin, the creature gains +5 to Armor against damage inflicted by fire.
Depletion: 1 in 1d100 (checked each time the user sustains fire damage)

Skin of Water Breathing

Level: 1d6 + 1
Form: When not affixed to a creature, this looks like a mass of diaphanous fabric. On a creature, it is almost invisible.
Effect: When stretched over a creature's normal skin, this organic material adheres and conforms to its body shape. While wearing the skin, the creature can breathe normally both in air and underwater, and is not adversely affected by extreme pressure or sudden changes in pressure.
Depletion: 1 in 1d100 (checked each day the skin is used)

Sky Chariot

Level: 8
Form: A large hollow head, about 30 feet (9 m) in diameter, made from stone. Characters can access the interior by crawling through its mouth. The inside has enough space to hold up to eight human-sized people. The head's interior features comfortable cushions on its floor and several cabinets containing foodstuffs, drinks, and toiletries that replenish each day.
Effect: The device hovers 3 feet (1 m) above the ground and remains there until activated by the pilot. A potential pilot must be inside the head and wear a headband that is connected to the device by a thick cord. The pilot can then fly the head by making Intellect rolls (level 3) each round. In combat, the pilot can use an action to move the head a long distance reach round. On extended trips, the head can fly up to 60 miles (97 km) per hour and reach an altitude of 5 miles (8 km).
Depletion: 1 in 1d20

Despite its name as the ring of Iron Wind, it is unknown whether this device actually protects from the Iron Wind or if that is just hopeful conjecture.

Iron Wind, page 135

Slugspitter, page 311

Spray, page 30
Arc Spray, page 31

A slave cap can be adjusted to affect automatons rather than organic living creatures with a task difficulty of 5.

Slave Cap

Level: 1d6 + 2
Form: A mesh skullcap that's placed on another creature and a handheld device that allows the user to control the creature
Effect: The cap shuts down all mental capacity by suffusing the wearer's mind with psychic static. If the wearer's level is equal to or lower than the artifact level, the wearer cannot take actions for one hour or until the cap is removed.

The user can use the handheld device to control the wearer as an action. The user may give the target general instructions, such as "Stand over there" or "Clean that room," or a specific instruction to take a particular action, such as to move or attack. In the case of general instructions, the wearer carries them out to the best of its ability until it completes the task. Then it stands in place until given new instructions.

When the effect ends, the wearer does not remember being controlled or anything that it did while controlled.
Depletion: 1 in 1d6

Slugspitter (Heat)

Level: 1d6 + 2
Form: A long device with a narrow metal tube
Effect: With a quiet sound like a puff of air, this device fires a tiny slug of metal with a range of 200 feet (61 m). It inflicts damage equal to the artifact level. A slug that strikes and does damage then grows very hot, so on the next round, the target automatically suffers the same amount of damage again from the heat.

This device is a rapid-fire weapon, and thus can be used with the Spray or Arc Spray abilities that some glaives and jacks have, but each "round of ammo" used or each additional target selected requires an additional depletion roll.
Depletion: 1–3 in 1d100

Slugspitter (Inorganic Phasing)

Level: 1d6 + 2
Form: A long device with a narrow metal tube
Effect: With a quiet sound like a puff of air, this device fires a tiny slug of metal with a range of 200 feet (61 m). It inflicts damage equal to the artifact level, but since the slug phases through inorganic matter, it ignores Armor. In fact, the slug can even pass through walls unhindered, although targeting through a solid wall provides its own challenges.

This weapon cannot harm inorganic targets (it passes through them).

This device is a rapid-fire weapon, and thus can be used with the Spray or Arc Spray abilities that some glaives and jacks have, but each "round of ammo" used or each additional target selected requires an additional depletion roll.
Depletion: 1–4 in 1d100

Slugspitter (Mass Increasing)

Level: 1d6 + 2
Form: A long device with a narrow metal tube
Effect: With a quiet sound like a puff of air, this device fires a tiny slug of metal with a range of 200 feet (61 m). Since the slug increases its mass as it travels, it inflicts damage equal to the artifact level + 4.

This device is a rapid-fire weapon, and thus can be used with the Spray or Arc Spray abilities that some glaives and jacks have, but each "round of ammo" used or each additional target selected requires an additional depletion roll.
Depletion: 1 in 1d20

Smart Boots

Level: 1d6 + 1
Form: A pair of boots
Effect: When activated, the boots allow the wearer to move across rough or difficult terrain, walk up walls, and even walk across liquids without penalty to movement for one hour. In a low-gravity or zero-gravity environment, the boots adhere to a surface and allow the wearer to walk normally.
Depletion: 1 in 1d100

Smart Cape

Level: 1d6 + 1
Form: Collared cape
Effect: It takes one round to slip into the cape, pull up the collar, and seal the front. When activated, the cape provides +3 to Armor against damage from fire, electricity, radiation, and most forms of energy.
Depletion: 1 in 1d100

Smart Gloves

Level: 1d6 + 2
Form: Gauntlets
Effect: When activated, these long gloves allow the wearer to safely handle objects that would otherwise inflict damage if held, such as burning items or items dripping with acid. He can also safely insert his arms up to the elbow into liquid that would otherwise inflict damage, such as lava.
Depletion: 1 in 1d100

Smart Helm

Level: 1d6 + 1
Form: Bulky silvery globe that encloses the wearer's head

Effect: When activated, the helm allows the wearer to breathe in any medium, including water, a poisonous atmosphere, or even the airless void, for one hour.
Depletion: 1 in 1d100

Smoke Helm

Level: 1d6
Form: A hood or helmet designed to be worn on the head
Effect: When worn, the helmet synthesizes a telepathic smoke from the wearer's breath.

If someone else inhales the smoke, they feel everything the wearer feels for one hour. (If two people wear the helmets, they can "trade" sensations with each other for one hour.)
Depletion: 1 in 1d20

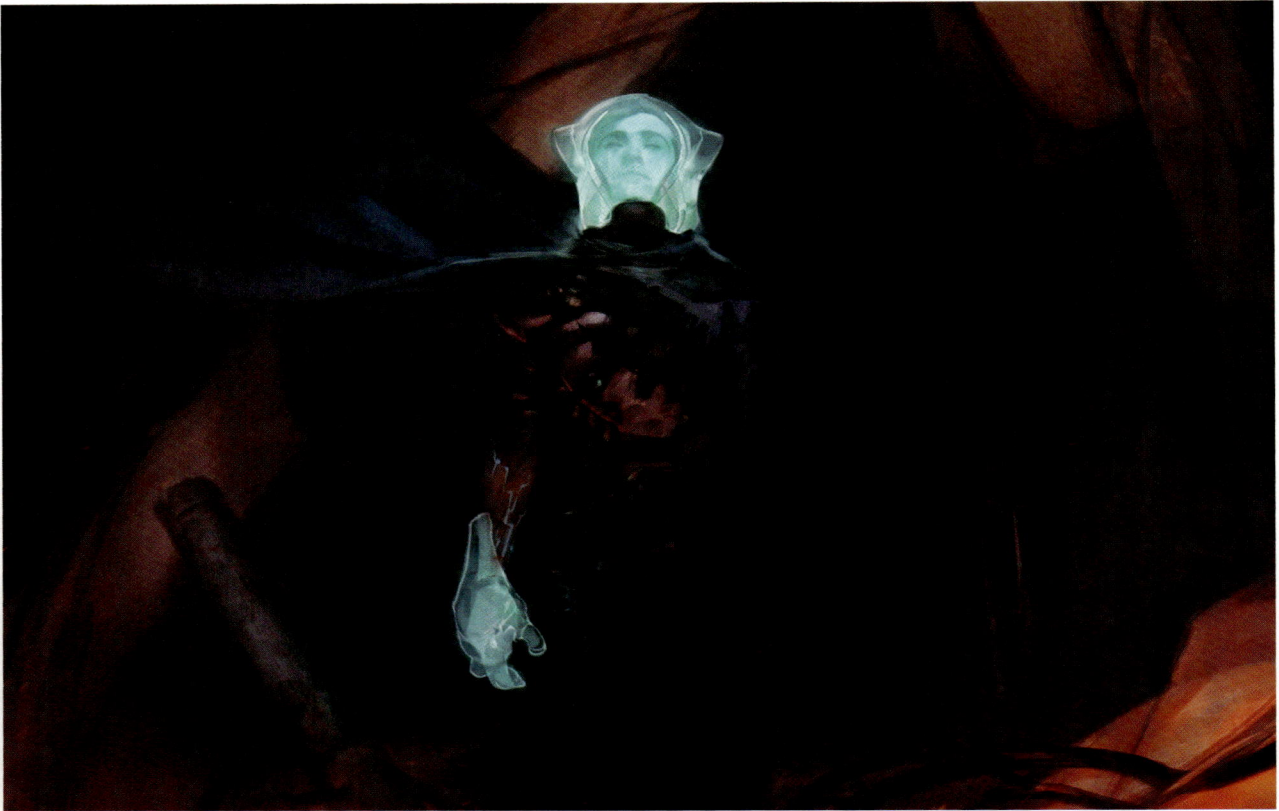

Snail shells come in many shapes and forms, including frogs with distended stomachs, large flowers with closed buds, and large purple fruit from the Ausren Woods. All secretly hold anywhere from one to four cyphers, and they are designed to seem like simple objects with no apparent purpose other than decorative. Whatever their design, they are still commonly called snail shells.

Snail Shell

Level: 1d6
Form: A sculpted snail with a hollow, insulated shell made of expandable, malleable metal
Effect: Up to two cyphers can be placed within the snail's shell, as long as each is no larger than a typical handheld device. Thanks to the specially designed material of the shell, these cyphers do not count against a character's cypher limit.

The metal shell has a built-in lock that requires a spoken password to open (set by the user). It's very difficult to tell from looking at the shell that it is anything more than a whimsical object.
Depletion: 1 in 1d20 (check each time a cypher is added to the shell)

Snuffler

Level: 1d6 + 2
Form: A 3-foot-tall (1 m) hairless, nearly mindless creature lacking any distinctive features beyond a gaping orifice in its head
Effect: This is a level 1 creature. It accompanies you and obeys your commands, but it's not capable of attacking. As a level 1 creature, it has a target number of 3 and 3 health. If you wave something in front of the snuffler's orifice, the creature inhales and

memorizes the scent. It can then unerringly track the scent until it gets a good sniff of something else. If the creature is reduced to 0 health, it is instantly slain.
Depletion: —

Solid Light Bindings

Level: 1d6 + 3
Form: Small metal cylinder
Effect: When activated, bonds of solid light entwine around a creature touched by the cylinder. It is possible to use this as a weapon in melee or at immediate range, but successfully capturing an opponent requires two attack rolls—one to touch him with the cylinder and the other to ensure that he is ensnared. The bonds last for up to 28 hours.
Depletion: 1 in 1d20

Solid Light Helm

Level: 1d6 + 1
Form: A metal collar
Effect: When the device is activated, the wearer's head is encased in solid light. If anything specifically attacks the wearer's head, he has 12 Armor. Moreover, he has breathable air while the helmet is active.
Depletion: 1 in 1d20 (check once each day)

Sonic Blade
Level: 1d6 + 1
Form: A dagger covered in glowing tracery
Effect: This blade functions as a normal dagger except that when used to make an attack, it vibrates at an ultrasonic frequency that lets it punch through physical armor and other defenses. The weapon inflicts 2 additional points of damage.
Depletion: —

Sphere Thrower
Level: 1d6 + 1
Form: Metal rod with a clawlike end
Effect: When activated, the clawlike end of the rod fills with a ball of roiling energy. If used as a melee weapon, this is a medium weapon that inflicts 2 additional points of damage from the energy, but this strike exhausts the energy and it must be reactivated.

More devastatingly, the sphere can be hurled from the rod up to long range, where it bursts in an immediate radius and inflicts damage equal to the artifact level.
Depletion: 1 in 1d20

Spider Harness
Level: 1d6 + 1
Form: Harnesslike belt
Effect: When activated, eight spindly, jointed metallic legs emerge from the belt and lift the wearer a few feet off the ground for a number of minutes equal to the artifact level. The legs give the wearer a long movement speed on the ground and a short movement speed when climbing on walls or ceilings. In addition, they provide an asset on any task involving running, balance, staying upright, climbing, and so on.
Depletion: 1 in 1d100

Spine Armor
Level: 1d6 + 3
Form: A synth belt with a toggle
Effect: When activated, a spine in the belt injects the wearer with a mutagen, causing her skin to grow a mass of protective spines over the course of a few minutes, providing +3 to Armor without any penalties associated with wearing armor. It can't be worn with other normal armor, which would be pierced and torn by the spines. Whenever a character wearing spine armor makes a successful Speed defense roll against a melee attack, the attacker takes 3 points of damage from the piercing spines. The spine armor lasts for four hours, after which the spines become brittle and break off.
Depletion: 1 in 1d20

Spinneret Ring
Level: 1d6
Form: Clear stronglass locket ring that houses a tiny biomechanical spider
Effect: When the stronglass is lightly stroked, the spider inside reacts by releasing a thin, incredibly strong steel cord through a small hole in the stronglass. Each cord is about 20 feet (6 m) long. If firmly attached to something, the cord can hold up to 300 pounds (136 kg). Additionally, it can be used as a snare, a whip, or a similar device to cause damage equal to the artifact level + 2.
Depletion: 1 in 1d6 for the spinner ability (after depletion, the ring can still be worn)

Spirit Call
Level: 1d6 + 2
Form: A metal glove
Effect: While worn, the user activates the glove by touching the face of a dead creature. If the creature's head is largely intact, the glove imbues the head with the semblance of life for 1d6 minutes. Although not alive, the head animates, and, if it still has a mouth, it can speak and answer questions put to it based on what it knew when it was alive. The head remains cooperative only until the last minute of the duration begins. At that point, the head realizes it is dead and spends the remaining time weeping and screaming for help.

This artifact can affect a particular corpse only one time.
Depletion: 1 in 1d10

Stasis Projector
Level: 1d6 + 4
Form: Handheld device
Effect: This device projects a wide ray at a target that is already immobile (perhaps a creature that is bound or willing). The target is placed in safe suspended animation within an energy sheath. The sheath floats about 4 feet (1 m) off the ground and can be pushed along easily, almost as if it were weightless. The sheath lasts for 28 hours and is impervious to attacks of a level lower than the artifact that created it.
Depletion: 1 in 1d10

Affixing a weapon nodule to a sonic blade requires a task with a difficulty of 4.

"I do not enjoy using device names that suggest something mystical, such as 'spirit call' or 'demonflesh.' I give such items my own names. In these specific instances, I might use the terms 'brain reactivator' and 'energized flesh,' respectively." ~Sir Arthour

Stimulation Stem

Level: 1d6

Form: Biological tube synthesized from living cellular tissue, with a toothed "mouth" at each end

Effect: This 3-foot-long (1 m) tube can be attached to the flesh of two biological, sentient creatures via the ever-grasping mouths. Once the teeth sink in, the tube is attached for five minutes (pulling it off before that kills the cellular tissue and renders the device useless). If both creatures are in agreement, one of them can siphon 1d6 Might points from the other via the tube. If the device senses that one or both participants are not amenable to the exchange, it draws 1d6 Might points from both creatures.

When not pulled tight, the tube self-coils for easy carrying.

Depletion: 1 in 1d20

Strangelight Torch

Level: 1d6 + 1

Form: Glowing sphere on the end of a synth rod

Effect: This device illuminates the immediate area regardless of barriers. It casts no shadows, and every nook and cranny in the area is well lit.

Depletion: —

Synthsteel Shield

Level: 1d6

Form: Synth shield

Effect: This shield is far hardier and still somewhat lighter than Ninth World smithing techniques could ever manage with steel. It grants an additional +1 bonus to Speed defense rolls in addition to the asset that shields normally grant.

Depletion: —

Telescopic Beast

Level: 1d6

Form: Pocket-sized cube that unfolds into a box-shaped automaton about 1 foot by 1 foot (0.3 m by 0.3 m) with four telescoping legs.

Effect: Once the creature is unfolded, the user may control it via voice for 28 hours. It can understand and carry out simple commands such as moving laterally, staying stationary, reforming into a cube, and telescoping up and down (it can raise its body up to 10 feet [3 m] with a single person standing on top of it). Action to unfold.

If you permanently combine a strangelight torch with a liminal scanner (task difficulty 6), you create an artifact that grants the user information as if she used the Scan esotery. Its depletion is 1 in 1d100.

Liminal scanner, page 121

Depletion: 1 in 1d6 for the telescopic abilities (after depletion, the creature continues to follow the other voice commands)

Temporal Armor

Level: 1d6 + 2

Form: Heavy armor of synth

Effect: This heavy armor has a field around it that is triggered when the wearer wishes (requiring an action) and lasts for ten minutes. During this time, the field causes incoming attacks to potentially stop suddenly or slow down before they strike. This adds +2 to the wearer's Armor.

Depletion: 1 in 1d6

Temporal Maul

Level: 1d6 + 1

Form: A metal and synth device placed at the end of a metal haft, turning it into a heavy weapon

Effect: This time-displacement device constantly shifts back and forth through moments in time, making it very difficult to defend against. All attacks made with the maul have an asset that decreases the difficulty of the attack by one step.

Depletion: 1 in 1d100

Tentacle Harness (Bladed)

Level: 1d6 + 2

Form: A heavy body harness equipped with two 15-foot (5 m) segmented metal tentacles that each end in a metal blade

Effect: Putting on the harness allows the wearer to control the tentacles as if they were extra limbs. The tentacles are fully prehensile and can be used to make attacks (each tentacle is a medium weapon) while the wearer's normal arms are free. The wearer is still limited by the normal number of actions she can take in a round.

Depletion: —

Tentacle Harness (Clawed)

Level: 1d6 + 2

Form: A heavy body harness equipped with two 15-foot (5 m) segmented metal tentacles that each end in a grasping claw

Effect: Putting on the harness allows the wearer to control the tentacles as if they were extra limbs. The tentacles are fully prehensile and have the same functionality as if they were the wearer's arms.

Depletion: —

Tentacle Helmet

Level: 1d6 + 3

Form: A smooth, lightweight synthsteel helmet with an octagon-shaped device on the back

Effect: When activated, a 9-foot (3 m) tentacle comes out of the device. This tentacle resembles that of a very large living creature, but it's also translucent, as it modulates between phase states. The tentacle can be used to pick up or manipulate small objects, push buttons, and so forth, but it has very little strength. It can't pick up an object that weighs more than 10 pounds (5 kg) and could never be used to make an effective attack. However, its most remarkable feature is that because of its pandimensional nature, the tentacle can move through energy fields, including solid force fields, as if they were not there.

Once activated, the tentacle lasts for ten minutes.

Depletion: 1 in 1d10

The Death by Angles

Level: 1d6 + 2

Form: Handheld device

Effect: This object can be used as a weapon that fires a beam of energy up to long range. The beam always bounces off of inorganic materials but not living tissue or organic materials. Thus, the weapon can be used only against living targets (or an organic nonliving target). However, the beam is harmless unless it ricochets off a surface first. Strangely, the beam never ricochets in the way that a character expects, so attack rolls with the weapon are two steps more difficult than normal. The beam inflicts 7 points of damage.

Particularly skilled users discover that if the beam reflects off of more than one surface, the damage increases. For every additional surface, the difficulty increases by one step, but the damage increases by 3 points (maximum 19 points).

Depletion: 1 in 1d20

Thought Storage

Level: 1d6 + 2

Form: Long organic rod with a number of crystal nodules

Effect: The user can store fifteen minutes' worth of mental images (real or imagined) and words that can be replayed by anyone who activates the rod again.

Depletion: 1 in 1d20

movement for a number of minutes equal to the artifact level.

Depletion: 1 in 1d20

Thunder Vocalizer

Level: 1d6 + 2

Form: A choker with a mechanical device that sits atop the user's throat

Effect: This device turns the user's words into powerful weapons. When it is activated, the user speaks and the device throws the sound to a spot within short range. A thunderous boom erupts from that spot and inflicts 4 points of ambient damage to everything within an immediate distance.

Depletion: 1 in 1d20

Time Machine

Level: 10

Form: A massive arch made of metal and equipped with a display and keyboard protruding from one side of the arch

Effect: Upon activation, an invisible barrier springs into existence out to a short distance around the device. The barrier shunts everything within it out of normal time so that within the barrier, time flows ten thousand times slower than it does outside the barrier. In other words, for each minute a person spends inside the barrier, about seven days pass outside the barrier.

For characters inside the barrier, time passes normally, though the environment outside the barrier may seem quite strange, as time there seems to pass very rapidly. If the artifact is outside, a day passes every 8.5 seconds. To creatures outside the barrier, people within seem frozen, though an extended viewing reveals that they are not in stasis but instead moving very slowly. Nothing can pass through the barrier while the device is in operation.

Depletion: 1 in 1d10 (check at the start of each hour of operation)

"Ah, a broken-down control panel. Or, as I like to call it, a treasure chest." ~Sir Arthour

Thoughtlight

Level: 1d6

Form: A small synth box that lights up on one side

Effect: When touching (or practically touching—through clothing, for example) a living, thinking creature, the thoughtlight gives off light like a torch, powered by the brain waves of the creature. The moment the user stops thinking (which is to say, is very likely dead), the light goes out.

Depletion: —

Thunder Boots

Level: 1d6 + 4

Form: A pair of boots

Effect: When activated, the boots allow the wearer to lift off the ground on a jet of flame, granting him the ability to fly with long

Tongue Snake

Level: 1d6 + 2
Form: Snakelike creature grafted onto a user's tongue
Effect: The creature must be surgically and permanently attached (a task equal to the artifact level), a procedure that takes about an hour in a skilled chiurgeon's hands.

Once the serpent is attached to the user's tongue, he can control it and attack with it. The serpent can attack targets within an immediate distance and inflicts poison damage equal to the artifact level (ignores Armor).
Depletion: —

Torment Wand

Level: 1d6 + 1
Form: Long black rod of metal and synth
Effect: The user can attack anyone within short range, inflicting horrendous pain. The victim moves one step down the damage track and cannot take actions. This lasts as long as the victim is within range and the user spends an action each round to continue the attack. Torment wands of level 6 or higher can continue to move the victim down the damage track each round (with a new Might defense roll each round to resist), which means that after three rounds, the target is dead.
Depletion: 1 in 1d10

Tracer Nodule

Level: 1d6 + 1
Form: A small crystal
Effect: When activated, the crystal adheres to any surface and transmits its location (distance and direction) to the user via a mental connection. The connection has a range of 100 miles (161 km) and lasts for a number of days equal to the artifact level.
Depletion: 1 in 1d20

Transdimensional Blade

Level: 1d6 + 2
Form: Broadsword
Effect: When activated, this blade exists on multiple levels of reality at once. The wielder can strike foes (or objects) that are out of phase or resistant to attacks or damage due to their ultraterrestrial or transdimensional nature as if they were normal targets. Each activation allows for a single attack, but activation is not an action.
Depletion: 1 in 1d20

Transformation Chamber

Level: 1d6 + 3
Form: Complex device 9 feet (3 m) tall and 10 feet (3 m) wide with a central open cylindrical area
Effect: The subject must stand within this device when it is activated. Doing so transforms the subject over ten painful minutes into another organic form of approximately the same size, chosen upon activation. The form can be (but does not have to be) extremely specific, but it must be well known to the operator of the device. For example, a human could be changed into a specific margr, if that margr is known. The transformation is permanent, although another activation can be used to change the subject back.
Depletion: 1 in 1d6

Traveling Coiffeur

Level: 1d6
Form: Large bubble-shaped helm that fits over a person's head and houses a complex chamber inside
Effect: Provides the user with the opportunity to completely change her hair style (including facial hair) via a complicated contraption of electronic blades, ray emitters, and modified hairspiders. A control panel along the side of the device shows myriad style options, from completely bald to long, spiderspun tresses in various colors. The user must choose her desired option ahead of time (28 hours prior to being used) to allow the device time to prepare.
Depletion: 1 in 1d20

Trio

Level: 1d6 + 2
Form: A metal rod with a splay of three prongs on the end
Effect: When activated, this fires three rays at once up to long range, each inflicting damage equal to the artifact level. Unless the target is very large, the rays never strike the same target, but instead potentially strike three targets standing near each other. Roll separately for each attack.
Depletion: 1 in 1d10

Truth Seeker

Level: 1d6 + 1
Form: Small synth square
Effect: When affixed to a user's forehead (perhaps with a headband), this device allows him to sense whether someone speaking

If you use any cypher or artifact that is a crystal (such as a weapon or armor nodule) and reconfigure it with a tracer nodule (task difficulty 8), you can have multiple tracer nodules functioning at once.

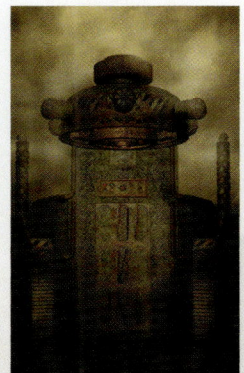

to him is lying. The speaker must be within immediate range and must be speaking in a language that the wearer understands.
Depletion: 1 in 1d6

Tunneling Gauntlets

Level: 1d6 + 1
Form: An oversized pair of metallic gauntlets with broad nails

Effect: It takes one round to slip into the gauntlets. When activated, they give the wearer an immediate burrowing speed for one hour. She can burrow through most soils and even some stone, but not material whose level is equal to or higher than the artifact level. Burrowing leaves behind a tunnel with a diameter of 5 feet (2 m) that remains stable for several hours. After that, the tunnel is subject to collapse.
Depletion: 1 in 1d20

Twin Mirrors

Level: 1d6
Form: Two 1-foot (0.3 m) diameter disks polished to a mirrorlike finish
Effect: When a character looks into one mirror, he sees out the other and vice versa regardless of the distance that separates them.
Depletion: —

Ultimate Grapnel

Level: 1d6 + 2
Form: A length of 100 feet (30 m) of synth rope with a glowing sphere at one end
Effect: The glowing sphere adheres to any surface or object until activated, which turns off the grip for one minute.
Depletion: 1 in 1d100

Ultra Armor

Level: 1d6 + 4
Form: A massive suit of metal and synth armor
Effect: This heavy armor provides +5 to Armor rather than +3. It boosts the wearer's strength and reflexes, increasing her Might Edge and Speed Edge by 1. She inflicts 2 additional points of damage with melee weapons and can jump twice as far as normal. The interior of the suit has its own oxygen, water, food supply, and environmental controls, sustaining the wearer in any environment indefinitely.

Depletion of this artifact is not standard. When depletion occurs, it then provides only +4 to Armor. Depletion must continue to be checked. When it occurs again, the Might Edge and Speed Edge bonuses fail, and the damage and jumping boosts are lost. When depletion occurs again, the sustenance and environmental protections break down. When it occurs one last time, the suit then provides only +3 to Armor, but depletion

need not be checked ever again, and the suit remains usable heavy armor.
Depletion: 1 in 1d10 (checked each day worn)

Urchalis Mask

Level: 1d6 + 2
Form: A distinctive mask of thin, curved strips
Effect: This mask has no function unless worn by someone with at least some mechanical components—automatons, characters who Fuse Flesh and Steel, characters with a mech eye or a mechanical arm, and so on. (Simply wearing a mechanical device is not enough—it must be a permanent part of one's body.) Such characters gain an asset when using their mechanical parts. This means that an all-mechanical being like an automaton gains an asset on almost every task.
Depletion: 1 in 1d20 (check each day worn)

Usurper

Level: 1d6
Form: A small handheld device with two prongs extending from the end
Effect: Activating the device causes the two prongs to fire at a target within immediate range. The target takes 1 point of electrocution damage, and if the target's level is equal to or less than the artifact level, the user takes control of the target for one minute provided that the user and the target are within an immediate distance of each other. If either exceeds this distance, the target regains control of itself.
Depletion: 1 in 1d6

Vision Snake

Level: 1d6 + 1
Form: A 3-foot-long (1 m) flexible synth tube that can be extended to 8 feet (2 m)
Effect: Looking through one end of this tube always allows the user to see through it to the other end, no matter how many twists or bends are in the tube.
Depletion: —

Void Clamp

Level: 1d6
Form: A metal bar with clamps on either end
Effect: The device activates when the clamps are placed on any object that can fit inside a 20-foot (6 m) cube. The clamps bond with the object and make it weightless. Anyone can lift it and move it by gripping the handle. The device can be detached at any time (not an action), and the object regains its normal weight.
Depletion: 1 in 1d20

Void Knife

Level: 1d6
Form: A cylinder about the size of a knife handle
Effect: When the device is gripped, an invisible blade extends out from the cylinder, allowing the wielder to use this device as a dagger.
Depletion: —

Vox Scrambler

Level: 1d6
Form: A mouthpiece secured with a thick strap that wraps around the head
Effect: Whenever the user speaks while wearing this device, her words sound normal to those within immediate range, but they sound like gibberish to those farther away.
Depletion: 1 in 1d100 (check once each day)

Water Finder

Level: 1
Form: A floating crystal that emits soft yellow light
Effect: For one hour after it's activated, the device vibrates whenever it is within a short distance of water. The closer the user gets to the water, the stronger the device vibrates.
Depletion: 1 in 1d100

Water Skimmers

Level: 1d6
Form: Black and silver covers for footwear sporting thick heels layered with hydrofuge hairs
Effect: Anyone wearing these water skimmers over their regular footwear can stride quickly across liquid surfaces up to 20 feet (6 m) deep without sinking or getting wet.

Wearing water skimmers while on land offsets the wearer's center of gravity, increasing the difficulty of all movement-based actions by one step.
Depletion: —

Wavesplitter

Level: 1d6 + 3
Form: A metal-and-glass vehicle that is 12 feet (4 m) long, 8 feet (2 m) wide, and 6 feet (2 m) tall. It hovers about 3 feet (1 m) above the ground. The vehicle has an access hatch on the side. Inside there is a seat and control panel for the pilot, plus three more seats for passengers. Numerous portholes allow occupants to look outside.
Effect: This vehicle can hold up to four characters and be piloted by someone who makes Intellect rolls (level 2) each round. In combat, the pilot can use an action to move the vehicle a long distance each round. On extended trips, it moves up to 40 miles (64 km) per hour.

The vehicle provides a breathable atmosphere for everyone inside, allowing occupants to breathe normally for up to seven hours.

The vehicle also sports six lamps on the exterior, one on each corner and two in front. The lamps light everything within a long distance. The pilot can shut off the lights or turn them on (not an action).

Although the vehicle can travel over land, it excels underwater and can move through liquids at half its ground speed. The device can descend to depths of 5 miles (8 km). If it goes any deeper, roll for depletion each round, with depletion in this case indicating that the walls buckle and spring leaks.
Depletion: 1–4 in 1d100

Weapon Mount

Level: 1d6
Form: A thin mechanical arm grafted to a person's back
Effect: The mount must be surgically and permanently attached (a task equal to the artifact level). The procedure takes about an hour in a skilled chiurgeon's hands.

Once attached, the mount can hold a light or medium weapon, and the user can attack with that weapon as if he was wielding it.
Depletion: —

Wheeled Porter

Level: 1d6 + 1
Form: A triangular device 4 feet (1 m) high and 5 feet (2 m) across with treads, sporting metal rods on top
Effect: Obeying verbal commands, this device will follow the user around, even over difficult terrain. It can create up to three force bubbles at the ends of the rods, which can contain up to 200 pounds (91 kg) of inanimate material or gear. The bubbles are only as large as they need to be to hold whatever they are given. Commanding the device to create or negate a force bubble is an action.
Depletion: 1 in 1d100 (check each day)

Whisperer in the Ether

Level: 1d6 + 1
Form: A small crystal
Effect: The bearer of this crystal has a direct line of telepathic communication with an immortal, artificial intelligence whose location is unknown (and may not even be relevant or comprehensible). The user can converse with the intelligence on an ongoing basis, but in general, the whisperer can share a useful bit of information, insight, or advice about once every 28 hours. Sometimes, this translates into an asset on one of the user's actions, as the intelligence suggests the right phrase to make friends with a shopkeeper to get a good deal, the right tools to use while tinkering with a device, or the right place to put a shield to deflect an incoming attack. Sometimes the information is more broad, such as the right road to take to reach the next town or why the abhumans are attacking the caravan.

The whisperer's willingness and ability to converse varies considerably. Sometimes it is quite chatty and offers advice. Other times, it must be convinced, cajoled, or tricked into giving information. Still other times, it is

entirely absent for reasons it will not explain. The whisperer's knowledge base is broad but not omniscient. It cannot see the future, but it can often predict outcomes based on logic. It has little or nothing of use (to a Ninth World inhabitant) to say about the distant past.
Depletion: 1 in 1d20 (check each day)

"While I enjoy working with numenera vehicles, I have found it safer for all involved to have someone else pilot them for me."
~Sir Arthour

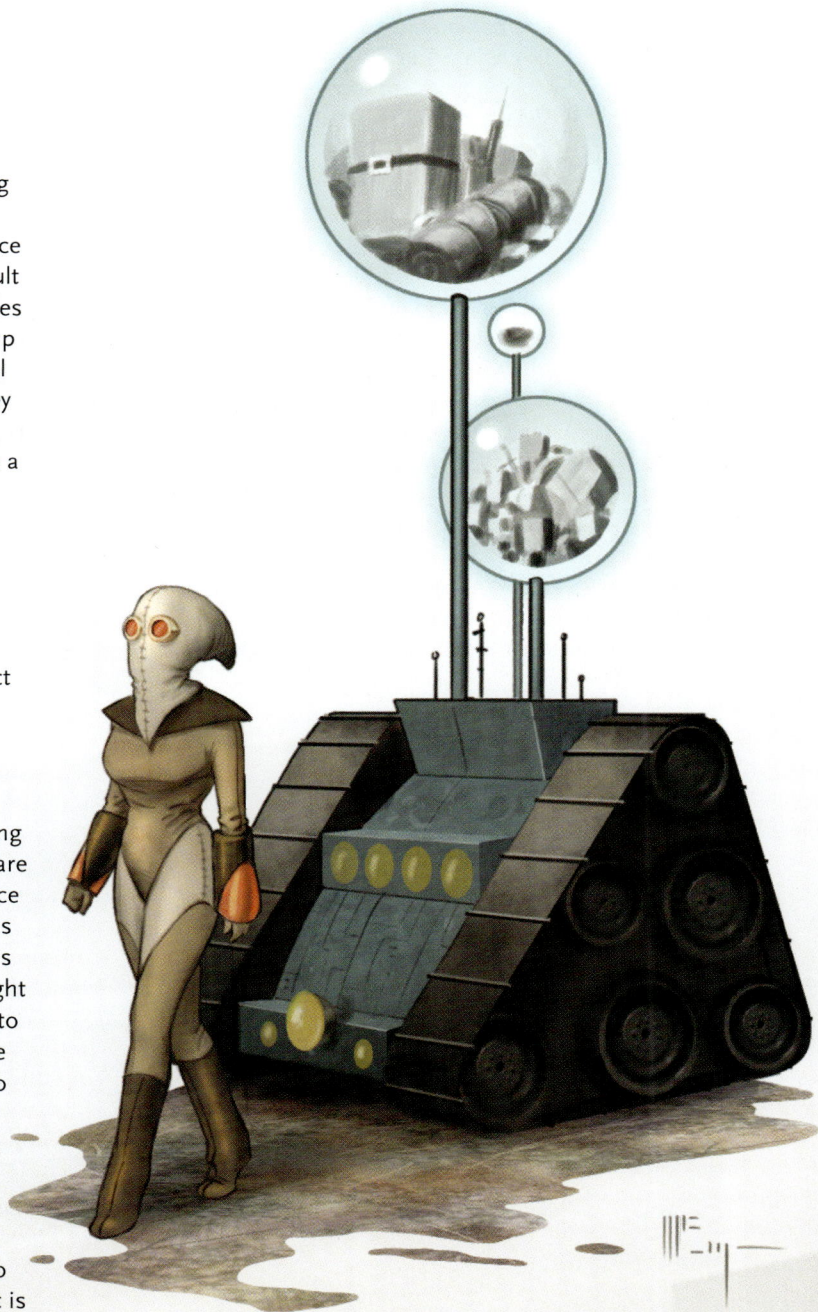

If you permanently combine a yarrin with significant parts from any other automaton cypher or artifact (task difficulty 7), you create an artifact that functions as a yarrin but with +2 to its level and the ability to attack two targets (if two creatures are attacking the user) with its beams as a single action.

Wing Blade

Level: 1d6 + 1
Form: A small winged insect with a lower body that tapers down to a sharp point
Effect: The user activates the insect by tossing it into the air. On each of the user's turns, the insect flies a short distance and attacks a target that she chooses. The device inflicts damage equal to half the artifact level. At the end of this time or when the user chooses, the insect flies back to her and attaches itself to one of her limbs.
Depletion: 1 in 1d10

Woodwind of the Broken

Level: 1d6
Form: A flutelike musical instrument
Effect: This musical instrument can be played normally, but it has one setting that produces no obviously audible noise. If a tune is played on this setting in any area open to dry wastes, temperate lowlands, or mountains, a pack of 2d6 + 6 broken hounds arrives within a few hours or less at the location where the instrument was played. Once summoned, the broken hounds revert to their normally vicious demeanor.
Depletion: 1 in 1d20

Yarrin

Level: 1d6 + 1
Form: A synth cube
Effect: The yarrin is a creature with a level equal to the artifact level, and it has 3 health per level and 3 points of Armor. When activated, the yarrin hovers in the air in orbit around the user and becomes invisible. If anyone within immediate distance attacks the user, the yarrin automatically intercepts and absorbs the attack. Assuming the attack does not destroy the yarrin, it immediately becomes visible and begins attacking the assailant with thin beams of energy (one per round) that inflict damage equal to its level.

The yarrin fights for one round per artifact level and then deactivates. However, until it intercepts an attack, it continues to hover invisibly, even as the user sleeps.
Depletion: 1 in 1d10

Yesterglass

Level: 1d6 + 4
Form: Glass panel
Effect: When held before the user's face, this panel allows her to see the last major activity that occurred in the area, even if it happened years or centuries earlier. The effect lasts for one minute per use.
Depletion: 1 in 1d6

CHAPTER 4

ODDITIES

Explorers return from investigating ancient ruins with many treasures. Some have wondrous abilities that make the explorers more powerful. Others are traded in towns and might change the lives of those that buy them.

And then there are the rest. The weird things that no one can seem to identify, find a use for, or even understand. These are oddities. They represent the vast array of strange things recovered from ancient technologies that are just... weird. Adding them into a Numenera game provides verisimilitude (not everything is a weapon or usable gear) and conveys the flavor of the setting.

Oddities can be traded, sold, used, or given as interesting gifts. Usually, their value is around 10 shins, but some oddities might fetch as much as 50 shins depending on their potential utility.

Many of the oddities listed here are intentionally left vague so the GM can tailor them as needed. The size, color, shape, and so on can be changed. Ninth World crafters might set some of the oddities into jewelry, on the end of a staff, or into items of clothing or armor. Many people like to incorporate oddities into their clothing, hair, or other possessions as a sign of fashion and prestige.

To determine an oddity randomly, roll on the chart below, which then indicates where to roll for your oddity.

01–25	Numenera corebook, page 314
26–50	Oddities Table 1
51–75	Oddities Table 2
76–00	Oddities Table 3

Many oddities are numenera objects worked into ordinary Ninth World items. For example, the stuffed seskii doll is of recent origin, but the growling device inside it is not.

ODDITIES TABLE 1

1. Tiny lidded box that opens, revealing the emptiness of space
2. Square of cloth that changes texture and color randomly
3. Neverending spray canister of harmless foam that evaporates quickly
4. Crystal antiprism about 4 inches (10 cm) across that is mildly repelled away from living flesh
5. Lenses that make everything appear upside-down
6. Lenses that tint everything pink
7. A pair of rose-colored spectacles that, when worn, cause everyone to appear to be in the prime of their lives or dead
8. Goggles with glowing lenses (although you can see through them normally)
9. A black box from which issue faint calls of "Hello?"
10. A bottle of clear liquid whose flavor changes to match whatever you most desire
11. A small blue stone that stays wherever you put it, even if you release it in the air, but it can hold no weight
12. A black wedge that weighs 1 pound (0.5 kg) and becomes 1 pound (0.5 kg) heavier each month it remains in your possession
13. An unbreakable clear crystal sphere filled with green smoke
14. A ceramic tile that etches itself with strange markings whenever someone speaks to it
15. A synth pyramid that gives off light for one hour at a random time each day
16. A tiny harp with strings made of glowing energy
17. A crystal that always hovers an inch above a metal ring
18. A pouch of six seeds that, when planted, grow over the next twenty days into hollow shelters large enough to accommodate one hound-sized animal each
19. A small metal box that makes a clicking noise when in the presence of smoke
20. A metal wand with a tip that glows in the dark
21. A 1-foot (0.3 m) length of silver cord with both ends neatly cut
22. A ring that makes the wearer's fingertips glow blue
23. An oblong metal object from which issues a faint ticking sound
24. A silver needle that always remains sharp but can puncture nothing
25. A wedge of glass that shows the image of three strangely garbed children playing and one frightened child watching you
26. Shoes that fit anyone who wears them but leave bizarre, seemingly random prints behind
27. A bottle of ink that never goes dry or runs out
28. A human-faced insect trapped in a piece of amber
29. A ceramic box holding a tiny worm with a head at each end
30. A mummified nonhuman hand that twitches as if still alive
31. A glass ball filled with fluid through which swims a bloodshot eye trailing its nerve endings
32. A small metal container that keeps liquid poured inside lukewarm but makes it bitter
33. A horn that, when blown, blows bubbles instead of making a sound
34. Three glowing synth rings that orbit whatever they are placed around (like a wrist)
35. A dozen small stones in a narrow, thin box that burst with vibrant colors when tossed into a fire
36. A leather belt with metal plates that glow faintly with light
37. A set of garish clothes that never get dirty or show signs of wear and tear
38. A pouch of six pellets that, when dropped into liquid, remove its flavor and color
39. A small metal box that produces sounds of hysterical laughter when shaken
40. A large piece of fabric that does not reflect in mirrors
41. A fist-sized glass sphere that floats through the air, never straying more than 2 feet (0.6 m) from a glass token
42. A glass jar filled with an edible, creamy white substance that fills back to the top each day at dawn
43. A vial of red liquid that causes anything that touches even a drop to turn bright purple for 28 hours
44. A metal wedge that always points east when placed on the ground
45. Small pink stone that, when placed under the tongue, causes harmless vapor to spill from your mouth
46. A synth hemisphere that occasionally puffs out harmless green mist
47. A tiny synth cube with two metal prongs on one side that hum
48. A metal baton that feels as though it is filled with fluid
49. A small metal box filled with blue powder that, when snuffed, causes profound feelings of ecstasy for about a minute, followed by painful cramps that are alleviated only by a messy and noisy bowel movement

50. A mirror that shows anything reflected in it, but something is always missing
51. A pair of eyes made of bronze that appear slightly human and occasionally blink
52. An invisible, empty, hollow cylinder that is 9 inches (23 cm) long
53. A powerful magnet that appears to be in the shape of a stylized spider
54. Bit of moldable synth that generates constant, soft static noise
55. Shoes that produce sound and light with each step
56. Synth sleeves that fit over one's fingertips
57. Cloth mask that makes each breath taste like mint
58. Small synth squares that taste good but are inedible
59. Metal sphere that floats like a balloon
60. Crystal pendant that causes the wearer's hair to stop growing
61. Five-inch (13 cm) square of cloth that is uncannily pleasant to touch
62. Synth paper that absorbs ink (and stains) after one hour
63. Six-inch (15 cm) synth string that stretches to 8 feet (2 m) without breaking
64. Unbreakable glass pyramid filled with what appears to be ice or snow
65. Synth sphere that is always warm
66. Glass cube that is always cold
67. Synth rod that changes color based on who holds it (always the same color for the same people)
68. Metal hemisphere with a glass handle that constantly repeats words in an unknown language
69. Glass panel that appears to show the surrounding area from a high vantage, but it is always completely wrong
70. Clear synth globe with an arrow inside it that always points at the sun
71. Synth panel about 8 inches (20 cm) square that shows meaningless, complex diagrams
72. Round pendant with a blinking red light that syncs with the wearer's heartbeat
73. Small jar that produces 1 ounce (28 g) of green paint when the sun rises
74. Synth panel that constantly shows unknown creatures cavorting in a woodland of unknown plants
75. Small metal container that produces a peculiar (but not unpleasant) odor when opened
76. Small, warm metal blade that gives a very close shave
77. Small metal disk with a crystal at its center that causes a buzzing noise in the ears of anyone holding it
78. Eight-inch (20 cm) length of synth cord that is invisible
79. Pea-sized sphere that reduces the pull of gravity within about 4 feet (1 m), just enough to notice
80. A pair of 1-foot-tall (0.3 m) metal stilts that can strap onto boots or shoes
81. A jar of putty that hardens after being exposed to air for one hour, but softens again if touched
82. A small disk that bears the image of the father of whoever is touching it
83. Six-inch (15 cm) wand of glass that can be bent and even tied in a knot
84. Small metal container that makes a loud (but brief) shrill tone when opened
85. A small sphere nested within a cube, but the cube exists out of phase and cannot be touched
86. Eye lenses that glow in the dark
87. Three shoes meant for an unknown, nonhuman creature
88. Seven-inch (18 cm) square of cloth to which nothing—dirt, muck, tar, adhesive, and so on—will adhere
89. Metal rod bent into a triangle that frightens off small animals with its mere presence
90. Glow-in-the-dark hair dye (enough for twenty uses)
91. Glove that, when worn, makes the wearer's voice sound very high and squeaky
92. Ring that reduces the wearer's sense of touch
93. Brush that produces a cleansing soap when used
94. Tiny box that produces a small synth figurine in the image of someone within immediate range at random times
95. Synth cup that turns any liquid placed within it purple (no other change is made)
96. Cloth mask that gives anyone who wears it itchy hives for one hour
97. Rod that projects the two-dimensional image of an unknown creature on any flat surface
98. Metal rod that makes anyone who touches it sneeze, but never more than once every few minutes
99. Two magnets that become one hundred times heavier when put together
00. Tiny glass cube that distorts visibility within 6 inches (15 cm) around it

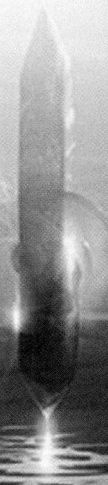

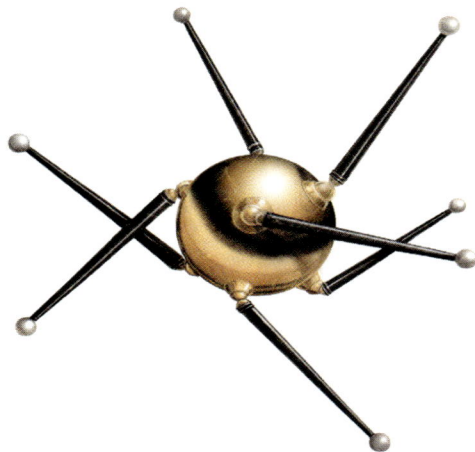

ODDITIES TABLE 2

1. A small cloth sphere that one can thrust a hand through to put things in the inside. The hole made always instantly repairs itself.
2. A metal cube that, when touched, turns to thick liquid for one minute
3. A ball of unbreakable twine that, when fully unraveled, is 100 feet (30 m) long
4. A tiny box with a button that makes a faint chiming noise when pressed
5. Twenty red cigarettes that, when smoked, let you exhale monstrous shapes
6. A coin stamped with the profile of a man that changes each month
7. A bag that always has twenty-seven marbles inside, no matter how many are removed
8. Small metal half-ring that forces anyone touching it to say "Fanoshil"
9. Device that makes everyone within immediate range experience the last one to two seconds again, though nothing can be changed
10. Silver pendant with an invisible chain
11. Small sphere that always remains 1 inch (3 cm) from the tip of a short rod, even though they are not physically connected
12. Crystal that pulses in time with the heartbeat of anyone holding it
13. Glowglobe that, if taken underwater, is never moved or disturbed by currents
14. A 1-inch (3 cm) square of folded black paper that can be unfolded until it becomes a 10-foot (3 m) square of paper
15. A black diamond that causes erotic dreams when it is placed under a sleeper's head
16. A box of twenty oddly shaped stones in different shades of red that can be used like chalk but never run out
17. A box of toothpicks that each have a different and sometimes strange flavor
18. A pouch of powder that can be sprinkled over rotten meat to freshen it and make it safe to eat
19. A cube of ice that never melts
20. A wooden ball that cannot be burned, but freezing it turns it to vapor
21. A plate of glass that turns frosty in freezing temperatures and sometimes shows handprints in the frost
22. A monocle that shows different colored auras around people depending on the time of day they were born
23. A metal box with a glass panel in the center that displays different undecipherable symbols each sunrise
24. A quivering mass of gelatin that hardens whenever it is about to storm
25. A 6-inch (15 cm) metal bar that is impervious to all damage
26. A fist-sized hunk of wet flesh that never dries out and makes a purring noise when stroked
27. A vial containing six droplets that, when added to a pile of excrement, turn it back into what it was before it was digested (though the droplets don't restore life to something that was killed by being eaten)
28. A metal ring that issues a faint ringing noise when rubbed
29. A dark glass trapezohedron that, if held behind someone's head, makes him state his name, even though he is unaware that he did so
30. A glass box containing a living, beating heart wrapped in a golden mesh of wires
31. A piece of flexible plastic that emits soft blue, green, or pink light when worn around the ankle or wrist
32. A clear elastic sheet, 7 feet (2 m) wide and 2 feet (0.6 m) long, of unknown waterproof material that sparkles under starlight
33. A rubber ball that, when thrown with any strength at all, flies for 1 mile (2 km) or until it comes into contact with a solid object and then falls

34. An oblong metal plate covered with strange inscriptions and diagrams
35. A fist-sized metal object filled with holes that gives anyone touching it a brief glimpse of an endless sea
36. A crystal that prevents the person holding it from perspiring
37. A glass ball that, when placed on the ground, rolls around in a circle until it's picked up
38. Shoes with such slippery soles that they are impossible to walk in
39. A tiny square of foil that always feels warm to the touch
40. A small metal box that changes the color of anything placed inside it
41. A sponge that can absorb up to 10 gallons (38 L) of liquid
42. Five synth-sealed edible bars that provide nourishment for seven days each
43. A porous stone that can be used like soap and has a fresh smell
44. A hat that disappears when the wearer wishes, but returns in a few hours
45. A cup that turns any liquid poured into it into alcohol
46. Oddly shaped plastic box with a button on one side that, when depressed, causes a random word in the viewer's language to appear in a tiny display
47. A rubber ball that, when thrown against a hard surface, creates a second rubber ball that lasts for a few minutes before disappearing
48. A piece of cloth that polishes any metal object it touches
49. A synth dodecahedron that allows one to see for about two seconds through the eyes of a person touched
50. A pomander that always smells of freshly baked bread
51. A metal rod that quickly melts ice touched to it, despite its cool temperature
52. The face of a person stretched and pressed between two panes of glass
53. A long piece of cloth never moved by the wind
54. A synth torc that makes the wearer so dizzy that it's almost impossible to walk a straight line
55. A metal sphere the size of a pebble that weighs 50 pounds (23 kg)
56. A ball of fur that squeals when submerged in water
57. A floating orb that removes all odors from the air for a few minutes
58. A crystal that creates a tiny flame when rubbed
59. A bottle of pills that have no nutritional value but take away feelings of hunger
60. Synth full helmet with six eyeholes and a buzzing sound within
61. A metal octahedron that, when held, causes the user's voice to change pitch
62. A synth bowl that nothing adheres to, so it's always dry and clean
63. A 1-foot (0.3 m) bar that has the weight of steel but the flexibility of rubber
64. A synth sphere that always displays the current temperature with a moving set of lines
65. A metal ring that grows warm in cool temperatures or cool in warm temperatures
66. Synth heptahedron that, when touched to other synth, makes everyone in an immediate radius very hungry
67. A device that fits over your ears and plays strange noises that sound like atonal, mostly unpleasant music
68. A pair of multifaceted lenses set into leather goggles that make the wearer see things as an insect would
69. An orange contact lens that occasionally lets you see a person's spoken words float above his head in written form
70. An asymmetrical polygon about the size of a fist that spins whenever placed on the ground with a particular side down
71. A gyroscopic toy top that spins indefinitely if undisturbed
72. A copper ring about the size of a bracelet. If spun around a small shaft (like a finger or a pen), it spins indefinitely.
73. Three separate silver lozenges about 1 inch (3 cm) long that attach to flesh (and can be pried off with difficulty), but only if all three are on the same creature
74. A slab of clear synth that encases a dozen items, most of which appear to be fossils of some kind. There is writing in an unknown language beneath each item.
75. A coated piece of paper about 1 foot (0.3 m) square that folds itself into a different complex design each day
76. A knitted square that adds a new row of stitches on its own
77. A synth honeycomb about 3 inches (8 cm) square that produces a tangy blue syrup
78. A small marble that howls in response to the sounds of laughter
79. A miniature ball on a chain that hovers in the air
80. Purple goo that sometimes shows a lit map of unknown constellations
81. A chime of synth objects that sounds like people talking
82. A belt made of unknown leather and metal that makes you feel full all the time
83. A glass prism that provides a kaleidoscope of scents
84. An incredibly soft pillow that sometimes cuts your hair while you sleep

85. An ankle bracelet that sometimes eases muscle aches
86. A needle with thread that never runs out but constantly changes color
87. A mass of gel that vibrates in time to any sound
88. A synth box that shows a new image of a place in the Ninth World every couple of days
89. A hairpiece that does not seem to have been made for humans
90. A tiny mirror that reflects your face exactly as it looked yesterday
91. A small grey bottle with a screw-off lid that looks like a piece of rock
92. A ceramic bird with a razor-sharp metal beak
93. A piece of felt that expands into a large, flat waterproof bowl
94. A piece of waterproof paper that can't be crumpled and shows a map of somewhere unknown
95. A clear synth hole punch that will make a tiny circular hole in almost any thin material
96. A stronglass shell that sometimes has a ghostly visage of a crab inside it
97. A ring that erases most scratches, scuffs, and ink when passed over them
98. A tube of purple smoke that changes to a liquid when exposed to sunlight
99. A lock of hair that whispers constantly
00. A bottle of liquid that releases bubbles that glow in the dark

ODDITIES TABLE 3

1.   A small stamp that creates a bizarre design on anything edible
2.   A small ring that can be scanned over anything and becomes the color of the item scanned
3.   A metal disk with a hole in it that reveals shapes in the clouds when you look through it
4.   An antler from an unknown creature that continues to slowly grow
5.   A clock face that marks the passage of time with unreadable and unsolvable equations
6.   A wooden tube with a creature carved inside it. Every few days, the creature moves into a different position.
7.   A ring that vibrates when the sun rises in your location
8.   A hat that rests just on top of your head but never blows or falls off
9.   A 3-inch (8 cm) tall tornado that never stops moving when you hold it in your hand
10. Two small blue disks that seem attracted to your skin and are hard to pull off when they come in contact with you
11. Teardrop-shaped object that forms salt crystals along the bottom surface
12. Button that seems to fit through any buttonhole
13. Living orange and green frog encased inside a clear stronglass bubble
14. Necklace that, when worn, temporarily turns your hair grey
15. Unbreakable stemmed glass that always looks empty, even when it's full
16. A petrified anomalous octopus with multiple branched arms
17. A can of liquid propellant that turns all dust in the air into rainbow colors
18. An empty hinged box that sounds like it's full of rocks when shaken
19. A tiny tube that, when blown through, produces small pebbles (and sometimes a surprisingly large rock)

20. An egg-shaped stone that, when cracked open, squeals and then puts itself back together
21. A bag of small green scales that sometimes seem to mold themselves into a tail
22. A bizarrely shaped paintbrush that, when licked, becomes coated with a sparkling clear substance that smells like the sea
23. A tube of lip gloss that temporarily makes the user's lips invisible
24. A winged circlet that whispers endlessly about jumping when worn
25. A leather headdress that turns your eyes black when worn
26. A small round mirror that reflects nothing during the day and reflects only the moon at night
27. A small, ornate bead that adjusts to fit over any diameter of rope or string
28. A mesh teabag shaped like a star that can be used over and over and never seems to get used up
29. A tiny tiara that seems too small for even a newborn baby
30. A tiny synth mouth that spits out words all day long, at random
31. A handful of small blue stones that randomly turn into sacs full of water. They appear to be drinkable if you open them while in their liquid state.
32. A long-handled spoon that brings everything in it to the perfect eating or drinking temperature
33. A living plant that turns into a different type of edible herb each night
34. A length of chain that glows blue if touched by sweat or salt water
35. A teardrop-shaped bauble that always leans to the south
36. A leaf pin that gradually turns different colors as time passes
37. A glob of chewing putty that never loses its flavor or texture
38. A slab of petrified wood that glows with a soft green hue
39. A preserved flower that lights up when you blow on it
40. A 5-foot (2 m) length of string that hangs perfectly horizontal without being tied to anything
41. Small stone that sings a lullaby in an unknown tongue when you rub your thumb over it
42. A small colored-glass sculpture of a bird that flaps its wings in sunlight
43. A net with holes so large you can't imagine what it's designed to capture
44. A leather mask that, when worn, causes you to hear meaningless voices in your head
45. A jar of face paint that starts out black and changes color to match your mood while you wear it
46. A feather necklace that seems to attract all small birds in the area to you
47. A small square of cloth that is always clean, cool, and slightly damp
48. A square of ice 3 inches by 3 inches by 1 inch (8 cm by 8 cm by 3 cm) that never melts, never feels cold, and cools liquids
49. A bit of yeast in an inflatable synth packet that occasionally expands. When placed in the sun for a day, it turns into a fully cooked loaf of bread. If eaten, a new bit of yeast appears inside the packet.
50. A glass pentagonal cupola 2 inches (5 cm) wide that makes one's hair stand on end if touched
51. A self-stick bandage that changes size to fit any wound up to 4 inches (10 cm)
52. A pair of black and blue feathers that float on the wind and flap in the presence of varjellens
53. A handheld rake that scratches only synthetic materials. If used on dirt or rock, it softens in your hands.
54. A piece of strong paper full of written symbols. Every few days, one of the symbols rises off the paper, becoming three-dimensional, and disengages from the paper. A new symbol appears on the page to take its place.
55. A jar full of glitter that always goes back into the jar in the morning, no matter what you used it on
56. A pillow in the shape of a creature's face that never bites you while you sleep
57. A skull of an unknown creature that is covered in ornate tattoos, one of which shows the face of someone you used to know
58. A small handheld box that projects a series of shadows on a flat surface. The shadows seem to be asking for help.
59. A wire sculpture of a flower that releases petals when you blow on it. The petals "grow" back eventually.
60. A crystalline stellated dodecahedron that changes color based on how much numenera is nearby (more numenera makes it redder)
61. A stub of paper with writing on it that says something different to everyone who looks at it
62. A metal bell that releases the scent of animal dung when you ring it
63. A synth bracelet with a tiny pocket that manufactures potable water every time it rains
64. A charm bracelet that randomly adds new charms (and occasionally shins)
65. A soft, big-brimmed hat that sometimes drips water when it's not raining
66. A rolled-up piece of synth that plays music when it gets warm
67. A scarf that releases a soothing odor when you're scared or hurt
68. A piece of natural stone that, when you press your ear to it, makes noise that sounds like people screaming
69. A pair of glasses that purr and coo softly when you breathe rapidly

70. A double-handled mug that appears to be made for nonhuman hands
71. A fossilized curled shell that sometimes uncurls
72. A sticky piece of synth that shows a series of bones and adheres to almost anything
73. A crystal that sometimes attracts living things, such as insects and plants, to its surface. The living things appear to be unharmed, and eventually they are released.
74. A tiny cage in which different things appear, sometimes living, sometimes not. There appears to be no way to open or break the cage.
75. A bit of synth that is full of holes. The holes collect and hold fluid, despite the fact that they go all the way through the material.
76. A synth star about 3 inches (8 cm) across that allows one to levitate about 1 inch (3 cm) for about three seconds, usable at random intervals (about once a day)
77. A mask with a set of eyes drawn on the outside. The eyes blink rapidly in bright sunlight.
78. A heart-shaped piece of synth that you can smoke through, and it always tastes faintly of wood
79. A pyramid made of heavy metal that always stands straight up from its narrowest end
80. A synth ball that perfectly camouflages itself to whatever it's touching. It turns white when you whistle at it.
81. A flexible synth mold of a creature you've never seen before, except in your dreams
82. A piece of lavarock that is cool to the touch but never stops flowing with bright red lava
83. A ceramic cup that lights up when it's full of liquid
84. A handheld shredder that seems to work only on plants
85. A synth flower that stays mostly in bud form but blooms when you place it under certain people's chins
86. A tiny hose made of rubber that squirms around, as if it's trying to connect to something
87. Two metal rings that sometimes become one
88. A tiny stuffed seskii doll that growls when you kiss it
89. A set of tassels that attach to your clothing and flutter when you're near someone you love
90. A set of stick-on nails that were clearly created for someone with much larger hands than a normal human
91. A stone with a mouth carved into it that sometimes has a pinkish tongue
92. A stone snail that grows edible mushrooms instead of a shell
93. A black metal box that makes the sound of a broken hound when you shake it
94. Shoes that make the ground ripple like water when the wearer walks
95. A mask made of a long jaw and sharp teeth. When you wear it, it makes your tongue numb.
96. A jar of oil that, when spread on metal, makes the metal glow with a faint radiance
97. Metal boots that sizzle and steam as if very hot, although their temperature is normal
98. Metal wristband that smells strongly of sugar
99. Rhomboid of solid stone that sometimes turns to liquid, but always reforms
00. Glowing, 6-inch (15 cm) elongated teardrop made of synth that seems to have no weight and very little substance

CHAPTER 5

ITEMS BY CATEGORY

SA = Sir Arthour's Guide
CB = Numenera corebook

ARTIFICIAL BODY PARTS/IMPLANTS

Name	Type	Source	Page
Biomorph	Cypher	SA	35
Breather symbiote	Cypher	SA	37
Comprehension graft	Cypher	CB	283
Electronic nose	Cypher	SA	50
Eyestalk graft	Cypher	SA	52
Foam limb	Cypher	SA	55
Head transference collar	Cypher	SA	60
Organ patch	Cypher	SA	77
Periscopic eye	Artifact	SA	126
Pincer arm	Artifact	SA	127
Poison brain implant	Artifact	CB	309
Remote sensorium	Cypher	SA	83
Replacement hand	Artifact	SA	130
Reproductive bud	Cypher	SA	83
Sleep watch	Cypher	SA	87
Telepathy implant	Cypher	CB	296
Tendril gloves	Cypher	SA	92
Tendril graft	Artifact	CB	312
Warmth projector	Cypher	CB	297
Weapon graft	Artifact	CB	313

AUTOMATONS

Name	Type	Source	Page
Access token	Cypher	SA	33
Automated cook	Artifact	CB	300
Chiurgeon sphere	Artifact	CB	302
Cicerone	Cypher	SA	38
Eyebug	Cypher	SA	52
Fangs of the reaver	Cypher	SA	53
Fluttering recorder	Cypher	SA	55
Glass scorpion	Cypher	SA	57
Harassing companion	Cypher	SA	60
Inflatable companion	Cypher	SA	63
Instant servant	Cypher	CB	288
Navigator daemon	Cypher	SA	75
Portable steed	Cypher	SA	80
Projectile drone	Artifact	SA	128
Remote clamp	Artifact	CB	310
Repair sphere	Artifact	CB	310
Repair unit	Cypher	CB	294
Snake in the grass	Cypher	SA	87
Steel sentinel	Cypher	SA	89
Task drone	Cypher	SA	92
Weaver drone	Cypher	SA	96

CRYSTAL DEVICES

Name	Type	Source	Page
Banishing nodule	Cypher	CB	282
Blue crystal	Cypher	SA	37
Crystal helmet	Artifact	SA	108
Crystal virus	Cypher	SA	41
Datasphere siphon	Cypher	CB	283
Density nodule	Cypher	CB	283
Disrupting nodule	Cypher	CB	285
Echo crystal	Cypher	SA	49
Fool killer	Cypher	SA	56
Heat nodule	Cypher	CB	287
Invisibility nodule	Cypher	CB	289
Tracer nodule	Artifact	SA	139

DATASPHERE DEVICES

Name	Type	Source	Page
Analysis daemon	Cypher	SA	33
Biometric reference	Cypher	SA	35
Cohesion stabilizer	Artifact	CB	303
Conflict advisor	Cypher	SA	40
Contingent subroutine	Cypher	SA	41
Data armor	Artifact	SA	109
Data flood	Cypher	SA	42
Data merge	Cypher	SA	42
Data spike	Cypher	SA	42
Datasphere siphon	Cypher	CB	283
Death messenger	Cypher	SA	43
Dreamachine	Cypher	SA	49
Interaction advisor	Cypher	SA	64
Remnant reader	Artifact	SA	129
Remote viewer	Cypher	CB	293
Secret finder	Cypher	SA	85
Silver ichor	Artifact	SA	131
Telepathy implant	Cypher	CB	296
Temporal viewer	Cypher	CB	296
Tracer	Cypher	CB	297

DETONATIONS

Name	Type	Source	Page
Bloom (fireflower)	Cypher	SA	36
Bloom (serpent)	Cypher	SA	36
Bloom (spore)	Cypher	SA	36
Detonation	Cypher	CB	284
Detonation (coma)	Cypher	SA	44
Detonation (crystal)	Cypher	SA	45
Detonation (desiccating)	Cypher	CB	284
Detonation (distress)	Cypher	SA	45
Detonation (electromagnetic)	Cypher	SA	45
Detonation (filament)	Cypher	SA	45
Detonation (flash)	Cypher	CB	284
Detonation (flashfire)	Cypher	SA	45
Detonation (flesh warping)	Cypher	SA	45
Detonation (foam)	Cypher	SA	45
Detonation (gravity)	Cypher	CB	284
Detonation (healing)	Cypher	SA	45
Detonation (living metal)	Cypher	SA	45
Detonation (matter disruption)	Cypher	CB	284
Detonation (plant transformation)	Cypher	SA	46
Detonation (pressure)	Cypher	CB	284
Detonation (singularity)	Cypher	CB	285

Detonation (smoke)	Cypher	SA	46
Detonation (sonic)	Cypher	CB	285
Detonation (spatial warping)	Cypher	SA	46
Detonation (spawn)	Cypher	CB	285
Detonation (stasis)	Cypher	SA	46
Detonation (suggestion)	Cypher	SA	46
Detonation (tendril)	Cypher	SA	46
Detonation (web)	Cypher	CB	285
Doomsday device	Cypher	SA	48
Exploding arrow	Artifact	CB	304
Gas bomb	Cypher	CB	287
Heartburst	Cypher	SA	61
Needleburst	Cypher	SA	76
Poison (explosive)	Cypher	CB	292

ENHANCEMENTS

ENHANCEMENTS (MOVEMENT)

Name	Type	Source	Page
Adhesion clamps	Cypher	CB	282
Airfins	Cypher	SA	33
Bounding boots	Artifact	CB	302
Buoyancy	Cypher	SA	37
Burrowing bubble	Cypher	SA	37
Cloudskimmer	Cypher	SA	40
Crawler tank	Artifact	SA	107
Drastic propulsion	Cypher	SA	48
Floating bubble	Cypher	SA	54
Flow	Cypher	SA	54
Flying cap	Cypher	SA	55
Ground orb	Cypher	SA	58
Instant boat	Cypher	SA	64
Light flyer	Cypher	SA	67
Lightwings	Artifact	SA	120
Portable steed	Cypher	SA	80
Seed boat	Cypher	SA	85
Suspensor belt	Artifact	CB	312
Windrider	Artifact	CB	313
Wing symbiote	Cypher	SA	97

ENHANCEMENTS (STEALTH)

Name	Type	Source	Page
Camouflage spray	Cypher	SA	38
Chameleon cloak	Artifact	CB	302
Cloaking pin	Cypher	SA	39
Colorless grease	Cypher	SA	40
Deployer (optical)	Cypher	SA	44
Eagleseye	Cypher	CB	285
Ghostly intruder	Cypher	SA	56
Ghostly veil	Cypher	SA	57
Sound dampener	Cypher	CB	295

ENHANCEMENTS (MIGHT)

Name	Type	Source	Page
Armored flesh	Artifact	CB	300
Augmenter harness	Artifact	SA	104
Battlesuit	Artifact	CB	301
Bone garden	Artifact	SA	105
Chemical factory	Cypher	CB	283
Growth harness	Cypher	SA	58
Living armor sheath	Artifact	CB	307
Pleasure center	Cypher	SA	79
Revealer dart	Cypher	SA	83
Second skin	Artifact	CB	310
Sheen	Cypher	CB	294
Silver ichor	Artifact	SA	131

Strength boost	Cypher	CB	295
Stronghold	Cypher	SA	90

ENHANCEMENTS (SPEED)

Name	Type	Source	Page
Chemical factory	Cypher	CB	283
Deployer (muscular)	Cypher	SA	44
Kinetic shield	Artifact	CB	306
Metabolism bud	Artifact	CB	307
Revealer dart	Cypher	SA	83
Speed boost	Cypher	CB	295
Suspensor belt	Artifact	CB	312
Visual displacement device	Cypher	CB	297

ENHANCEMENTS (INTELLECT)

Name	Type	Source	Page
Atmospheric hyperskin	Cypher	SA	34
Brain bud	Artifact	CB	302
Chemical factory	Cypher	CB	283
Data armor	Artifact	SA	109
Intellect enhancement	Cypher	CB	288
Motion sensor	Cypher	CB	291
Nightvision goggles	Artifact	CB	308
Recorder headband	Artifact	CB	309
Second sight symbiote	Cypher	SA	84
Signal detector	Cypher	SA	87

GRAVITY DEVICES

Name	Type	Source	Page
Bounding boots	Artifact	CB	302
Gravity dampener	Cypher	SA	58
Gravity nullifier	Cypher	CB	287
Gravity-nullifying spray	Cypher	CB	287
Hover belt	Artifact	CB	305
Hover square	Artifact	CB	305
Reality spike	Cypher	CB	293

HARD LIGHT DEVICES

Name	Type	Source	Page
Data merge	Cypher	SA	42
Data vault	Cypher	SA	43
Echo crystal	Cypher	SA	49
Hard light cutter	Artifact	SA	118
Hard light goggles	Artifact	SA	118
Light binder	Cypher	SA	66
Light spike	Artifact	CB	306
Light steed	Cypher	SA	67
Photonic fabricator	Cypher	SA	78
Photonic hand	Cypher	SA	78
Photonic smasher	Cypher	SA	78
Radiant web	Cypher	SA	82
Solid light bindings	Artifact	SA	134
Solid light gloves	Cypher	SA	88
Solid light helm	Artifact	SA	134
Solid light retribution	Cypher	SA	88
Tendril gloves	Cypher	SA	92

HEALING DEVICES

Name	Type	Source	Page
Artificial leech	Cypher	SA	34
Brain lightning	Cypher	SA	37
Chiurgeon sphere	Artifact	CB	302
Detonation (healing)	Cypher	SA	45
Ecstasy glass	Cypher	SA	50

Name	Type	Source	Page
Essence transfer	Cypher	SA	51
Exalted vapor	Cypher	SA	51
Healing nodule	Cypher	SA	60
Healing sword	Artifact	CB	305
Health viewer	Cypher	SA	60
Regrow	Cypher	SA	83
Rejuvenating shield	Cypher	SA	83
Rejuvenation field	Cypher	SA	83
Rejuvenator	Cypher	CB	293
Remake	Cypher	SA	83
Repair sphere	Artifact	CB	310
Repair unit	Cypher	CB	294
Restoration pod	Artifact	SA	130
Speed heal	Cypher	SA	89
Stimulation stem	Artifact	SA	136
Talio's compass	Cypher	SA	92
Tranquility pod	Cypher	SA	93

MAGNETIC DEVICES

Name	Type	Source	Page
Blood magnet	Cypher	SA	36
Countermeasure (magnetic)	Cypher	SA	41
Instant bridge	Artifact	CB	306
Kinetic shield	Artifact	CB	306
Magnetic master	Cypher	CB	290
Magnetic shield	Cypher	CB	290
Metamagnetizer	Cypher	SA	72
Talio's compass	Cypher	SA	92

NODULES

NODULES (ARMOR)

Name	Type	Source	Page
Armor patch	Cypher	SA	34
Blinking nodule	Cypher	CB	282
Controlled blinking nodule	Cypher	CB	283
Force nodule	Cypher	CB	286
Invisibility nodule	Cypher	CB	289
Retaliation nodule	Cypher	CB	294

NODULES (WEAPON)

Name	Type	Source	Page
Banishing nodule	Cypher	CB	282
Density nodule	Cypher	CB	283
Disrupting nodule	Cypher	CB	285
Echo crystal	Cypher	SA	49
Explosive nodule	Cypher	SA	52
Fast hail	Cypher	SA	53
Gravity nodule	Cypher	SA	58
Hand of the conqueror	Cypher	SA	59
Healing nodule	Cypher	SA	60
Heat nodule	Cypher	CB	287
Heat sheath	Cypher	SA	61
Living weaponmaster nodule	Cypher	SA	67
Shock nodule	Cypher	CB	294

NUMENERA ENHANCEMENTS

Name	Type	Source	Page
Amulet of safety	Artifact	CB	300
Battle vapor	Cypher	SA	35
Biometric patch	Artifact	SA	104
Cypher replicator	Cypher	SA	41
Cypher seed	Cypher	SA	42
Death messenger	Cypher	SA	43

Name	Type	Source	Page
Detonation delay	Cypher	SA	46
Detonation trigger	Cypher	SA	47
Device enhancer	Cypher	SA	47
Echo crystal	Cypher	SA	49
Energy module	Cypher	SA	50
Hidden reviver	Cypher	SA	62
Hover module	Cypher	SA	63
Mind module	Cypher	SA	72
Numenera analyzer	Cypher	SA	76
Numenera net	Cypher	SA	76
Parous cypher ball	Cypher	SA	78
Parous oddity box	Cypher	SA	78
Projectile module (homing)	Cypher	SA	80
Projectile module (mind blasting)	Cypher	SA	81
Projectile module (poison)	Cypher	SA	81
Projectile module (teleport)	Cypher	SA	81
Repair sphere	Artifact	CB	310
Solar reviver	Cypher	SA	87
Spatial warp	Cypher	CB	295
Time delay	Cypher	SA	93
Trigger trap	Artifact	CB	313

ORGANIC/BIOTECH DEVICES

Name	Type	Source	Page
Brain bud	Artifact	CB	302
Butterfly drone	Cypher	SA	38
Clone tank	Cypher	SA	39
Ear worm	Cypher	SA	49
Fallback clone	Cypher	SA	53
Fungal garden	Cypher	SA	56
Growth serum	Cypher	SA	59
Growth stimulator	Cypher	SA	59
Grub armor	Cypher	SA	59
Health symbiote	Cypher	SA	60
Instant companion	Cypher	SA	64
Instant guardian	Cypher	SA	64
Internal detector	Cypher	SA	65
Living solvent	Cypher	CB	289
Lutin (bioengineered insects)	Cypher	SA	68
Mental thieves	Cypher	SA	71
Poison (emotion)	Cypher	CB	291
Poison (explosive)	Cypher	CB	292
Poison (mind-controlling)	Cypher	CB	292
Poison (mind-disrupting)	Cypher	CB	292
Portable biolab	Cypher	SA	79
Purgspitter	Cypher	SA	81
Second sight symbiote	Cypher	SA	84
Seed of knowledge	Cypher	SA	85
Skill boost	Cypher	CB	294
Skill bud	Artifact	CB	311
Sleep inducer	Cypher	CB	295
Transformation torque	Cypher	SA	94
Visage changer	Cypher	CB	297

PROTECTION

GENERAL PROTECTION

Name	Type	Source	Page
Armored flesh	Artifact	CB	300
Battle armor	Artifact	CB	300
Battlesuit	Artifact	CB	301
Bezoar discharge	Cypher	SA	35
Blinking nodule	Cypher	CB	282
Bone dress	Cypher	SA	37
Catholicon	Cypher	CB	282
Chameleon cloak	Artifact	CB	302
Chitin colony	Cypher	SA	38

Name	Type	Source	Page
Concrete casting	Cypher	SA	40
Contingent subroutine	Cypher	SA	41
Controlled blinking nodule	Cypher	CB	283
Countermeasure (membrane)	Cypher	SA	41
Countermeasure (technological)	Cypher	SA	41
Cyberflesh	Cypher	SA	41
Dimensional armor	Artifact	CB	303
Displacement cloak	Cypher	SA	48
Filtration straw	Artifact	CB	304
Fireproofing spray	Cypher	CB	285
Flame catcher	Cypher	SA	53
Flame-retardant wall	Cypher	CB	286
Floating bubble	Cypher	SA	54
Food scanner	Artifact	CB	305
Force dome	Artifact	CB	305
Force nodule	Cypher	CB	286
Gel suit	Cypher	SA	56
Grub armor	Cypher	SA	59
Health symbiote	Cypher	SA	60
Heat stone	Cypher	SA	61
Heliolithic halo	Cypher	SA	61
Hoop staff	Artifact	CB	305
Indestructible oil	Cypher	SA	63
Inertia shield	Cypher	SA	63
Inflatable suit	Cypher	SA	63
Instant shield	Cypher	SA	64
Invulnerable mesh	Cypher	SA	65
Kinetic shield	Artifact	CB	306
Light shield	Cypher	SA	66
Liquid armor	Artifact	CB	306
Living armor sheath	Artifact	CB	307
Lobal sheath	Cypher	SA	68
Lotus paste	Cypher	SA	68
Orbital armor	Cypher	SA	77
Overwatch defender	Cypher	SA	77
Perma-damp	Cypher	SA	78
Personal environment field	Cypher	CB	291
Plant jar	Artifact	CB	309
Poison brain implant	Artifact	CB	309
Prismatic field projector	Cypher	SA	80
Protection amulet	Artifact	SA	128
Psycap	Artifact	SA	128
Purity	Cypher	SA	81
Ranged protector	Cypher	SA	82
Redlight clip	Artifact	CB	309
Rejuvenating shield	Cypher	SA	83
Repulsion field	Cypher	SA	83
Ring of Iron Wind	Artifact	SA	130
Safe corridor	Artifact	CB	310
Sheen	Cypher	CB	294
Skin of water breathing	Artifact	SA	131
Snow lens	Cypher	SA	87
Solid light retribution	Cypher	SA	88
Spatial distorter	Cypher	SA	88
Stasis projector	Artifact	SA	135
Stone form	Cypher	SA	90
Subdual field	Cypher	CB	296
Teleport seal	Cypher	SA	92
Telltale glass	Artifact	CB	312
Temporal sheath	Cypher	SA	92
Time dilation nodule (defensive)	Cypher	CB	296
Visual displacement device	Cypher	CB	297
Warmth projector	Cypher	CB	297

ARMOR

Name	Type	Source	Page
Armored flesh	Artifact	CB	300
Armoring cloth	Artifact	SA	103
Battle armor	Artifact	CB	300
Battlesuit	Artifact	CB	301
Crystal armor	Artifact	SA	108
Dimensional armor	Artifact	CB	303
Fireproofing spray	Cypher	CB	285
Liquid armor	Artifact	CB	306
Psychic helmet	Artifact	CB	309
Rynrad skin	Cypher	SA	84
Skin of fire sloughing	Artifact	SA	131
Smart cape	Artifact	SA	133
Spine armor	Artifact	SA	135
Ultra armor	Artifact	SA	140

RAY PROJECTORS

Name	Type	Source	Page
Cellular disruptor	Artifact	CB	302
Erosion ray	Cypher	SA	51
Image projector	Cypher	CB	288
Inferno wall projector	Cypher	CB	288
Pyrolytic pulser	Cypher	SA	82
Ray emitter	Cypher	CB	293
Ray emitter (molecular rearrangement)	Cypher	SA	82
Ray emitter (numbing)	Cypher	CB	293
Ray emitter (paralysis)	Cypher	CB	293
Shrink ray	Cypher	SA	86
Terrorizer	Artifact	CB	390
Transdimensional ray projector	Artifact	CB	313

SMART FLUID DEVICES

Name	Type	Source	Page
Gel suit	Cypher	SA	56
Liquid armor	Artifact	CB	306
Liquid sword	Artifact	CB	307
Memory gel	Cypher	SA	71

SOUND/SONIC DEVICES

Name	Type	Source	Page
Communication disks	Cypher	SA	40
Deployer (hypersound)	Cypher	SA	44
Dissonance cube	Cypher	SA	48
Electromagnetic projector	Artifact	SA	111
Emoacoustic weapon	Cypher	SA	50
Psychic whistle	Artifact	CB	309
Screaming madness	Cypher	SA	84
Sonic blade	Artifact	SA	135
Sonic hole	Cypher	CB	295
Sound amplifier	Cypher	SA	88
Sound dampener	Cypher	CB	295
Thunder cannon	Artifact	CB	312

TIME DEVICES

Name	Type	Source	Page
Reset	Cypher	SA	83
Temporal maul	Cypher	SA	136
Temporal viewer	Cypher	CB	296
Time auger	Cypher	SA	93
Time capsule	Cypher	SA	93

Time dilation nodule (defensive)	Cypher	CB	296
Time dilation nodule (offensive)	Cypher	CB	296
Time machine	Artifact	SA	138

DIMENSIONAL/PHASE DEVICES

Name	Type	Source	Page
Controlled blinking nodule	Cypher	CB	283
Demonsphere	Cypher	SA	43
Dimensional armor	Artifact	CB	303
Ghostly duplicate	Cypher	SA	56
Growth harness	Cypher	SA	58
Multidimensional blade	Artifact	CB	308
Phase changer	Cypher	CB	291
Phase disruptor	Cypher	CB	291
Phasing piton	Artifact	CB	309
Quadraturin	Cypher	SA	82
Reality spike	Cypher	CB	293
Secret pocket	Cypher	SA	85
Sidestep portal	Cypher	SA	86
Summoning staff	Cypher	SA	90
Teleport seal	Cypher	SA	92
Teleport trap	Cypher	SA	92
Teleporter (bounder)	Cypher	CB	296
Teleporter (mass)	Cypher	SA	92
Teleporter (traveler)	Cypher	CB	296
Tentacle helmet	Artifact	SA	137
Transdimensional gate	Cypher	SA	93
Transdimensional ray projector	Artifact	CB	313

WEAPONS

MELEE WEAPONS

Name	Type	Source	Page
Bloodblade	Artifact	SA	104
Cacophony blade	Artifact	SA	105
Despoiler, the	Artifact	CB	157
Disruption blade	Artifact	CB	303
Disruptive sword	Artifact	SA	110
Drill spear	Artifact	CB	304
Instant weapon	Cypher	SA	64
Kinetic rod	Cypher	SA	66
Light spike	Artifact	CB	306
Lightning whip	Artifact	SA	120
Malady maker	Cypher	SA	70
Mephitic staff	Artifact	CB	307
Miniaturized weapon	Cypher	SA	73
Monoblade	Cypher	CB	291
Multidimensional blade	Artifact	CB	308
One perfect cut	Cypher	SA	76
Phase axe	Artifact	SA	127
Phasing piton	Artifact	CB	309
Poisoner's touch	Artifact	SA	127
Power glove	Artifact	SA	128
Pyroclastic staff	Artifact	SA	129
Repulsion field	Cypher	SA	83
Shock manacles	Artifact	CB	311
Shocker	Cypher	CB	294
Sonic blade	Artifact	SA	135
Sphere thrower	Artifact	SA	135
Spinneret ring	Artifact	SA	135
Tendril graft	Artifact	CB	312
Tentacle harness (bladed)	Artifact	SA	136
Tongue snake	Artifact	SA	139
Transdimensional blade	Artifact	SA	139

Void knife	Artifact	SA	141
Vuechi	Artifact	CB	313
Weapon graft	Artifact	CB	313
Windslice blade	Artifact	CB	313

RANGED WEAPONS

Name	Type	Source	Page
Cellular disruptor	Artifact	CB	302
Ecstasy paralyzer	Artifact	CB	304
Fearmaker	Artifact	CB	304
Fiery hellmaker	Artifact	CB	304
Flame hand	Cypher	SA	53
Flesh eater	Cypher	SA	54
Foam sprayer	Cypher	SA	55
Fool killer	Cypher	SA	56
Gas bomb	Cypher	CB	287
Hunter/Seeker	Cypher	CB	287
Jolter	Cypher	SA	65
Launcher	Artifact	CB	306
Lightning lance	Cypher	SA	67
Lutin (bioengineered insects)	Cypher	SA	68
Lutin (combos)	Cypher	SA	68
Lutin (engineered spores)	Cypher	SA	68
Lutin (light drops)	Cypher	SA	69
Lutin (metal shrapnel)	Cypher	SA	69
Lutin (nanites)	Cypher	SA	69
Magnetic attack drill	Cypher	CB	289
Mental scrambler	Cypher	CB	290
Mind killer	Cypher	SA	72
Murder globe	Artifact	CB	308
Nano-needler	Artifact	CB	308
Needler	Artifact	CB	308
Overwatch slayer	Cypher	SA	77
Photon igniter	Cypher	SA	78
Photonic smasher	Cypher	SA	78
Portable vortex	Cypher	SA	80
Pulse staff	Artifact	SA	128
Pyroclastic staff	Artifact	SA	129
Pyrolytic pulser	Cypher	SA	82
Ranged retaliator	Cypher	SA	82
Remote scarificator	Cypher	SA	83
Root spike	Cypher	SA	84
Rynrad skin	Cypher	SA	84
Screaming madness	Cypher	SA	84
Sensory disruptor	Cypher	SA	86
Shatter wand	Artifact	CB	311
Skull blaster	Artifact	CB	311
Slug thrower	Artifact	CB	250
Slugspitter	Artifact	CB	311
Slugspitter (heat)	Artifact	SA	132
Slugspitter (inorganic phasing)	Artifact	SA	132
Slugspitter (mass increasing)	Artifact	SA	133
Snipewand	Artifact	CB	311
Sparkle	Cypher	SA	88
Sphere thrower	Artifact	SA	135
Standstill	Cypher	SA	89
Stasis field emitter	Cypher	SA	89
Stunner	Artifact	CB	312
Terrorizer	Artifact	CB	390
Tether	Cypher	SA	93
The death by angles	Artifact	SA	137
Thunder cannon	Artifact	CB	312
Transdimensional ray projector	Artifact	CB	313
Vuechi	Artifact	CB	313
Water weapon	Cypher	SA	96
Wrist launcher	Cypher	SA	97

NEED YOUR NINTH WORLD FIX?

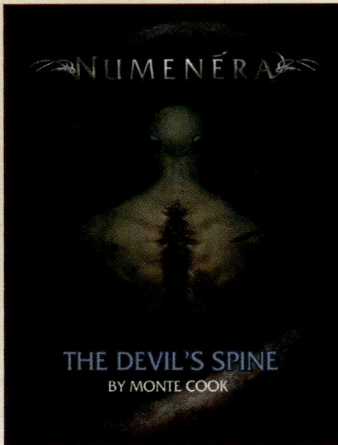

THE DEVIL'S SPINE
This collection of linked-but-separate adventures showcases the narrative structure of Numenera, and offers new creatures, characters, and items to add to any campaign.
96 pages. $24.99 MCG003

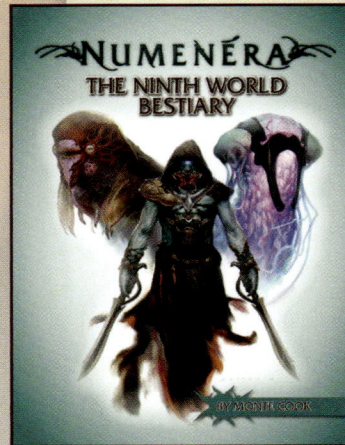

THE NINTH WORLD BESTIARY
This full-color hardcover creature book is lavishly illustrated, featuring creatures and some unique characters to use in Numenera games. A must-have for any Numenera GM.
160 pages. $39.99 MCG004

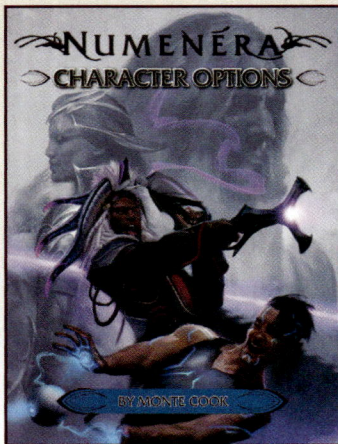

NUMENERA CHARACTER OPTIONS
Numenera Character Options is brimming with new material and new choices to help make Numenera character creation even more fun, more interesting, and more weird, including more than 40 abilities for each character type, 40 new descriptors, and dozens of new foci.
96 pages. $24.99. MCG019

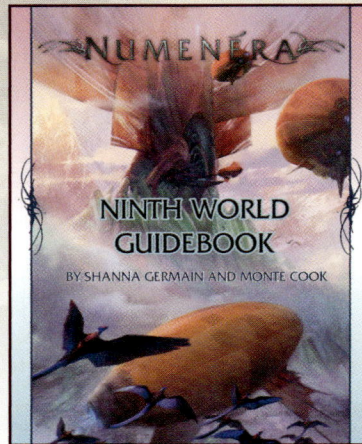

THE NINTH WORLD GUIDEBOOK
This full-color hardcover setting guide, building on what's in the Numenera corebook, brims with art and maps, presented in the style of a traveler's guide. Full of new adventures, creatures, and items, it also provides great ideas, stories, characters, and concepts for creating your next amazing campaign.
256 pages. $49.99 MCG006